HENRI POINCARÉ
A Biography Through the Daily Papers

HENRI POINCARÉ
A Biography Through the Daily Papers

Jean-Marc Ginoux
LSIS, CNRS, Université de Toulon, France
Archives Henri Poincaré, CNRS, Université de Nancy, France

Christian Gerini
Université du Sud Toulon Var, France
& Université Paris-11 Orsay, France

World Scientific

NEW JERSEY · LONDON · SINGAPORE · BEIJING · SHANGHAI · HONG KONG · TAIPEI · CHENNAI

Published by

World Scientific Publishing Co. Pte. Ltd.
5 Toh Tuck Link, Singapore 596224
USA office: 27 Warren Street, Suite 401-402, Hackensack, NJ 07601
UK office: 57 Shelton Street, Covent Garden, London WC2H 9HE

British Library Cataloguing-in-Publication Data
A catalogue record for this book is available from the British Library.

HENRI POINCARÉ
A Biography Through the Daily Papers

ISBN 978-981-4556-61-3

"Thought is only a flash between two long nights, but this flash is everything."

— H. Poincaré[1]

---

[1] *The Value of Science.*

Foreword

Henri Poincaré is known all over the world as a famous astronomer, mathematician, physicist and philosopher. He has been dubbed by Eric Temple Bell as the "Last Universalist". As a mathematician and physicist, he made many original fundamental contributions to pure and applied mathematics, mathematical physics, and celestial mechanics.

In his seminal works "On the curves defined by differential equations" Poincaré (1881-1886) was led to define what is nowadays called a "dynamical system" to model the evolution of phenomena by using ordinary differential equations (O.D.E.). Then, he developed many tools to analyze the behavior (stability) of the solutions of such systems including "characteristic exponents" and "first return maps" which has since been named in his honor as "Poincaré maps". In 1889, Poincaré won the Prize Competition sponsored by the king Oscar II of Sweden and Norway proving thus the efficiency of his new mathematical concepts to establish the stability of the Solar system. Unfortunately, very few months later, the Swedish mathematician Lars Edvard Phragmen responsible for proofreading, discovered a mistake in the memoir (entitled: "On the three body problem and the problem of dynamics") sent by Poincaré. The Editor in Chief, Gösta Mittag-Leffler informed Poincaré of this problem in July 1889 and here is what he answered in December 1889:

> "I thought that all these asymptotic curves (homoclinic orbits) after moving away from a closed curve representing a periodic solution would then asymptotically approach the same closed curve. What is true is that there is an infinity of them that enjoy this property. I will not conceal from you the distress that this discovery has caused me."

It has since been noticed (see the works of J.-C. Yoccoz) that this "fruitful mistake" led Poincaré to the discovery of deterministic chaos. His letter to Mittag-Leffler ends with this sentence:

> "I will write more when I see a little clearer in my works."

It will take ten years for Poincaré to "see a little clearer" in his works. Ten years during which he wrote his famous "New Methods of Celestial Mechanics" (1892-1899). In the third volume, Poincaré (1899) wrote about the homoclinic orbits which nowadays is considered as the signature of chaos:

> "The complexity of this figure will be striking, and I shall not even try to draw it."

Thus, as briefly recalled above, Poincaré's contribution to Dynamical Systems Theory and more particularly to Chaos Theory is obviously of great importance. In my own works concerning Nonlinear Circuit Theory and Cellular Automata, Poincaré's methods were the foundations upon which some of my demonstrations are based on. As an example, in an article entitled: The Double Scroll family (Chua et al., IEEE, 11, pp. 1073-1118, 1986), I used the Poincaré and half-return maps to establish a Rigorous Proof of Chaos in my electronic circuit (Chua's circuit). Although the importance of Poincaré's works is universally recognized in Pure and Applied Mathematics, in Physics, in Astronomy and in Philosophy, and in spite of the fact that many works have been devoted to them, very few biographies have been written about his life. In the middle of the thirties Eric Temple Bell (1937) included in his book *Men of Mathematics* a chapter entitled "Henri Poincaré: the last universalist" in which he told many anecdotes about him. Here is one:

> "One phase of Poincaré's absent-mindedness resembles something quite different. Thus (Darboux does not tell the story, but it should be told, as it illustrates a certain brusqueness of Poincaré's later years), when a distinguished mathematician had come all the way from Finland to Paris to confer with Poincaré on scientific matters, Poincaré did not leave his study to greet his caller when the maid notified him, but continued to pace back and forth – as was his custom when mathematicizing – for three solid hours. All this time the diffident caller sat quietly in the adjoining room, barred from the master only by flimsy portières. At last the drapes parted and Poincaré's buffalo head was thrust for an instant into the room. "Vous me

derangez beaucoup" (You are disturbing me greatly), the head exploded, and disappeared. The caller departed without an interview, which was exactly what the "absent-minded" professor wanted." (Bell, 1937, p. 588)

Regarding his working method, Bell said, quoting Gaston Darboux who was the President of the jury of the thesis:

"Poincaré was an intuitionist. Having once arrived at the summit he never retraced his steps. He was satisfied to have crashed through the difficulties and left to others the pains of mapping the royal roads destined to lead more easily to the end." (Bell, 1937, p. 592)

The above anecdotes provide some insight on Poincaré's personality and allow us to better understand his work and his thought. Indeed, the work of a genius is an inexhaustible source of knowledge in which we should go over with a fine-toothed comb in order to draw the ideas that lead to new theories.

Leon Chua
University of California, Berkeley
Technische Universität, München

Note from the translator

Many different lives in one man's life – this is the general feeling when going though a work like *Henri Poincaré : Une biographie au(x) quotidien(s)*, Ellipses, 2012. Henri Poincaré was polyvalent, to say the least, considering his accomplished works in fields as various as mathematics, physics, astronomy, philosophy and literature. He was a man of science and a man of letter, and both these qualities made him part of controversies which the press of his time did not fail to write about throughout his life. The book being written on the basis of what the newspapers of the time had to say about him, its chapters are therefore as diversified as Poincaré's life itself. And this made the translation of this book as interesting as it made it challenging. How to rightly translate a biography as multiple as Poincaré's? Surely by becoming a specialist in all the fields in which he distinguished himself. This is what I had to keep in mind while doing my research translation, but time was obviously missing to fully reach this purpose. And however faithful and clear I tried to remain, I would therefore like to apologize for the passages where the translation might not be perfectly accurate.

My objective was to make the reading as convenient as possible, the original book, *Henri Poincaré : Une biographie au(x) quotidien(s)*, Ellipses, 2012, includes many references to books written by Henri Poincaré himself, or by other French scientists and scholars of the time, as well as many titles of newspaper and journal articles. Most of Henri Poincaré's writings have been translated, and the English titles can therefore easily be found. However, as the English titles and the French titles often both appear in the various bibliographies, I usually leave the original title in French, followed by the translated English title into brackets. This was in my opinion the best way for a reader that would want to look further into the subjects mentioned in the book to have all the information he would need to do his research. As for the losses due to translation, I am deeply sorry that I had to leave out a whole part of the book. The reason for this decision lies in the fact that the original section deals with the variations on the name "Poincaré" itself. It is actually filled with many references and press articles playing with the "point" (in English point) and the "carré" (in English square) that make the name "Poincaré". There would then have been no point translating this chapter into English. However pleasant it is to read it in French, it surely would have been absolutely tiresome and of very little interest for the English-speaker readership. Considering how universal Henri Poincaré's work is, translating this book felt like an obvious and natural thing to do. And what I truly focused on during the whole process was to make it accessible to the largest possible number of readers. And I believe that one of the purposes of this book was to go beyond the exclusive circle of scholars and reach the general public, as did Poincaré himself – and the book emphasizes it well – when he began to work towards a "scientific popularization". Translating the book in line with its very essence was a beautiful and noble purpose, and I hope to have served it well.

Selma Naëck,
Master's Degree,
Institut de Traducteurs, d'Interprètes et de Relations Internationales,
Université de Strasbourg,
selma.naeck@gmail.com

Preface

On July 17, 2012 the centenary of Henri Poincaré's death was commemorated. His name is associated with so many fields of knowledge that he was considered as the *Last Universalist*. In Pure and Applied Mathematics, in Physics, in Astronomy, in Engineering and in Philosophy his works had a great influence all over the world.

So, Poincaré acquired in his lifetime such a reputation, both nationally and internationally, which made his life and career the object of various articles in daily papers in France and also in the U.S.A. Some of his philosophic concepts have even caused sharp controversies in the Press as we will discover in this book. Thus, it seemed appropriate and interesting to reconstitute in a certain way Henri Poincaré's biography through the press of his time and through the eyes of the XIXth century and of the beginning of the XXth century reader who would conceive the portrait of a man through newpaper articles alone.

This approach or, more precisely this concept, that could be also used for studying the biography of other scientists, led to the publication of a book (in French) entitled: *Henri Poincaré : une biographie au(x) quotidien(s)*, Ellipses, 2012 in which we only focused on the French daily papers.

The present work is much more than a simple translation of the French version because it has required the same level of research and this time included the American press.

Many American newspaper articles extracted from *The New York Times, The San Francisco Sunday Call, The Times, The Sun, The Washington Post*, ...) could have been consulted and downloaded from the website of the Library of Congress (http://chroniclingamerica.loc.gov/) and from the online archives of *The New York Times* (http://query.nytimes.com/search/sitesearch/?vertical=/).

The comparison between both studies (in France and in U.S.A.) has provided an insight into the dissemination of information at the time – some information crossing the Atlantic Ocean whilst others remaining anchored in the French news.

This was also the case for the Prize of King Oscar II of Sweden and Norway for which we found[2] no reference in the American newspapers although there were many articles concerning the King Oscar II. On the contrary, The New York Times reported extensively on his commitment in the Dreyfus affair as well as on his election at the Académie française. Moreover, his philosophical writings were also analyzed in the main U.S. daily papers.

Thus, this work presents an original portrait of Henri Poincaré from various unknown anecdotes of his life (his first name was not Henri, but Henry, he obtained his high school diploma in sciences with zero in mathematics, ...) and from what the newspapers of his time wrote of him.

Many of Poincaré's biographies have already been written by focusing on some aspects of his immense work but none can aspire to the exhaustiveness.

Although, this work remains unfinished,we feel nevertheless that the collected information illustrate well enough the way with which the personality and the work of Henri Poincaré were received in the press of his time.

Jean-Marc Ginoux,
Ph.D. in Applied Mathematics and Ph.D in History of Sciences,
Senior Lecturer at Université du Sud.
`ginoux@univ-tln.fr`

Christian Gérini,
Ph.D. in History and Philosophy of Sciences and Degree in Mathematics,
Senior Lecturer at Université du Sud.
`gerini@univ-tln.fr`

---

[2]This does not necessarily mean they do not exist, just that they are not yet online.

Acknowledgments

Here we want to show our gratitude to World Scientific editions – and particularly to Professor Phua Kok Khoo – for the confidence he has given to our project and made possible the publication of this book.

We also wish to thank all the people and all institutions without which this work would not have been possible and would not be what it is.

First, we would like to thank Miss Selma Naëck who spent long hours translating the French version of this book and Mr. Appasamy Danen for his helpful comments. Miss Gaëlle Chapdelaine (librarian) who provided us many original articles. Then, Michel Brunel who developed the design of the cover.

We also express our gratitude to all those who have encouraged us: Professor Leon Chua (University of California, Berkeley) who proposed this project to the editor and who gave us the honor and friendship to write the foreword of this book. Then, the PROTEE laboratory of the Université du Sud which supported the translation of the French version of our book.

Thank you also to Professor June Barrow-Green (United Kingdom) Mikael Ragstedt, Institut Mittag-Leffler (Sweden) and to all the members of the Archives Henri Poincaré in Nancy (France) for having so kindly and so quickly agreed to provide us unpublished documents that we have could reproduced in our work.

Finally, we wish to thank very warmly all our loved ones who have helped, advised and borne throughout the development of this biography through the daily papers.

To my family and my wife who have supported me in this work I would like to extend my gratitude and love.

Contents

List of Figures

PART 1

The early years

A scientist worthy of the name, above all a mathematician, experiences in his work the same impression as an artist; his pleasure is as great and of the same nature.

— H. Poincaré —

Chapter 1

The Poincaré Family

In the ducal town of Nancy is the Hotel Martigny, located at number 2, rue de Guise and at the corner of la Grande Rue[1]. On July 5, 1913, the Alumni Association of Nancy, Metz, Strasbourg and Colmar's high schools had a plaque affixed on the façade on which one can read this inscription:

> "In this house was born on April 29, 1854, Henri Poincaré, member of the Académie Française and of the Académie des Sciences, died in Paris on July 17, 1912."

The date of this event is definite and correlates with references in the French press such as *Le Gaulois* and *Le Matin*, released on Saturday the 5th of July, 1913. On the following day, the newspaper *Le Temps* makes "In honor of Henri Poincaré" one of its titles, and at last, the *Journal des débats politiques et littéraires* wrote:

> "It is probable that on the 15th of July, at the time of its prize distribution, Nancy's high school will be given the name of Lycée Henri Poincaré."

Indeed, just one week later, on Saturday the 12th of July, the Nancy's boys high school would from that day onwards take the name of Lycée Henri Poincaré, in accordance with the decree published in the official newspaper. The Poincaré family have had some illustrious members between the end of the 19th century and the beginning of the 20th. To help defining how all of them are related, here is a simplified version of their family tree[2] (see Fig. 1.2).

---

[1] In 1854, this street was called "rue Ville-Vieille".

[2] A more complete genealogy is presented in: André Bellivier, *Henri Poincaré ou la vocation souveraine*, coll. "Vocations" N° IV, Gallimard, Paris, 1956, p. 22-23 and Jean-Sebastien Joly, Léon Poincaré (1828-1892): Un nom célèbre, une œuvre oubliée, PhD Thesis Université Henri Poincaré, Nancy I, May 2000, p. 32.

Fig. 1.1   Commemorative plaque on Henri Poincaré's native house.

1.1   The Grandfather: Jacques-Nicolas Poincaré

Henri's paternal grandfather, Jacques-Nicolas Poincaré, was a pharmacist in Neufchâteau (Vosges region of France). He moved to Nancy in 1820, and acquired the hotel Martigny in 1833, in which there was already a pharmacy (see Fig. 1.4). There, he kept on working as a chemist until he died in 1865. Three children from his marriage with Catherine Rollin (1797-1880) were born in that hotel: Clémentine (1823-1902), Antoni (1825-1911) and Léon Poincaré (1828-1892), Henri's father.

1.2   The Uncle: Antoni Poincaré

Antoni, Léon's elder brother, studied at Polytechnic School (X 1845)[3] and became a mining engineer. He spent most of his career being General Inspector for the civil works in Bar-le-Duc. He wrote many articles on meteorology, as well as a notice on the mathematician Edmond Laguerre

---

[3]We use here the classical notation indicating the year the student leaves the École Polytechnique, also called "X".

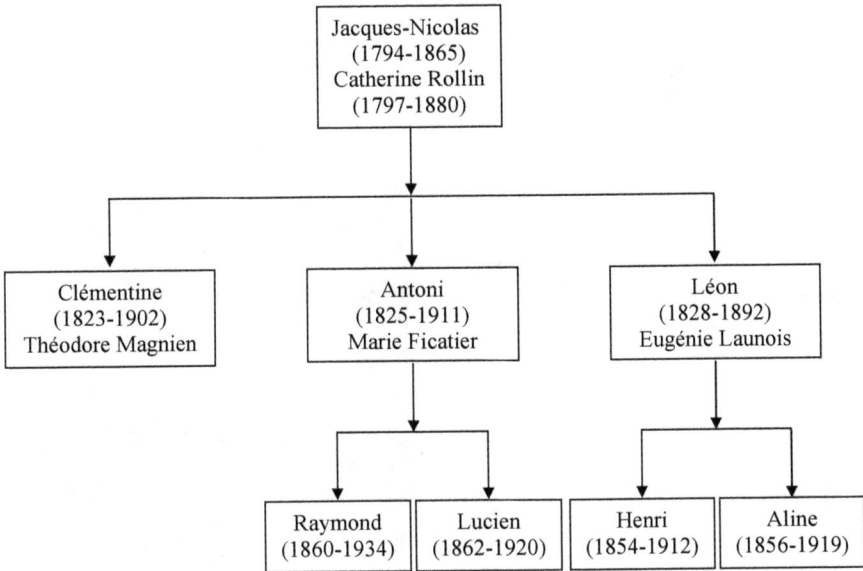

Fig. 1.2 Simplified genealogy of the Poincaré family.

Fig. 1.3 Léon Poincaré (*A.H.P.*, Nancy).

(1834-1886), who was also a native of Bar-le-Duc[4]. Two children were born from his marriage with Nanine-Marie Ficatier (1838-1915): Raymond (1860-1934) and Lucien (1862-1920). Raymond was a lawyer in Paris before becoming President of France in 1913. Lucien was Inspector General for Secondary Education in Physics, he then became rector of the Paris Academy.

---

[4]See Jean-Sebastien Joly mentioned above, p. 31.

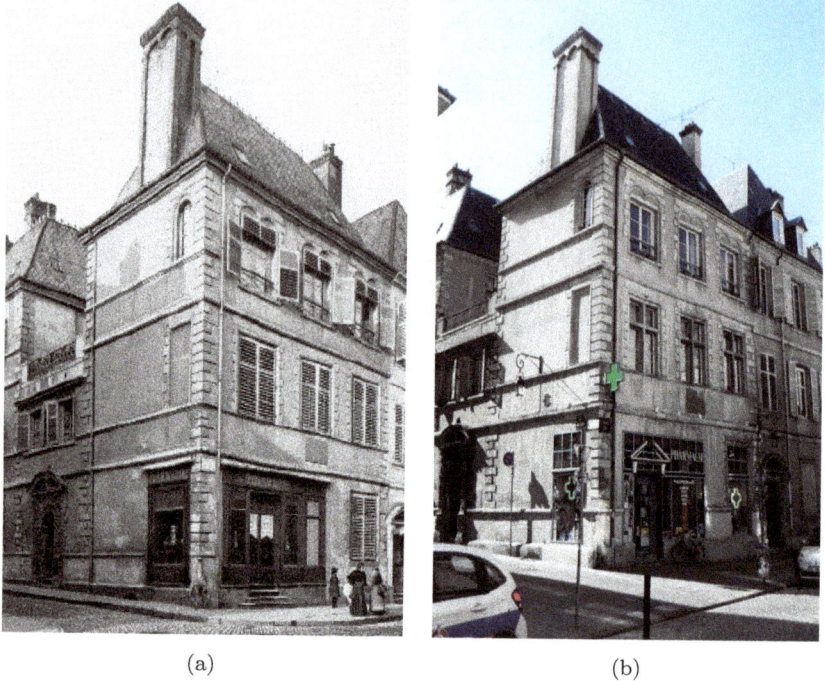

(a)   (b)

Fig. 1.4 Henri Poincaré's native house (*A.H.P.*, Nancy): (a) from the Archive Henri Poincaré, (b) in color in 2012.

1.3   The Father: Léon Poincaré

Although his father wanted him to take over the drugstore he ran, Léon preferred to take the entrance examination to become a surgeon in the Military Health Service, which he passed in 1848. At the military hospital of Metz, he came first in his year in 1848 and 1849, but was forced to finish his medical studies in Paris, after the Val-de-Grâce military hospital closed in may 1850. On July the 3rd, 1852, he defended a thesis entitled "On the purulent ophtalmia of the infants". In order to pursue his career in the Health Department, the young doctor had to get into the Val-de-Grâce school of military medicine, which was created in 1850. He finally decided not to, and went back to Nancy, his native town. He then started to work as a private practitioner as early as 1852, while carrying some medical and social duties (welfare office, vaccination) as well as teaching (head of medical clinic at the école de Médecine). The *Journal de la Meurthe et des Vosges* paper of March 31st, 1854, wrote about the devotion of many

doctors of the charity medical service, among which was Léon Poincaré[5].
The year before, he had married Eugénie Launois (1830-1897) who gave
him a son named Jules Henry, born on April the 29th, 1854, and a daughter
named Aline, born on January the 14th, 1856. Very soon, an intellectual
and affectionate complicity grew between the two children, as can be seen
from Aline's diary[6].

It is interesting to notice that the first name of the one who was to
become the illustrious scientist and man of letters immortalized by History,
is here written with an "y". In May 1858, Léon Poincaré was appointed
assistant professor of Anatomy and Physiology at the École de Médecine,
he was also in charge of Physiology from 1858 to 1872. From 1873 to
1876, he published *Leçons sur la physiologie normale et pathologique du
système nerveux* and *Le Système Nerveux Périphérique au point de vue
Normal et Pathologique[7]*", which all important contemporary physiologists
consider to be great works. From that moment on, he turned his research
towards Hygiene. He thus became the first to occupy the chair of Hygiene
at the University, from 1879 to 1892. Throughout his life as an "inflexible
worker[8]", he never stopped publishing and communicating his research.
Young Henri Poincaré probably did suffer from these unremitting efforts,
as can be seen from a letter he addressed to his mother:

> "He'll end up dead if he keeps on swotting and tormenting him-
> self; I know him well."

---

[5] Amusing detail that will come up soon, Poincaré is spelled with two "r" in the newspaper. See below.

[6] See Aline Poincaré-Boutroux, *Vingt ans de ma vie, simple vérité*. La jeunesse d'Henri
Poincaré racontée par sa sœur published in 2012 by Laurent Rollet, Hermann publications, Paris. The book is actually the diary of Aline Poincaré: extensive excerpts of it
can be found in André Bellivier's book referred to above.

[7] See Léon Poincaré, *Leçons sur la physiologie normale et pathologique du système
nerveux*, Berger-Levrault & Co., J. B. Baillière & Fils, Paris, 1873-1874 (2 volumes)
and Léon Poincaré, *Le Système Nerveux Périphérique au point de vue Normal et
Pathologique, Leçons de Physiologie*, professed at Nancy Berger-Levrault & Co, Paris,
1876, which follows the two previous volumes.

[8] The expression is from André Bellivier p. 59.

EXTRAIT des Registres des Actes de l'Etat civil de la commune de *Nancy*, déposés au Greffe du Tribunal de première instance de Nancy, département de Meurthe-et-Moselle.

L'an mil huit cent *cinquante-quatre*, le *premier mai* à *onze* heures du *matin*, pardevant nous *Adjoint au* Maire, faisant fonctions d'Officier de l'Etat civil de la commune de *Nancy*, arrondissement de *Nancy*, département de *la Meurthe*, a comparu M. *Léon Emile Poincaré* âgé de *vingt-cinq* ans, profession de *Docteur en médecine* domicilié à *Nancy*, lequel nous a présenté un enfant du sexe *masculin*, né le *vingt-neuf avril* mil huit cent *cinquante-quatre* à *une* heure du *matin en la maison rue St. Pierre N°. 2,* et nommé *Jules Henry* fils légitime *du comparant et de Marie Piérette Eugénie Launois, son épouse,* âgée de *vingt-trois ans.*

Lesquelles déclaration et présentation ont été faites en présence de MM. *Auxence Théodore Magnien,* âgé de *trente-sept* ans, profession de *Pharmacien,* domicilié à *Nancy* de *André ? Cinzelin,* âgé de *trente trois* ans, profession de *Directeur de l'Ecole Supérieure,* domicilié à *Nancy,* lesquels après lecture ont signé le présent acte avec nous et le déclarant.

Signé: (*suivent les signatures*)

ACTE DE NAISSANCE.

Pour extrait certifié conforme par le Greffier soussigné.

Vu pour légalisation de la signature de M. *Le Bon* Greffier du siège. Nancy, le *Dix mai* mil huit cent soixante-*treize*. Le Président du Tribunal civil de Nancy,

Fig. 1.5   Henri Poincaré's birth certificate (*A.H.P.*, Nancy).

Unfortunately, his mother was right. As demonstrated by the eulogy from Doctor Hyppolite Bernheim[9] at the funeral of Poincaré:

> "For many years, this unremitting overwork had been wearing down his sturdy constitution; he knew he was affected, but he never failed to honor his duties as a doctor and a professor. A few weeks ago, he unhappily fell down and had a serious head injury[10]. Weakened by an important haemorrhage, he refused to take the moral rest he needed. But could he have done so, considering his passionate nature, continuously in demand by an ever-moving spirit? His old sickness started up again, serious and threatening, though it seemed averted. He fought most energetically to stand up on his feet, to support his floating thoughts, to maintain his mental vigor, which had become a little failing due to the inexorable ache. He did succeed for a few days. But all of a sudden, the spring broke! And this grand intelligence has passed away! This sagacious and penetrating mind is gone! This generous heart has stopped beating!"

He adds:

> "He died while still doing the work he always did, victim of being always busy, overcome before the end by a life of sacrifices and abnegation."

During the following days, his death was announced in the main newspapers. In *Le Figaro* of September 21, 1892, one can read:

> "The funeral took place among a large crowd. Doctor Poincaré was a very esteemed man in Nancy."

The following day, the sad news was reported by the papers *Journal des débats politiques et littéraires*, *Le Temps* and *La Presse* as well. Therefore, the name of Poincaré rose to fame, and lots of chroniclers got interested in its origin. In 1913, the philologist, historian and medievalist Antoine Thomas (1857-1935) finally fixed its etymology in the paper *Le Temps*, on the occasion of the election of the new president of France: Raymond Poincaré.

---

[9]See Hyppolite Bernheim, Charles and Leon Benoit Vallois, Docteur Léon Poincaré (1828-1892): *Discours prononcés à ses obsèques, le 16 septembre 1892*, Berger-Levrault & Co., Paris, 1893.

[10]During the summer of 1892, while contemplating an eruption of Mount Etna, Leon Poincaré fell down and had a serious head injury with heavy bleeding. His diabetes got worse and caused his sudden death on September 15, 1892: he was 64 years old.

1.4   Origin of the Name Poincaré

In the originally French version of the book, this part is dedicated to the origin of the name Poincaré, with some variations on the French words "Point" (point) and "Carré" (square).

Henri Poincaré, the missed mathematician of genius but inexperienced philologist, seemed to have suffered from his family name, in which he thought to have found a grave distortion. When Frederic Masson welcomed him at the Académie Française on the 28th of January, 1909, he enjoyed himself teasing him about it.

> "Among those who bore your name – Pontcarré, rather than Poincaré, for as you said, one can imagine a pont carré (square bridge) but not a point (point) – there were magistrates, scholars, etc."

The philologists felt concerned about what had been said under the Dome of the Académie. They looked into the archives and found that there was a student of the Langres diocese at the university of Paris in 1403 whose Latin name was Petrus Pugniquadrati; they also found that in 1418, there was a man called Jehan Poingquarré, who was the secretary of the Queen Isabeau de Bavière and the Duke Jean sans Peur. So this strange family name is not about a pont (bridge) or a point (point), but a poing (fist). The word poing is still part of some picturesque locutions where he combines with past participles, as in the expressions dormir à poings fermés (be sound asleep), pieds et poings liés (hands and feet tied). But the poings carrés cannot be found anymore. It was different in times past, and this explains the forming of this family name.

Chapter 2

Childhood and Studies

Henri and his sister Aline, who was two years younger than him, spent a happy and cherished childhood at the hotel Martigny. Their parents and grandparents also lived there at the time, and the hotel was the scene of all their games, as Aline wrote in her diary[1].

2.1 An Almost Peaceful Golden Childhood

The peaceful happiness of their childhood was nonetheless disturbed during the winter of 1859, when Doctor Poincaré diagnosed his five-year-old son with diphtheria. Because of this illness, Henri's legs and larynx were paralyzed for nine months. This incapacitating disease made him become even closer to his little sister; they quickly instituted some sign system that allowed them to communicate. This "forced" rest that obliged him to live in isolation had a double effect: it not only contributed to modify his temper and physical constitution, but it also helped develop his ability to memorize as well as his intellectual curiosity through his passion for reading.

Among the many books that came out at that time, Gaston Darboux (1842-1917) said that one of Henri's favourites[2] was *La Terre avant le déluge* by Louis Figuier (1810-1894), of which its first illustrated edition was published in 1862. It is also probable that he read *Les Grandes Inventions anciennes et modernes, dans les sciences, l'industrie et les arts*, published in 1861 by the same author. In this book the principle on which the electric telegraph works is explained, which Henri understood without any help, as reported by André Bellivier[3].

---

[1] See Aline Poincaré-Boutroux mentioned above.
[2] As reported by Bellivier, p. 33 referred to above.
[3] As reported by Bellivier, p. 37. This fact is also reported by Aline Poincaré-Boutroux in her diary.

Henri Poincaré et sa sœur Aline.

Fig. 2.1   Henri Poincaré and his sister Aline (*A.H.P.*, Nancy).

The second half of the 19th century was marked by many scientific liter-ature publications, where popular works[4] like those of Camille Flammarion (1842-1925) and the novels of Jules Verne (1828-1905) intermingled. It is then highly probable that all these publications that enthused the young people of that time had an influence on young Henri Poincaré as well. This fact was underlined once again by André Belliver[5]:

> "The memories of his first readings accompanied him to the end of his life: in 1910, along with Paul Painlevé and other scientists, he wrote in the beautiful publication *Au seuil de la vie*[6] that Hachette was publishing!"

---

[4]A few years later, popular science journals appear. *La Nature* was founded in 1875 by Gaston Tissandier (1843-1899) and *La Science Illustrée* is created the same year by Adolphe Bitard, Elysee Reclus and Louis Figuier.

[5]As reported by Bellivier, p. 39, referred to above.

[6]See Poincaré, *Ce que disent les choses*, five chapters published in the children's journal *Au seuil de la vie*, Hachette, Paris, 1910 and republished by Hachette in 1911 in the

The following year, Léon Poincaré asked his neighbor, M. Alphonse Henzelin (1834-1911), a retired schoolteacher and friend of the Poincaré family, to teach his children. Thus, it was only in October 1862 that Henri started the ninth grade at Nancy's high school[7]. He was a brilliant pupil, and top of his class until the seventh grade. The way he worked puzzled his classmates. One of them, Paul Xardel (1854-1933) said that Henri came and went in the apartment, took part to the conversations and always seemed busy doing everything but his homework.

> "And suddenly, he would come near the table, and without sitting, putting one knee on the chair, he would take his pen with his right or left hand, and write a few words or lines, then get back to his comings and goings and the conversations he had left[8]."

After making several trips to his chair, the homework is done, and remarkably well done. It seems that he was in 4th grade when his predispositions for mathematics was revealed. Apparently, his professor told his mother this:

> "Henri is going to be a mathematician. I mean a really great one[9]."

However, Poincaré was also gifted in literature, so much so that one of his teachers encouraged him to study it. At that time, the students specialized as early as the 10th grade, and after the 9th grade, they had to make a choice corresponding to this branching (called a "bifurcation" in french)[10]. Poincaré then went into a literary tenth grade. During that period of time, on the 19th of July, 1870, the Franco-German war (or Franco-Prussian war) broke out. The battle of Sedan, during which Napoleon the IIIrd (1808-1873) was made prisoner, led to the fall of the French Empire and to the

---

eponymous book *Ce que disent les choses*. Republished by Christian Gerini, Henri Poincaré: *Ce que disent les choses*, Hermann, Paris, 2010.

[7]Renamed as Lycée Henri Poincaré in his honor on July 12, 1913. See above.

[8]As reported by Appell, *Henri Poincaré*, Librairie Plon, Paris, 1925, p. 15.

[9]As reported by Appell, p. 16 referred to above and Bellivier, p. 78 referred to above.

[10]It is probable that this terminology has been taken over by Henri Poincaré in his mathematical work when he introduced the concept of "bifurcation". See Henri Poincaré, "Sur l'équilibre d'une masse de fluide animée d'un mouvement de rotation," *Acta Mathematica*, vol. 7, 1885, p. 259-380.

Armistice, which for the Eastern region of France, was signed on the 28th of January, 1871[11].

2.2   Zero at the Math Test of the Baccalaureate

On the 5th of August, 1871, Henri Poincaré passed his literary baccalaureate with honors (see Fig. 2.2: the tests were marked out of 5 points[12].)

BACCALAURÉAT ÈS LETTRES

SUBI LE 5 AOUT 1871 PAR POINCARÉ (JULES-HENRI)

		Coefficients	Notes
Épreuve écrite.	Composition latine	1	4
	Version latine	1	2
	Composition française...	1	3
Épreuve orale.	Explication d'un auteur { grec	1	3
	latin	1	2
	français...	1	2
	Philosophie	1	2
	Histoire et géographie...	1	2
	Éléments de sciences....	1	3
		1	3
	Épreuve facultative d'allemand	1	3
			29

Note maximum : 5.
Mention : Bien.

Fig. 2.2   Henri Poincaré's marks for the literary baccalaureate.

Ten days later, Charles of Prussia's troops and his forty thousand soldiers march into occupied Nancy. That year, the students went back to school as late as the 17th of October. This is what Poincaré's sister wrote:

---

[11]The General Armistice, which occurred in February 15, 1871 resulted in the annexation of Alsace-Lorraine.
[12]As reported by Appell, p. 18, referred to above.

"He was ready to take the scientific baccalaureate as well, but the University professors refused that he took it without the proper training. Henri was intimidated and decided to postpone the exam until November[13]."

Exempted from the literary exams, Poincaré passed his scientific baccalaureate with honors on the 7th of November, 1871, despite getting a zero out of five in math[14]. (See Fig. 2.3).

BACCALAURÉAT ÈS SCIENCES
SUBI LE 7 NOVEMBRE 1871 PAR POINCARÉ (JULES-HENRI)

	Coefficients	Notes
Épreuve écrite. Composition scientifique.	1	0
	1	2
Épreuve orale. Mathématiques	1	3
	1	4
Sciences physiques	1	2
	1	4
		15

Mention : Assez bien.

Fig. 2.3   Henri Poincaré's marks for the scientific baccalaureate.

The story of this 'zero' mark was told by André Bellivier and Paul Appell[15]. Poincaré was a little late to the math written test on geometric progressions, and probably misread the wording, for he answered a question which had nothing to do with the one that was set. Without the benevolence of the examiners who knew how brilliant Poincaré normally was, this mark would have been disqualifying. A few weeks later, Henri went into the Elementary Mathematics class (which is now called Advanced Mathematics class) and attended the courses of M. Lecomte. On the 12th of August, 1872, he got the honour prize at the General Contest. He was then top of

---

[13]As reported by Aline Poincaré-Boutroux referred to above.
[14]Reported by Appell, p. 18 referred to above.
[15]See Bellivier and Appell referred to above.

his class and ranked first at the academic contest, which granted him the press' honours.

In November 1872, he got into the Special Mathematics class and met Paul Appell (1855-1930), who had also taken the scientific and the literary baccalaureate in Nancy in 1871. Back then, as reported by Bellivier and Appell[16], Poincaré found the solution to the wording set at the entrance contest to the École Polytechnique all alone.

Poincaré and Appell studied under the direction of Victor Elliot, former student of the École Normale Supérieure (year 1866) and qualified in Maths[17]. Right from the beginning of the lessons, Poincaré distinguished himself by his attitude[18]:

> "Poincaré, a little stooped already, sitting on the upper steps like all the new students, pulled a funeral announcement from his pocket and used it as a notebook. We thought it was an oversight, but the following days, we were astonished when we saw him scribble a few lines on the same sheet, which was easily recognizable by its border. Obviously, the newcomer was not serious! We had to make sure, because after all, he did come first in the General contest! At the end of the course, we sent a 4th year student to ask him for an explanation about something he had found particularly vague. Poincaré immediately explained it all, without thinking one minute, then left, leaving the student and the witnesses so amazed that one of them asked: How does he do that?"

People were first annoyed by Poincaré, but his intellectual influence and his great humility soon earned him sympathy. During the Easter holidays, M. Elliot, who was then visiting Paris, told his friend Louis Liard (1846-1917) that Poincaré will become director of the Higher Education at the Ministry of Education in 1884 and vice-rector of the Academy of Paris in 1902:

> "I have in my class a legendary figure of mathematics[19]."

At the end of the school year, Poincaré was again awarded the Honorary Prize at the Concours Général, but this time in Special Mathematics, and

---

[16] See Bellivier p. 106 and Appell, p. 20 referred to above.

[17] On 29 July 1876, along with his pupil Appell, Elliott defended a thesis entitled *Détermination du nombre des intégrales abéliennes de première espèce* at the Faculty of Sciences in Paris before MM. Puiseux (foreman), and Hermite and Briot (examiners)

[18] See Bellivier, p. 109 referred to above.

[19] See Bellivier, p. 110 and Appell, p. 21 referred to above.

Appell was awarded the second accessit (certificate of merit). The jury members who reviewed Poincaré's examination script were none other than Constant Rollier (1811-1876), the University's Inspector General for secondary education, Victor Puiseux (1820-1883), Charles Briot (1817-1882) and Jean-Claude Bouquet (1819-1885). A few years later, the latter was foreman of the examining board for the thesis defended by Henri Poincaré at the Faculty of Sciences in Paris in 1879.

A few weeks before that, Poincaré and Appell had taken the entrance exam for the École Normale Supérieure and for the École Polytechnique between the 4th and the 6th of August. Poincaré came in first at the entrance for the École Polytechnique and fifth at the École Normale Supérieure one, behind Appell, who came second, surprising all who knew Poincaré. As reported by Appell:

> "At the École Normale Supérieure, one of the examiners, who is now dead, found indeed that Poincaré expressed himself badly and would not be a good teacher: he then gave him a mark that made him come fifth, surprising us all. This shows the strange fate of the genius that cannot fit into the classifications of ordinary men[20]."

The journal *Le Figaro* on Thursday, October 23, 1873 indicated in a paragraph on the front page:

> "We have just seen the list of the successful candidates for the entrance to the École Polytechnique, in order of merit. The top candidate is Mr. Jules Henri Poincaré."

Poincaré chose the École Polytechnique, succeeding his uncle Antoni (year 1845). Aware of the reasons that made young Poincaré come fifth, Pierre-Augustin Bertin-Mourot, Deputy Director of the École Normale Supérieure, expressed his regrets to him through a call from Appell (who had got into the École).

2.3 "Poincarré" at The École Polytechnique

On November 2, 1873, Poincaré entered the École Polytechnique as Jules Henri Poincarré (see Fig. 2.5 & 2.7), for the Secretary of the School had

---

[20] As reported by Bellivier, p. 117 referred to above.

Fig. 2.4   Henri Poincaré at the École Polytechnique (*A.H.P.*, Nancy).

misspelled the name for two consecutive years without Poincaré bothering about it[21].

He followed the courses with no difficulty, maintaining his rank but complaining about the military rigor of the School:

> "The work we have to do here will be of no use to me for what I will be doing later."

And he added:

> "Here one uses only two faculties of his mind: memory and speech; everyone can understand a course with some work, and that is why everyone can swot up[22] if they really want to[23]."

This excerpt reveals his concern about losing his ranking of top of his year. This was indeed going to be the case: he was finally second, just behind Marcel Bonnefoy (1854-1881), when he came out of the École Polytechnique. However, if Poincaré lost his first place, it was not for lack of work but because of the "foolishness of some men[24]". Indeed, as reported

---

[21] As reported by Bellivier, p. 48 referred to above. The list of students admitted in the École Polytechnique included the same spelling error (see Fig. 2.5 & 2.7) as well as did the announcement in *Le Figaro* newspaper, which had actually made fun of it.

[22] To swot up means working hard to pass an examination or a competitive examination.

[23] As reported by Bellivier, p. 131 referred to above.

[24] As reported by Bellivier, p. 137 referred to above.

by Bellivier, Poincaré and Jules de la Gournerie (1814-1883), examiner in stereonomy[25], quarrelled[26] over a mathematical question. Ossian Bonnet[27] (1819-1892), academic dean, summoned Colonel Mannheim to settle the disagreement, but both Poincaré and Gournerie stood their ground. However, because Gournerie and Mannheim[28] were close friends, Poincaré got a 10 in the final examination of stereotomy, and Bonnefoy got a 20.

École Polytechnique.

Concours d'admission en 1873.   Ville d'examen. Nancy

N° du Certificat d'admissibilité. 255

M. Poincarré Jules, Henri

Désignation des Épreuves	N.	n.	P.	N.	n.	p.	S.	Observations
Examens oraux Algèbre. Géométrie analytique	20	52	1040					
Arithmétique. Géom" et Trigonométrie	20	50	1000					
Physique et Chimie	19	40	760					
Langue Allemande	18	8	144					
			2944				2944	
Compositions écrites Composition mathématique				20	15	300		
Composition de Géométrie descriptive				14	13	182		
Résolution de triangle. Calcul logarithmique				17	5	85		
Composition française				14	14	196		
Dessin				12	12	144		
Lavis				1	4	4		
Immunité de 50 points attribuée aux Bacheliers ès-lettres						50	961	1
							3905	

Fig. 2.5   Henri Poincaré's marks at the entrance exam to the École Polytechnique (*A.H.P.*, Nancy).

---

[25] Science on the size and cut of building materials, where descriptive geometry finds its origin.

[26] There are references to this quarrel in Henri Poincaré's correspondence. See the website of Henri Poincaré Archives.

[27] Ossian Bonnet as well was part of the jury for Poincaré's thesis, which was also dedicated to him. See Henri Poincaré, *Sur les propriétés des fonctions définies par les équations aux différences partielles*, Thesis of the Faculty of Sciences in Paris, 1879.

[28] This dispute with Mannheim found a better outcome for Poincaré when he was elected to the Académie.

Coeffi-cients		Poin-carré[1] Jules-Henri	Petit-didier Jules	Bonnefoy Marcel	Appell Paul
	Écrit.				
15	Mathématiques	20	20	13	15
13	Géométrie descriptive .	14	19	19	16
5	Calcul logarithmique. .	17	12	14	17
14	Composition française .	14	14	12	12
12	Dessin.	12	16	15	16
4	Lavis	1	16	16	15
	Oral.				
52	Algèbre, géométrie ana-lytique	20	15	18	16
50	Arithmétique, géomé-trie, trigonométrie . .	20	15	17	18
40	Physique, chimie . . .	19	16	15	18
8	Allemand.	18	17	9	16
	Baccalauréat ès lettres (bonification)	50	—	—	50
	Total	3.905	3.365	3.370	3.568

Fig. 2.6   Henri Poincaré's marks at the outlet exam of the École Polytechnique
(According to Bellivier, p. 116 quoted above).

This episode did not prevent Poincaré from submitting a few months be-fore, his first article to the the Annals of Mathematics. The article entitled "Démonstrations nouvelles des indicatrices d'une surface[29]" was published in October 1874.

As soon as he came out of the École Polytechnique in October 1875, Poincaré got into the École des Mines as indicated in the newspaper *La Presse* on Sunday October 31, 1875:

---

[29]See Henri Poincaré, "Démonstration nouvelle des propriétés de l'indicatrice d'une surface," *Nouvelles annales de mathématiques*, vol. 13, 1874, p. 449-456.   These Nouvelles Annales (new annals) were recently digitized and are available on the site http://numdam.org

École Polytechnique
2ᵉ Division
1873/74.

Classement général de fin d'année.

M. Poincaré

Cours.	Indication des épreuves diverses subies par l'élève sur les matières de chaque cours	Numéro de mérite obtenu sous chaque matière épreuve	Coefficient d'influence calculé à chaque matière épreuve	Nombre de points obtenu chaque matière 3 quasés	Nombre total de points obtenu chaque matière 3 épreuve	Observations
Analyse	Interrogation particulière	14	15	225	} 225	
	Interrogation générale	20	15	200		
Mécanique	Interrogations particulières	14 14	15		} 30	
	Travaux graphiques		8			
Géométrie descriptive	Interrogations particulières	11 60	10	116		
	Interrogation générale	19	10	190	} 494	
	Travaux graphiques	12 80	10	128		
Physique	Interrogation particulière	18 33	15		} 274 91	
Chimie	Interrogations particulières	18 24	10	182 6		
	Interrogation générale	20	10	200	} 449 11	
	Manipulations	13 33	8	16 66		
Stéréotomie	Interrogation particulière	18 33	15	274 91	382 91	
	Travaux graphiques	13 10	8	108 2		
Littérature française	Composition	16	12		192	
Langue allemande	Interrogation particulière	19	5	95	} 190	
	Interrogation générale	19	5	95		
Dessin		11 80	10		118 11	
Lavis		11 24	8		40 11	
					3945 86	
Examen de fin d'année.	Analyse	20	30		600	
	Mécanique	18	30		540	
	Géométrie descriptive	16 16	20		330	
	Physique	19	25		475	
	Chimie	19	20		380	
	Stéréotomie	10	25		250	
				Total	6620 86	

Fig. 2.7   Henri Poincaré's rank at the École Polytechnique (*A.H.P.*, Nancy).

"By decree, the three outgoing students of the École Polytechnique whose names follow were appointed engineering students of the third class at the Corps des Mines: MM. Bonnefoy, Poincaré, Petitdidier."

2.4 The École Des Mines – The Thesis

When getting into the École des Mines which was located on Boulevard Saint Michel, in the heart of the Latin Quarter (Paris), Poincaré turned to mathematical research. He planned to juggle his classes at the Mines and a university course. The Director of the School, Gabriel Auguste Daubree (1814-1896), professor of mineralogy, tried to dissuade him from doing so, as can be seen from the letter he wrote to his mother Eugenie shortly before Christmas 1875, and in which he explains:

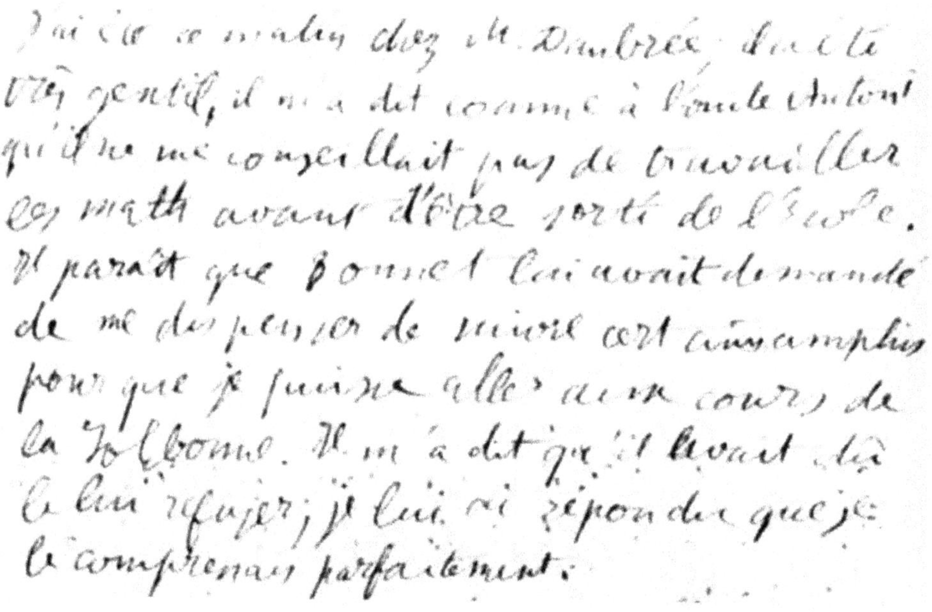
J'ai été ce matin chez M. Daubrée, il a été très gentil, il m'a dit comme à l'oncle Antoni qu'il ne me conseillait pas de travailler les math avant d'être sorti de l'École. Il paraît que Bonnet lui avait demandé de me dispenser de [illegible] pour que je puisse aller aux cours de la Sorbonne. Il m'a dit qu'il avait dû le lui refuser; je lui ai répondu que je le comprenais parfaitement.

Fig. 2.8 Poincaré's letter to his mother (*A.H.P.*, Nancy).

"I was this morning at Mr. Daubrée; he was very nice; he told me, as he told Uncle Antoni, that I shouldn't work on the math before I left the School. Apparently Bonnet had asked him to excuse me from following certain lectures so that I could go to courses at the Sorbonne. He told me he had to refuse; I told him that I totally understood."

Poincaré took classes at the École des Mines without caring about the ranking[30]. In parallel, he prepared a Bachelor of Science at the Sorbonne that he submitted on August 2, 1876. Once he got his degree, he turned to the PhD, but he first had to take two study trips abroad as required by the regulations of the School.

He then went to Austria-Hungary in the summer of 1877 with his classmate Leon Lecornu (1854-1940) and wrote two memoirs (now lost): one on the exploitation of the coal mines of the Staatsbahn in Hungary and the other on the metallurgy of tin in Banat. The following year, he went to Sweden with Marcel Bonnefoy[31], then to Norway, and wrote two other memoirs, lost as well, on mining in the Scandinavian countries.

It was during this second year at the École des Mines that he began to write a thesis at the Faculty of Science in Paris. It seems that he chose the subject of the thesis after reading a memoir[32] by Briot and Bouquet[33] entitled: "Recherches sur les propriétés des fonctions définies par des équations différentielles" (Research on the properties of functions defined by differential equations), which inspired him. He submitted his thesis in the course of the year in 1879 and defended it at the Faculty of Sciences in Paris on the 1st of August, 1879, before an examination board composed of MM. Jean-Claude Bouquet (foreman), Ossian Bonnet and Gaston Darboux[34](examiners). Having come in third of the year in the School (see Fig. 2.10 & 2.9), he was appointed inspector of mines in charge of the mineralogical sub-district of Vesoul, located in the Franche-Comté region of Eastern France.

Note in this transcript (Fig. 2.9) that the name of Poincaré is once again spelled with a 'y'. His classification is indicated in the bottom margin.

---

[30] He is now third behind Petitdider and Bonnefoy, as reported by Appell, p. 29 referred to above.

[31] He was killed on May 30, 1881 by a firedamp explosion during the inspection of a mine shaft in Champagnac.

[32] As reported by Bellivier, p. 181 referred to above.

[33] Charles Briot and Jean-Claude Bouquet, "Recherches sur les propriétés des fonctions définies par des équations différentielles," *Journal of the École Polytechnique*, the 36th book, vol. XXI, 1856, p. 133-198.

[34] At the entrance exam to the École Normale Supérieure in 1873, it was Darboux who was the examiner to Poincaré's oral test in mathematics and gave him the mark 19 out of 20. See Bellivier, p. 118 referred to above.

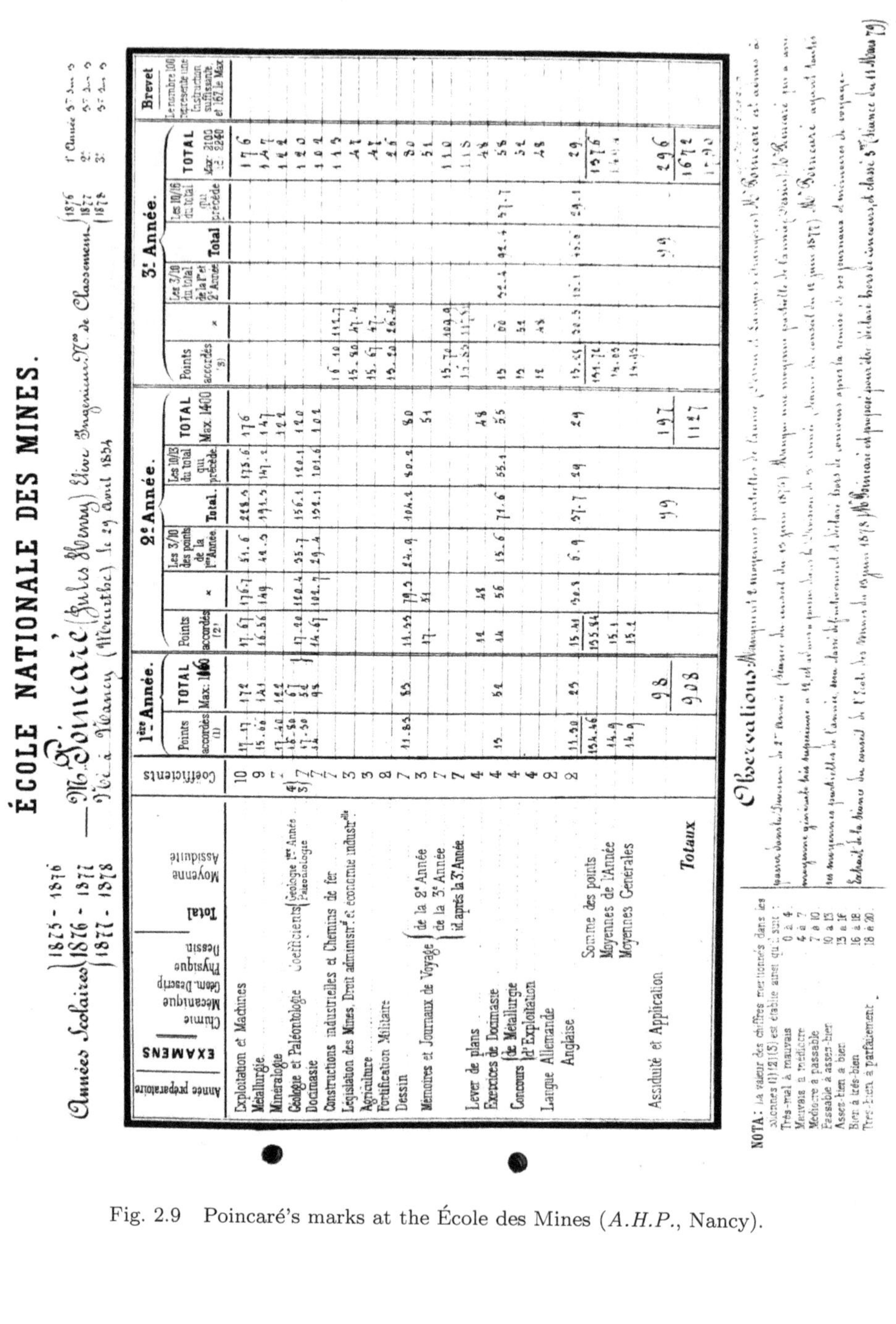

ÉCOLE NATIONALE DES MINES.

Années Scolaires 1875 - 1876, 1876 - 1877, 1877 - 1878 — Mr Poincaré (Jules Henry) Élève Ingénieur. Nos de Classement 1876 1e Année 3e ..., 1877 2e 3e ..., 1878 3e 3e ...

Né à Nancy (Meurthe) le 29 Avril 1854

EXAMENS (Année préparatoire: Chimie, Mécanique, Géom. Descrip, Physique, Dessin, Total, Moyenne, Assiduité)	Coefficients	1re Année Points accordés (1)	1re Année TOTAL Max: 1160	2e Année Points accordés (2)	×	Les 3/10 des points de la 1re Année	Total.	Les 10/13 du total qui précède	TOTAL Max. 1400	3e Année Points accordés (3)	×	Les 3/10 du total de la 1re et 2e Année	Total	Les 10/16 du total qui précède	TOTAL Max: 2100 id: 2240	Brevet (Le nombre 100 représente une instruction suffisante, et 167 le Max)
Exploitation et Machines	10	17.17	172	17.67	176.7	51.6	228.3	175.6	176						176	
Métallurgie	9	15.66	141	16.56	149	42.3	191.3	147.2	147						147	
Minéralogie	7	17.40	122						122						122	
Géologie et Paléontologie (Coefficients: Géologie 1re Année 4, Paléontologie 3)	7	15.80 / 17.50	67 / 52	17.20	120.4	35.7	156.1	120.1	120						120	
Docimasie	7	14	98	14.67	102.7	29.4	132.1	101.6	102						102	
Constructions industrielles et Chemins de fer	7									16.10	112.7				113	
Législation des Mines, Droit administr.f et économie industr.elle	3									15.80	47.4				47	
Agriculture	3									15.67	47.				47	
Fortification Militaire	8									13.20	26.4				26	
Dessin	7	11.83	83	11.33	79.3	24.9	104.2	80.2	80						80	
Mémoires et Journaux de Voyage de la 2e Année	3			17.	51				51						51	
de la 3e Année	7									15.70	109.9				110	
id. après la 3e Année	7									16.85	117.9				118	
Lever de plans	4			12	48				48						48	
Exercices de Docimasie	4	13	52	14	56	15.6	71.6	55.1	55	15	60	32.4	92.4	57.7	58	
Concours de Métallurgie	4									13	52				52	
Concours d'Exploitation	4									12	48				48	
Langue Allemande	2															
Langue Anglaise	2	11.50	23	15.41	30.8	6.9	37.7	29	29	15.25	30.5	10.1	40.6	25.1	29	
Somme des points		154.46		155.84						141.72					1576	
Moyennes de l'Année		14.9		15.1						14.05					1494	
Moyennes Générales		14.9		15.1						14.45						
Assiduité et Application			98				99		197				99		296	
Totaux			908						1127						1672 / 1790	

NOTA: La valeur des chiffres mentionnés dans les colonnes (1) (2) (3) est établie ainsi qu'il suit :

Très-mal à mauvais	0 à 4
Mauvais à médiocre	4 à 7
Médiocre à passable	7 à 10
Passable à assez-bien	10 à 13
Assez-bien à bien	13 à 16
Bien à très-bien	16 à 18
Très-bien à parfaitement	18 à 20

Observations: Manquent 2 moyennes partielles de l'année (Dessin et Langues étrangères). Mr Poincaré est admis à passer dans la Division de 2e année (Séance du conseil du 15 juin 1876). Manque une moyenne partielle de l'année (Dessin). Mr Poincaré qui a une moyenne générale très supérieure à 12, est admis à passer dans la Division de 3e année (Séance du conseil du 12 juin 1877). Mr Poincaré ayant toutes ses moyennes partielles de l'année, sera classé définitivement et déclaré hors de concours après la remise de ses journaux et mémoires de voyage. Extrait de la séance du conseil de l'École des Mines du 13 juin 1878. Mr Poincaré est proposé pour être déclaré hors de concours, et classé 3e (Séance du 11 Mars 79)

Fig. 2.9 Poincaré's marks at the École des Mines (*A.H.P.*, Nancy).

Fig. 2.10 Henri Poincaré at the École des Mines (*A.H.P.*, Nancy).

Chapter 3

Inspector of Mines in Vesoul

Native of the Lorraine Basin, Henri Poincaré was thus inspector of mines in Vesoul for a very short time (eight months in 1879). He was therefore in the French department that was the closest to the Meurthe department where he was born. It became the Meurthe et Moselle in 1871 and remained French when a part of Alsace and Lorraine was annexed by the Germans at the end of the Franco-Prussian War of 1870-1871. This was Poincaré's first appointment and thus the beginning of his professional life.

For the centenary of his birth, in 1954, Maurice Roy and René Dugas recounted in detail this aspect of his career[1]. Roy and Dugas spoke of "the conscientiousness with which he fulfilled the duties of his office." Indeed, although Henri Poincaré was an engineer in charge of supervising and ensuring the smooth running of the mines near Vesoul, especially the mine of Ronchamp, he did not hesitate to lower himself into the wells where he regularly and accurately took notes. Roy and Dugas wrote:

> "It should be noted that Poincaré has continued throughout his life, to belong to the Corps des Mines, while sent on secondment at the Sorbonne and the École Polytechnique for his teaching functions. Thus, he was appointed chief engineer on July 22, 1893 and Inspector General on June 16, 1910."

It is true that such a course – secondment from the Corps des Mines to which one belongs for his whole career – is not uncommon. But in the case of Poincaré, his experience during the eight months he spent in Vesoul, as well as his writings about it over thirty years later, show that this was not simply formal or institutional to him. He was deeply affected by the explosion at the well of Magny on September 1st, 1879, that resulted in

---

[1] Available for consultation on http://www.annales.org/archives/x/poinca2.html# roy.

"9 widows and 35 orphans" according to the professional and detailed report he wrote at the time. He used the words of an expert, although he did let his emotions show in his writing, as can be seen from these few lines:

> "It was unfortunately very certain that we would find nothing but corpses, for the state of the first victims we discovered left us no doubt in this regard. What was most urgent was to get the draft back, by replacing the destroyed doors by dams. We did not restore them under the same conditions as before the accident because the workers had to stand in the assembly, which therefore had to be carefully ventilated. (...) Rescuers continued to walk forward as the restoration of ventilation allowed them, and they found another two corpses. But they were soon stopped by a landslide that obstructed the assembly at the seventh crosspiece and needed clearing. After this operation, we were able to get to the top of the ramp, where we discovered the bodies of the five unfortunate workers[2]"

During those eight months in Vesoul, Henri Poincaré could then experience the reality of the dangers and the working conditions of miners. Being an engineer did not shelter him from these risks. Marcel Bonnefoy, appointed inspector of mines along with Poincaré, as seen above, was not as lucky as him: on May 30, 1881, in identical circumstances that occurred in the mines of Champagnac, he succumbed to a second gas blast that fired when he was inspecting the damage caused by the accident that had just happened.

To show how traumatized he was by the Magny accident (and certainly by Bonnefoy's death as well two years later), it was interesting to read the chapter devoted to mining that Henri Poincaré wrote in 1910 in the magazine *Au seuil de la vie*, which was intended for the children of upper primary schools. Asked by the publisher Hachette to write five texts on science, he imposed this mining chapter which was *a priori* far from the subject of *Ce que disent les choses* (the section he was supposed to write for). In 1911, Hachette published a book called *Ce que disent les choses* out of this section. Besides Poincaré's commitment for popularizing science for children, one can find in there some personal traces of his earlier traumatic experiences. He insisted, in particular, on the dangers of firedamp explosions, on how useful the Davy lamp is, and some passages of the text were full of an emotion that one could feel was engrained in him for a long time.

---

[2]The statement is reproduced in its entirety on the Annals of Mines website: `http://www.annales.org/`.

Fig. 3.1   Well of Magny.

His text was very clear from the start. His description of the drillings made to find deposits was extremely detailed when it came to the composition and working of a drill bit.

This applied to the passages on wells and on the pumps used for their drying as well (and even the freezing technique of wet sand), and to his description of the construction of galleries, the general plan of a mine, the methods of excavation (blasting, sinking), the timbering and backfilling.

In the part of his text entitled "Le roulage et l'extraction" (the rolling and extraction), he puts us in the position of visitors: "here we are, at the bottom of the well, we must now go back to the top." It feels as if he was remembering his own explorations in the mines of St. Charles, St. Pauline, St. Joseph, Magny, etc.. in 1879: it is even probable that he re-read the notes he wrote about them, as well as his long expert's report after the Magny accident. Human intervention was mentioned ceaselessly, along with its harsh conditions, the dangers, the division of labor, and even the performance-related pay:

"The workers are forced to work while lying on their side" ("Ce qu'on retire des mines"); "Sometimes you have to lower

Fig. 3.2   Davy lamp.

some cast iron tubes into the hole to stabilize the grounds and prevent them from caving" ("Comment on découvre une mine"), "workers have to work with water up to their knees" ("Les puits"), "Even in the biggest galleries, you must be careful not to bump into the frameworks, for they are high enough for a horse, but not for a man"("Comment on abat la houille"), "the worker must constantly keep an eye on his roof; whenever a crack appears, he puts wood patches on it. If he doesn't put enough of them, he might get killed, and if he puts too many of them, he wastes his time, he doesn't cut down enough coal and is not paid enough" ("Boisage et remblayage"); we load it in trucks that young workers push on small railroads" and "We have to prevent the disasters that would occur if the cable broke down while the workers lowered themselves into the well" ("Le roulage et l'extraction"); "One of the minor's enemies is water" ("L'épuisement des eaux"); "the mines have to be ventilated; to allow the workers to work in a breathable air, but mostly to progressively remove the firedamp, as it emerges from the coal" ("L'aérage").

He praised the lamp invented by Davy nearly a century earlier, in 1816, and which bears his name; he roughly described how it works. Thanks to this lamp, there was an important diminution of the firedamp explosions caused by the lighting in the galleries: as he said, not only does the wire that surround the lamp prevent "a great flame that fills it entirely" from getting out, but he failed to mention that in addition to that, a change in the color of the flame can prevent an explosion, for this change indicates a high concentration of firedamp in the surrounding air. This invention was of great benefit in the XIXth century, at the time of the industrialization. Indeed, mine mortality due to firedamp – which had become unbearable at the beginning of the century – immediately fell, and coal production rapidly increased.

But if Poincaré so strongly praised the vital interest of this object – illustrated in the very first paragraph of his chapter on mines – it is certainly in memory of his 1879 report, where he concluded that the lamp no. 476 was damaged because of a human error, which caused the explosion, according to his assessment.

> "We should naturally suspect the lamp 476 that was found in that place to be responsible for the gas ignition and the disaster. The state of the lamp radically confirms these suspicions. Indeed, the tear we can observe at the bottom of the metal cylinder is very clear and its shape, like its dimensions, reminds us of the pickaxe section of the workers, so that no minor, when seeing it, has hesitated to recognize a pickaxe stroke. We did not encounter any collapse in the neighborhood that could make us suppose that the hole was produced by the shock of a stone falling from the roof. The lamp has not been violently thrown, which would explain this degradation, for it was found hanging from a timber."

Poincaré had probably read Zola. But what is certain is that his visit at the Magny well had profoundly marked him, and he indirectly spoke of it in a very humane and apprehensive way in the last section (entitled "Les accidents") of the chapter written for children. Besides, the main illustration of this text was also a superb anonymous drawing representing academically (for the time), yet realistically, a firedamp explosion. The illustration is reminiscent of this extract from Germinal, chapter IV, seventh book:

> "No doubt Zacharie, infuriate with the feeble vacillating light, which delayed his work, committed the imprudence of opening

his lamp, although severe orders had been given for leakages of firedamp had taken place, and the gas remained in enormous masses in these narrow, unventilated passages. Suddenly, a roar of thunder was heard, and a spout of fire darted out of the tube as from the mouth of a cannon charged with grapeshot. Everything flamed up and the air caught fire like powder, from one end of the galleries to the other. This torrent of flame carried away the captain and three workers, ascended the pit, and leapt up to the daylight in an eruption which split the rocks and the ruins around."

An extract from Zola's description that can be compared to the description given by Poincaré himself in the latter part of his 1910 text reads:

"...there is an explosive mixture of firedamp and air that fills the whole atmosphere of the mine and even the workers' lungs. It only takes one spark to ignite the mixture, and I give up on trying to describe the horrors that follow: hundreds of unfortunate men killed instantly by the explosion, while others, even more miserable, horribly burned and surviving for a few hours of a few days; others asphyxiated by the combustion products."

It is quite understandable then that this sad experience led Poincaré to really insist about the dangers of the mine in this. He obviously mainly spoke about the firedamp explosions, be he did not forget to mention all "other accidents" that the miners had to face: landslides, delayed explosions, floods. Roy and Dugas described:

"Poincaré shows that he had never stopped feeling concerned about the issue of mine safety, for in this article, he outlines the danger of dust, which was still unknown at the time he was in Vesoul: "There are mines where there are no firedamp; it is not safe yet though; sometimes the atmosphere is filled with some fine dust, and that dust, when it is mixed with air, can cause explosions just as gas does"."

In any case, the still vivid memory of his career as a mine inspector in Vesoul thirty years before, as well as his way of expressing it in a publication meant for children, is another demonstration of his profound humanism.

PART 2

The Professor and the Savant

The scientist does not study nature because it is useful to do so. He studies
it because he takes pleasure in it, and he takes pleasure in it because it is
beautiful. If nature were not beautiful it would not be worth knowing, and
life would not be worth living.

— H. Poincaré —

Chapter 4

From the University of Caen to the Sorbonne

On November 19, 1879, Henri Poincaré sent a letter[1] to Charles Freycinet (1828-1923), then Minister of Public Works, in which he sought a detachment of the Mines Department and a provision of the Department of Public Instruction in order to obtain the chair of "Calcul Différentiel et Intégral" at the Faculty of Science of Caen (Normandy). The answer came quickly and Poincaré was appointed lecturer at the Faculty of Science of Caen on December 1, 1879. However, he had to stay in Vesoul until the 12th of December to stand in for his successor, and waiting for him to take over. Thus, he arrived in Caen no earlier than the middle of December. He was then much more concerned about his mathematical research than his teachings as underlined in a confidential report by the new director of education of the Académie, Charles Capmas (1818-1898):

> "Mr. Poincaré is a very deserving mathematician, always obsessed with the subject of his research[2]."

4.1 The Discovery of the Fuchsian Functions

It was indeed during that period of time that Poincaré discovered some functions that he named "Fuchsian" and "Kleinian" in tribute to the German mathematicians Lazarus Fuchs (1833-1902) and Felix Klein (1849-1925) with whom he kept up a very active correspondence. While Fuchs seemed somewhat taken aback by how quick Poincaré was to establish this result, Klein was much more reluctant to see his functions being given the name of Fuchs, even if Poincaré wrote in a letter dated June 15, 1881:

---

[1] This letter is stored at the Archives Nationales.
[2] As reported by Appell, p. 34 referred to above.

"Sir,

Your letter shows me that you were the first to find some of the results I obtained in the theory of the Fuchsian functions. I am not at all surprised, for I know how much you know about the non-Euclidian geometry which is the real key to the problem we are dealing with. I will do you justice in this regard the day I will publish your results."

But apparently, Klein was not satisfied with this answer. The fact that Poincaré first credited Fuchs with the discovery made Klein question its legitimacy. The correspondence became aggressive and Poincaré wrote to Klein in a letter dated June 22, 1881:

"As for the name of the Fuchsian functions, I will not change it. The consideration I have for Mr. Fuchs does not allow me to do so. Moreover, it is true that the views of the geometrician scientist from Heidelberg is completely different from yours and mine, it is also certain that his work provided the starting point and basis for everything that has been done since in this theory. It is therefore only fair that his name remains linked to these functions which play such an important role in all this work."

The controversy reached its climax when Klein, having accepted to publish an article by Poincaré in *Mathematische Annalen*, added a footnote at the end of it in which he wrote:

"Einmal nämlich bewegen sich alle die Untersuchungen, welche Hr Schwarz und ich in der betreffenden Richtung bislang veröffentlicht haben, auf dem Gebiete der "fonctions fuchsiennes", über die Hr Fuchs selbst nirgends publicirt hat[3]."

Poincaré reacted very strongly to this "slipped" addendum without his knowing at the end of his article in a letter to Klein on March 30, 1882:

"You have lately been kind enough to have my work on the uniform functions that reproduce by linear substitutions inserted in the *Mathematische Annalen* (Vol. XIX, p. 553-564) and you had it followed with a note in which you expose the reasons why

---

[3]See Henri Poincaré, "Sur les Fonctions Uniformes qui se reproduisent par des Substitutions Linéaires," *Mathematische Annalen*, XIX, 1882, p. 553-564:

"And one day, all the research findings that Mr. Schwarz and myself had published up to now in this field, are gathered under the name of "Fuchsian functions", which are functions on which Mr. Fuchs himself has never published anything, anywhere."

you find the names I gave to these transcendental functions unsuitable. Let me say a few words to defend these names which were not randomly chosen[4]."

He finally closes the debate with his letter on April 4, 1882 in which he wrote:

"If I gave your name to the Kleinian functions, it is for the reasons I already mentioned, and not, as you insinuate, zur Entschädigung; for I don't have to compensate you for anything; I will be willing to accept an ownership as prior to mine only when you will be able to show me that the discontinuity of groups and the uniformity of functions in an ever so slightly general case were studied before, and that a series-expansion was drawn from these functions."

These findings, which "gave Poincaré the keys to the algebra world[5]", were seen after the Franco-Prussian War (see above) as a victory of French science over the German Schools of Göttingen and Berlin[6]. These exchanges of letters highlight the intellectual honesty that Poincaré has shown throughout his life. Indeed, when he presented a note to the *Comptes Rendus hebdomadaire des séances de l'Académie des Sciences* "Sur la dynamique de l'électron" ("On the dynamics of the electron")[7] on June 5, 1905, in which he introduced a transformation of coordinates which leaves the equations of the electromagnetic field invariant, he gives the name of transformation de Lorentz (Lorentz transformation):

"The importance of the issue made me decide to take it over; the results I obtained are in accord with those of Lorentz on all important points; I only had to modify and complete them in a few minor points. The essential point, established by Lorentz, is that the equations of the electromagnetic field are not altered by a certain transformation (which I will call transformation of Lorentz) ...[8]"

---

[4] See *Acta Mathematica*, vol. 39, (1923), p. 118 and Bellivier, p. 207 referred to above. At Poincaré's request, that letter was published in full in *Mathematische Annalen*, XX, 1882, p. 52 to 53.

[5] According to mathematician George Humbert (1859-1921), see Bellivier, p. 208 and Appell, p. 44 referred to above.

[6] During Henri Poincaré's inaugural speech at the Académie française on January 28, 1909, Frederic Masson talked about "kidnapping". See below.

[7] See Henri Poincaré, "Sur la dynamique de l'électron," *CRAS*, June 5, 1905, vol. 140, p. 1504 to 1508.

[8] *Ibid.*

Later, Poincaré told the story of his discovery of the "Fuchsian functions" himself, in a chapter of his book Science and Method[9].

When the book was published in 1908, the newspaper *The San Francisco Sunday Call*, summed the story up in an article published on November 29, 1908:

THE SOURCE OF INSPIRATION

"INSPIRATION is generally the result of a preliminary effort." So says a recent French writer, discussing some remarkable autobiographical passages from an article by Henri Poincare, the eminent French mathematician.

Almost every one has noticed that after long and fruitless mental effort the result after which one has been striving will come to him suddenly while he is thinking of something else. The preliminary mental work has borne its fruit subconsciously.

Poincare reports that many of his most abstruse mathematical discoveries have come to him in just this way. Once, after working on a difficult problem for two weeks, the solution came to him spontaneously at night while he was trying to get to sleep; another came to him while he was entering an omnibus, his mind apparently remote from all mathematical thoughts. Again an important conclusion forced itself upon him "with brevity, suddenness and immediate certitude" while he was resting on the sea beach after a long period of apparently futile cogitation.

The striking part of all this is the appearance of spontaneous illumination, which may be taken as the sign of long subconscious deliberation. Experiences of the kind would appear to be very common with mathematicians, and, indeed, with all whose work requires long periods of mental concentration.

Fig. 4.1   *The San Francisco Sunday Call* of November 29, 1908.

"For a fortnight I had been attempting to prove that there could not be any function analogous to what I have since called Fuchsian functions. I was at that time very ignorant. Every day I sat down at my table and spent an hour or two trying a great number of combinations, and I arrived at no result. One night I took some black coffee, contrary to my custom, and was unable

---

[9]See Henri Poincaré, *Science et Méthode*, dans la collection "Bibliothèque de Philosophie scientifique" de Gustave Le Bon, Flammarion, Paris, 1908, p. 50 et suivantes. See Henri Poincaré, *Science et Méthode*, in the series "Bibliothèque de Philosophie scientifique" of Gustave Le Bon, Flammarion, Paris, 1908, p. 50 and following.

to sleep. A host of ideas kept surging in my head; I could almost feel them jostling one another, until two of them coalesced, so to speak, to form a stable combination. When morning came, I had established the existence of one class of Fuchsian functions, those that are derived from the hypergeometric series. I had only to verify the results, which only took a few hours. Then I wished to represent these functions by the quotient of two series. This idea was perfectly conscious and deliberate; I was guided by the analogy with elliptical functions. I asked myself what must be the properties of these series, if they existed, and I succeeded without difficulty in forming the series that I have called Theta-Fuchsian. At this moment I left Caen, where I was then living, to take part in a geological conference arranged by the School of Mines. The incidents of the journey made me forget my mathematical work. When we arrived at Coutances, we got into a break to go for a drive, and, just as I put my foot on the step, the idea came to me, though nothing in my former thoughts seemed to have prepared me for it, that the transformations I had used to define Fuchsian functions were identical with those of non-Euclidian geometry. I made no verification, and had no time to do so, since I took up the conversation again as soon as I had sat down in the break, but I felt absolute certainty at once. When I got back to Caen I verified the result at my leisure to satisfy my conscience."

In 1880, the competition subject given by the Académie des Sciences for the "Grand Prix des Sciences mathématiques" was presented as follows: Perfectionner en quelque point important la théorie des équations différentielles linéaires à une seule variable indépendante (Perfect in one major point the theory of linear differential equations with one independent variable). Poincaré submitted an anonymous dissertation under the motto of his hometown: *non inultus premor* (see Fig. 4.2 & 4.4).

Although Henri Poincaré did not get the Grand Prix (awarded to George Halphen[10]), the rapporteur of the mathematics price, Edmond Becquerel[11], praised the work of the young mathematician.

---

[10]Mathematician Georges Halphen (1844-1889) was Poincaré's tutor at the École Polytechnique.

[11]Edmond Becquerel (1820-1891) belonged to a famous family of physicists and mathematicians. His son Henri Becquerel (1852-1908) discovered radioactivity. After discovering polonium and radium along with Pierre Curie (1859-1906) and Marie Curie (1867-1934), he shared the Nobel Prize in Physics with them in 1903.

Fig. 4.2   Poincaré's dissertation for the Grand Prix de mathématiques 1880
(*Archives Académie des Sciences*, Paris).

Between 1879 and 1880, Poincaré had in fact sent five papers to the
Académie des Sciences[12], which shows how enthusiastic he was for his mathematical research while taking on his studies and his job as an Inspector of
mines:

- Sur quelques propriétés des formes quadratiques (On some properties of quadratic forms)[13]
- Sur les formes quadratiques (On quadratic forms)[14]
- Sur les courbes définies par une équation différentielle (On the
  curves defined by a differential equation)[15]
- Sur les formes cubiques ternaires (On ternary cubic forms)[16],
- Sur la réduction simultanée d'une forme quadratique et d'une forme
  linéaire. (On the simultaneous reduction of a quadratic form and
  a linear form.)[17]

---

[12]See   http://www.academie-sciences.fr/activite/archive/dossiers/Poincare/
Poin_publi.htm.
[13]*Comptes rendus hebdomadaires de l'Académie des sciences*, T.89 (1879), p. 344-346.
[14]*Ibid.* T.89 (1879) p. 897-903.
[15]*Ibid.* T.90 (1880) p. 673-675.
[16]*Ibid.* T.90 (1880) p. 1336-1339.
[17]*Ibid.* T.91 (1880) p. 844-847.

On October 19, 1881, Henri Poincaré was appointed lecturer at the Faculty of Sciences in Paris by ministerial order, filling in for Guillaume Lemonnier-Hippolyte (1820-1882) who was then lecturer for the mathematical analysis class of the Faculty of sciences in Caen. On April 20, 1881, while he was staying in Normandy, Poincaré married Louise Poulain d'Andecy (see Fig. 4.3), who was the great-granddaughter of the naturalist étienne Geoffroy Saint-Hilaire (1772-1844).

Fig. 4.3   Louise Poulain d'Andecy (1857-1934) (*A.H.P.*, Nancy).

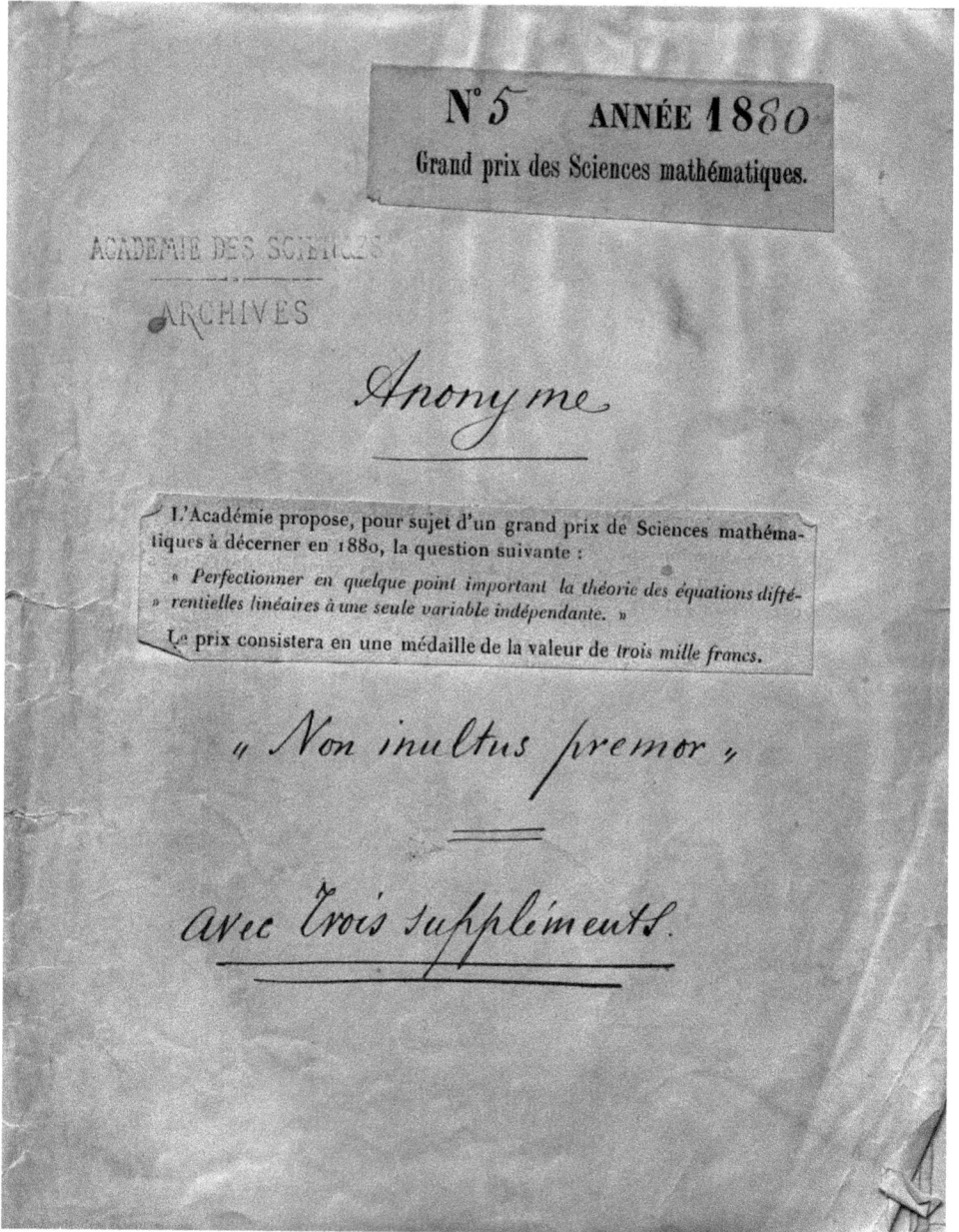

Fig. 4.4   Poincaré's dissertation for the Grand Prix de mathématiques 1880 (*Archives Académie des Sciences*, Paris).

Chapter 5

From the Sorbonne to the Académie

Henri Poincaré arrived in mid-December 1879 at the Faculty of Sciences in Caen, met Léon Lecornu – one of his classmates from the École Polytechnique and the École des Mines – as we have already mentioned, who then invited him for Christmas Eve. Later, Lecornu described the evening as follows:

> "At that time, he was more distracted than ever. I had invited him to have supper at my parents' on December 31, 1879, and I can still see him spending the evening walking back and forth, not hearing what he was told or barely replying in monosyllables, and forgetting what time it was, so much so that after midnight, I decided to gently remind him that we were in 1880. At that moment he seemed to come down to earth, and decided to take leave from us. A few days later, he met me on the port quay in Caen, and he casually said: I know now how to integrate all the differential equations. The Fuchsian functions were just born, and I knew then what he was thinking about when going from 1879 to 1880[1]."

A quarter of a century later, the newspaper *Le Figaro* of March 4, 1903 echoed this attitude.

Fig. 5.1   *Le Figaro* of March, 4, 1903.

---

[1] As reported by Appell, p. 33 and Bellivier, p. 215 referred to above.

Indeed, in an article dedicated to the geometric concerns of Minister Charles Freycinet (see above), the journalist wrote:

> "One is always surprised to see a man of action concerned with ideology: we meet indeed with so many men of action with so little powers of thinking! And on the other hand, how many thinkers live in the midst of realities as if they did not exist! Have you ever dined with Mr. Poincaré, the prodigious mathematician? It is marvelous to see how he ignores his soup and continues his terrible meditations where the food has absolutely no place. This brilliant mind lives beyond the sensible world."

The newspaper *The Advertiser* of November, 6, 1912 reported on Poincaré's absent-minded:

Fig. 5.2   *The Advertiser* of November, 6, 1912.

> "The late M. Henri Poincaré, the eminent French scientist was incorrigibly absent-minded. When, as a young graduate he went on his travels, his mother, knowing his weakness, furnished his pocket book with bells, which might serve to attract his attention when he dropped it, as she was sure he would. The great mathematician did, indeed, bring back his pocket-book, but he brought back something else, viz. a bed cover which he had carefully folded and placed in his port-manteau, under the impression that it was one of his shirts. One day when he reached his home, M. Poincaré was surprised to find that he was carrying a wicker-work cage in his hand. Returning by the way he had come, he discovered a gap in the goods displayed by a basket-maker, which his cage, when replaced, admirably filled. When he was received into the Académie Française M. Frederic Masson prophesied that these fits of abstraction would one day be as famous as those of Newton and of Kant."

Poincaré's distraction has since become legendary. Nevertheless, Adolf Bühl, (1878-1949) who defended a thesis in 1901 at the Faculty of Sciences in Paris entitled *Sur les équations différentielles simultanées et la forme aux dérivées partielles adjointe* ("On the simultaneous differential equations and

the form with attached partial derivatives") before the jury composed of
Gaston Darboux, Henri Poincaré and Paul Appell, wrote as follows:

> "Why focus on the distractions of a brilliant mind when it is
> obvious that they are out of this mind; what should rather
> be offered to public admiration is the work produced by this
> intelligent man when he happened to lose consciousness of the
> vulgar world. I can easily imagine that such a man must often
> have the feeling that he was nothing but a thought[2]."

Poincaré's production was considerable during this period of time (1879-
1887). He published three monographs (his course called *Cinématique et
Mécanique des Fluides* and the one called *Théorie du Potentiel* professed
at the Faculty of Sciences in Paris) and submitted more than a hundred
notes to the *Comptes rendus hebdomadaire des séances de l'Académie des
sciences (C.R.A.S.)*. Thus, Poincaré literally invaded the mathematical
scene of his time by flooding most journals like the *Journal de l'École Polytechnique*, the *Journal de mathématiques pures et appliquées*, the *Bulletin
de la Société mathématique de France* ... with papers and articles in which
he addressed the most various issues. He consistently provided answers to
all specific questions, and thus initiated some unsuspected perspective that
later generated loads of research. It would obviously be futile to try to
recount the importance of his contributions in just a line.

5.1 The Discovery of a *Terra Incognita*

However, among the many subjects addressed, one of them seems to con-
stitute a base to focus one's research on: that of the differential equations.
In 1880, his memoir on the Fuchsian functions for the Grand Prix des Sciences mathématiques led him to lay the basis for a general theory of the
automorphic functions, allowing him, among other things, to integrate the
linear differential equations with algebraic coefficients. From 1881 to 1886,
he published a series of four memoirs entitled "Sur les courbes définies par
une équation différentielle" (On curves defined by an differential equation[3])

---

[2]See Appell, p. 90, referred to above.
[3]See Henri Poincaré, "Sur les courbes définies par une équation différentielle," *Journal
de mathématiques pures et appliquées*, (III) 7, 1881, p. 375-422, Henri Poincaré, "Sur
les courbes définies par une équation différentielle," *Journal de mathématiques pures et
appliquées*, (III) 8, 1882, p. 251-296, Henri Poincaré, "Sur les courbes définies par une
équation différentielle," *Journal de mathématiques pures et appliquées*, (IV) 1, 1885,

which are the foundations for what was to become the *Théorie des Oscillations Non Linéaires* (Nonlinear Oscillations Theory) then the *Théorie des Systèmes Dynamiques* (Dynamical Systems Theory.) In these memoirs, of which one extract[4] was first presented at the 22nd of March session at the Académie des Sciences in 1880, Poincaré wrote about the nonlinear differential equations[5] for which a solution can generally be obtained only through the series-expansion method.

It then put forward a new approach, consisting of "constructing the curve defined by a differential equation" and making it a geometric study[6] he called "qualitative". When writing a note on his own scientific work[7] in 1886, in order to submit an application to the Académie des Sciences, he stressed the importance of this study in a field where he would soon be distinguishing himself:

> "Besides, this qualitative study will be of first-rate interest itself. Several very important issues of Analysis and Mechanics can indeed be related to it. Let's take for example the three body problem: can we not wonder if the distance between two bodies will increase or decrease endlessly, or if it will remain within certain limits? Can we not ask ourselves a thousand questions of this kind, that will all be solved when the way to qualitatively construct the trajectories of the three bodies will have been figured out? And, if we consider a larger number of bodies, what is the issue regarding the invariability of the planets' elements, but a real qualitative geometry issue, since showing that the major axis has no secular variation is showing that it constantly oscillates within certain limits? That is the range of discoveries that opens before the geometricians[8]."

A few years later, he clarified once more his vision of the problem when he wrote an analysis of his work in 1901, which was requested by mathe-

---

p. 167-244, Henri Poincaré, "Sur les courbes définies par une équation différentielle," *Journal de mathématiques pures et appliquées*, (IV) 2, 1886, p. 151-217.

[4]See Henri Poincaré, "Sur les courbes définies par une équation différentielle," *CRAS* (*Comptes rendus hebdomadaire des séances de l'Académie des Sciences*), April 24, 1880, vol. 90, p. 673-675.

[5]They are either equations with terms of degree superior to one or transcendental functions.

[6]See Christian Gilain, *La théorie géométrique des équations différentielles de Poincaré et l'histoire de l'analyse*, PhD Thesis, Université de Paris I, 1977.

[7]See Henri Poincaré, *Notice sur les Travaux Scientifiques de Henri Poincaré*, Paris : Gauthier-Villars, 1886.

[8]*Ibid.*

matician Gösta Mittag-Leffler (1846-1927) and would only be published in the journal *Acta Mathematica* after the end of the First World War.

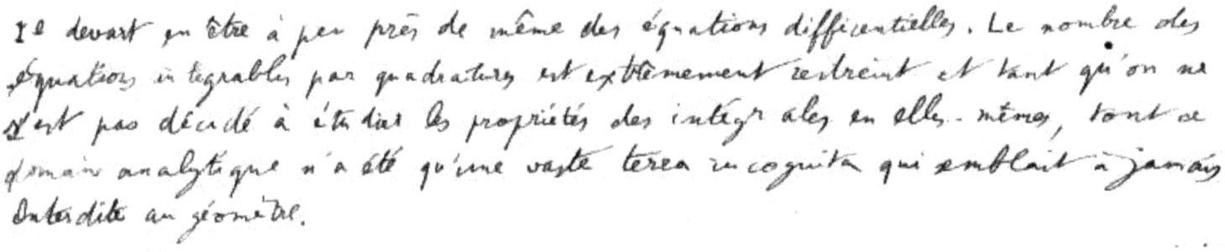
Il devait en être à peu près de même des équations différentielles. Le nombre des équations intégrables par quadratures est extrêmement restreint et tant qu'on ne s'est pas décidé à étudier les propriétés des intégrales en elles-mêmes, tout ce domaine analytique n'a été qu'une vaste terra incognita qui semblait à jamais interdite au géomètre.

Fig. 5.3 Manuscript of the Analysis of Henry Poincaré's Scientific Works (*A.H.P.*, Nancy).

> "It had to be the same for the differential equations too. The number of square-integrable equations is extremely limited and as long as we keep on not studying the integrals' properties in themselves, then all this analytical field was nothing but a vast *terra incognita* from which the geometrician seemed to have been forever banned."

It is in this same mathematical journal in spring 1885 that the announcement of the prize of King Oscar II of Sweden and Norway[9] was made

> "HIS MAJESTY OSCAR II, willing to give another proof of HIS interest in the advancement of the mathematical sciences, and HE has shown such interest before by encouraging the publication of the journal Acta Mathematica which is under HIS august protection, has resolved to reward an important discovery in the field of mathematical analysis with a prize, on the 21st of January 1889, sixtieth anniversary of HIS birth. The award will consist of a medal, of the eighteenth modulus, with the effigy of HIS MAJESTY and having a value in gold of a thousand francs, and of a sum of two thousand and five hundred gold Kronor (1 Krona = about 1 franc 40 cents)[10]."

[9]Many other scientific journals also announced the creation of this award: *Nature* (32, 1885, p. 302-303), *Comptes rendus* (101, 1885, p. 531-533), *Revue scientifique* (36, 1885, p. 318-319), *Giornali di matematiche* (23, 1885, p. 244-246), *Quaterly Journal of Mathematics* (21, 1886, p. 209-212), *Deutsche Litteraturz* (6, 1885, p. 1254-1255), *Astronomische Gesellschaft* (20, 1885, p. 210-213), *Cronica Cientifica* (9, 1886, p. 34-36), ...

[10]See "Mittheilung, einen von Knig Oscar II gestifteten mathematischen Preis betreffend," *Acta Mathematica*, Vol. 7 (1), 1885, p. I-IV.

One of the problems given in the competition was presented as follows:

"Given a system of arbitrarily many mass points which attract each other according to NEWTON's law, try to find, under the assumption that no two pointsever collide, a representation of the coordinates of each point as a series in a variable that is some known function of time and for all of whose values the series converges uniformly. This problem, whose solution would significantly extend our understanding of the solar system, would seem solvable using analytical methods presently at our disposal; we can at least suppose as much, since LEJEUNE-DIRICHLET, communicated shortly before his death to a geometer of his acquaintance, that he had discovered a method for integrating the differential equations of Mechanics, and that by applying this method, he had succeeded in demonstrating the stability of our planetary system in an absolutely rigorous manner. Unfortunately, we know nothing about this method, except that the theory of small oscillations would appear to have served as his point of departure for this discorvery[11]."

The memoirs had to be anonymously submitted (before June 1, 1888) and were then identified by their respective epigraph, as it had been the case for the Grand Prix des Sciences Mathématiques (see above). On May 17, 1888, Poincaré submitted a document with the motto *Nunquam praescriptos transibut sidera* (*The stars will never transcend the predicted limits*) and entitled: *Sur le problème des trois corps et les équations de la dynamique* (On the three body problem and the equations of dynamics). On January 26, 1889, the French mathematician Charles Hermite (1822-1901), who was one of the three members of the Commission[12] responsible for examining the submitted memoirs, wrote to Poincaré to inform him that the prize of King Oscar II of Sweden and Norway had just been awarded to him (see Fig. 5.4).

Two years before, on February 1, 1887, Henri Poincaré was elected at the Académie des Sciences in the Geometry section, in the chair of Edmond Laguerre (1834-1886).

For Poincaré, this election had a taste of revenge, since he was elected in Colonel Amédée Mannheim's place (1831-1906), because of whom he had

---

[11]KUMMER, "Gedächtnissrede auf Lejeune-Dirichlet," Abhandlungen der K. Akademieder Wissenschaften zu Berlin, 1860, p. 35.

[12]The other two members were the Swedish mathematician Gösta Mittag-Leffler (1846-1927) and the German mathematician Karl Weierstrass (1815-1897) who wrote in his report: "This memoir is of such importance that its publication will open a new era in the history of Celestial Mechanics."

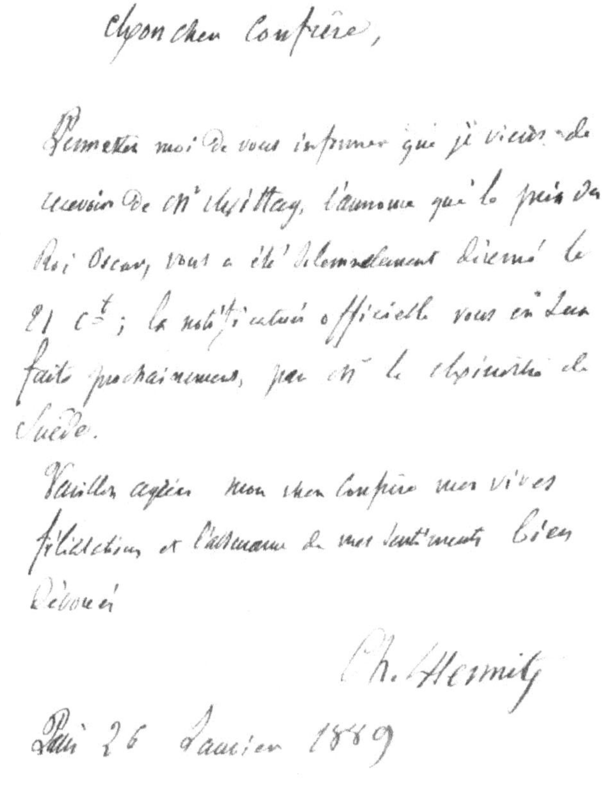
Mon cher Confrère,

Permettez moi de vous informer que je viens de recevoir de Mr Mittag, l'annonce que le prix du Roi Oscar, vous a été solennellement décerné le 21 ct; la notification officielle vous en sera faite prochainement, par Mr le Ministre de Suède.

Veuillez agréer mon cher Confrère mes vives félicitations et l'assurance de mes sentiments bien dévoués

Ch. Hermite

Paris 26 Janvier 1889

Fig. 5.4 Letter from Charles Hermite to Henri Poincaré (*A.H.P.*, Nancy).

lost his entrance ranking at the École Polytechnique (see above). He was a professor of descriptive geometry at the École Polytechnique, and wrote many books on this field[13]. Nevertheless, as reported by Appell:

> "In spite of a significant age difference between the two competitors, the Académie named H. Poincaré, compelled recognition because of his great work[14]."

[13]See A. Mannheim, *Transformation des propriétés métriques des figures à l'aide de la théorie des polaires réciproques*, Paris, Mallet-Bachelier, 1857; *Cours de géométrie descriptive de l'École Polytechnique*, Paris, Gauthier-Villars, 1879, 2nd ed., 1886; *Principes et développements de la géométrie cinématique*, Paris, Gauthier-Villars, 1893. Mannheim also created an innovation on the "slide rule" to which he added in 1851 a movable pointer (cursor). See A. Mannheim, *Règle à Calculs modifiée par M. Mannheim*, Grande Imprimerie Forézienne, Paul Roustan, Roanne, December 1851.

[14]See Appell, p. 109 referred to above.

Chapter 6

The Prize of King Oscar II
of Sweden and Norway

Based on the law of universal gravitation and the fundamental principle of dynamics formalized by Isaac Newton (1642-1727), it can be established that a planet subject to the sole attraction of the Sun would forever describe an elliptical orbit around it. Nevertheless, a planet in our Solar System may also undergo the attraction of the other ones. Thus, the path of the planets will, over the years, be gradually deviated from their elliptical orbits. Therefore, the problem is whether or not these successive deviations will radically change the shape of planetary orbits, which amounts to questioning the stability of the Solar System[1]. When limiting the number of planets to three, this issue is called the "three body problem", for which Poincaré won the prize of King Oscar II of Sweden and Norway.

Less than a month after the announcement made by Hermite, that was widely spread in the newspapers, Gösta Mittag-Leffler officially informed the Académie des Sciences about the prize results in a letter dated February 18, 1889 and addressed to the Permanent Secretary, Joseph Bertrand (1822-1900) who disclosed its content during the session of February 25[2]. The French press immediately got hold of the news.

6.1 From Success to Triumph

The press of his day, announcing his success in the Prize Competition instituted by King Oscar II of Sweden and Norway, did play a major role

---

[1] For further details see the article by F. Béguin, "Le mémoire de Poincaré pour le prix du roi Oscar" (Poincaré's memoir for the prize of King Oscar), in The Scientific Legacy of Poincaré, ed. Charpentier, Ghys, Lesne, History of Mathematics, 36, Providence: AMS, 2010.

[2] See *Comptes Rendus hebdomadaires des séances de l'Académie des Sciences*, 1889, Volume 108, p. 387.

in making the name of this young thirty-five-year-old geometrician famous; but the astronomer Camille Flammarion (1842-1925) made this success a triumph, as indicated by the title Poincaré gave to the summary of the memoir he presented to the *Société Astronomique de France* (Astronomical Society of France) during the session of June 5, 1889. On July 4, 1889, the contents of the Bulletin issued at the end of the session were detailed in the *Revue bibliographique* of the newspaper *Le Temps*.

6.2   A Fruitful Mistake

No sooner had Poincaré began to savor his success that it was undermined. Indeed, as soon as the beginning of July 1889, the Swedish mathematician Lars Edvard Phragmén (1863-1937), responsible for reviewing Poincaré's manuscript prior to its publication in the journal *Acta Mathematica*, reported a number of obscure points to Mittag-Leffler[3]. The latter immediately informed Poincaré of the fact of the letter dated July 16. It was only on December 1, probably after re-writing several of his demonstration, that Poincaré wrote back to Mittag-Leffler (see Fig. 6.1 & 6.2):

> "My dear friend,
> I have written this morning to M. Phragmén to tell him of an error I have made and doubtless he has shown you my letter. But the consequences of this error are more serious than I first thought."

He then went on about the "doubly asymptotic curves[4]" which were the solutions to the three body problem:

> "I had thought that all these asymptotic curves, having moved away from a closed curve representing a periodic solution, would then asymptotically approach the same closed curve. What is true, is that there is an infinity which enjoy this property[5]. I will not conceal from you the distress this discovery has caused me. He ended his letter as follows: I will write to you at length when I can see things more clearly."

---

[3]See June Barrow-Green, "Poincaré and the three-body problem" (1997), AMS-LMS History of Mathematics, Vol. 11, 1997, and Jean-Christophe Yoccoz, "Une erreur féconde du mathématicien Henri Poincaré," *Gazette de la Société Mathématique de France*, No. 107, January 2006, p. 18 to 26.

[4]These curves represent asymptotic solutions to the problem in the future, that is to say, as time passes but also in the past by time reversal.

[5]See L. P. Sil'nikov, "A case of the existence of a denumerable set of periodic motion," *Sov. Mat. Dokl.* 6, (1965) p. 163-166.

It actually took Poincaré almost ten years to be able to see "things more clearly". He presented his results in three imposing volumes of his *Méthodes nouvelles de la Mécanique Céleste* (New Methods of Celestial Mechanics[6]) in which he gave those "doubly asymptotic curves" the name of homoclinic[7] solutions, which have since been considered the "signature" of chaos[8]. Thus, as reported by Umberto Botazzini[9]: "What Poincaré had outlined with "distress" to Mittag-Leffler was the discovery of "deterministic chaos"."

This "fruitful mistake" Poincaré made had however not resulted in a reconsideration of the award of King Oscar II of Sweden and Norway, in so far as the memoir he had submitted was much better than those of his competitors. Nevertheless, since the memoir's printing and spreading had already begun, Mittag-Leffler then had to "recover" all the copies and destroy them. He invited Poincaré to be as discreet as possible[10] about it, and asked him to bear the costs of reprinting the "corrected version" of his memoir. That sum was one thousand crowns more than the prize he had received.

6.3   A Secret Not So Well Kept

According to Professor June Barrow-Green who has kindly transmitted to one of us (JMG) most of the information presented in this section, the existence of Poincaré's mistake was clearly well-known within the mathematical community when his memoir was published.

In a letter written by Weierstrass to Gösta Mittag-Leffler (see Fig. 6.3-6.6), dated 8 March 1890, he tells Mittag-Leffler that people are talking about the mistake in Poincaré's memoir, and that the news had come to Berlin via Hugo Gyldén and Wolf (probably the astronomer Max Wolf (1863-1932) who was in Stockholm c.1889-90). The most interesting part of this letter has been translated below:

---

[6] See Henri Poincaré, *Les Méthodes Nouvelles de la Mécanique Céleste*, Paris, Gauthier-Villars, 1892-93 -99.

[7] *Ibid.*, tome 3, 1899, p. 384 and following and Jean-Christophe Yoccoz referred to above.

[8] See L. P. Sil'nikov, *Ibid.*

[9] Umberto Bottazzini, "Poincaré : philosophe et mathématicien," Les Génies de la Science, novembre 2000.

[10] This is probably the reason why nothing had filtered through the press.

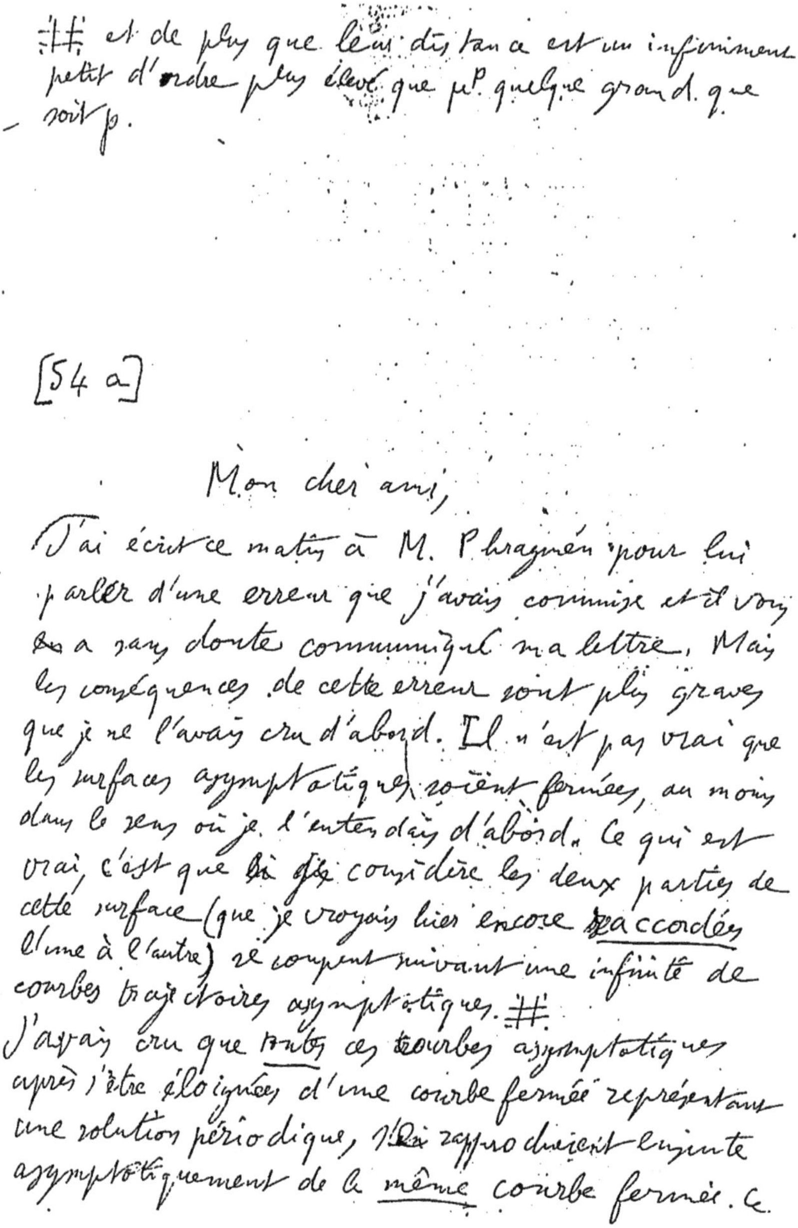

⧻ et de plus que leur distance est un infiniment petit d'ordre plus élevé que p^n quelque grand que soit p.

[54 a]

Mon cher ami,

J'ai écrit ce matin à M. Phragmén pour lui parler d'une erreur que j'avais commise et il vous a sans doute communiqué ma lettre. Mais les conséquences de cette erreur sont plus graves que je ne l'avais cru d'abord. Il n'est pas vrai que les surfaces asymptotiques soient fermées, au moins dans le sens où je l'entendais d'abord. Ce qui est vrai, c'est que si qqe considère les deux parties de cette surface (que je croyais liées encore raccordées l'une à l'autre) se coupent suivant une infinité de courbes trajectoires asymptotiques. ⧻ J'avais cru que toutes ces courbes asymptotiques après s'être éloignées d'une courbe fermée représentant une solution périodique, se rapprochent ensuite asymptotiquement de la même courbe fermée. C.

Fig. 6.1   Henri Poincaré's letter to Gösta Mittag-Leffler
(*Institut Mittag-Leffler*, Stockholm).

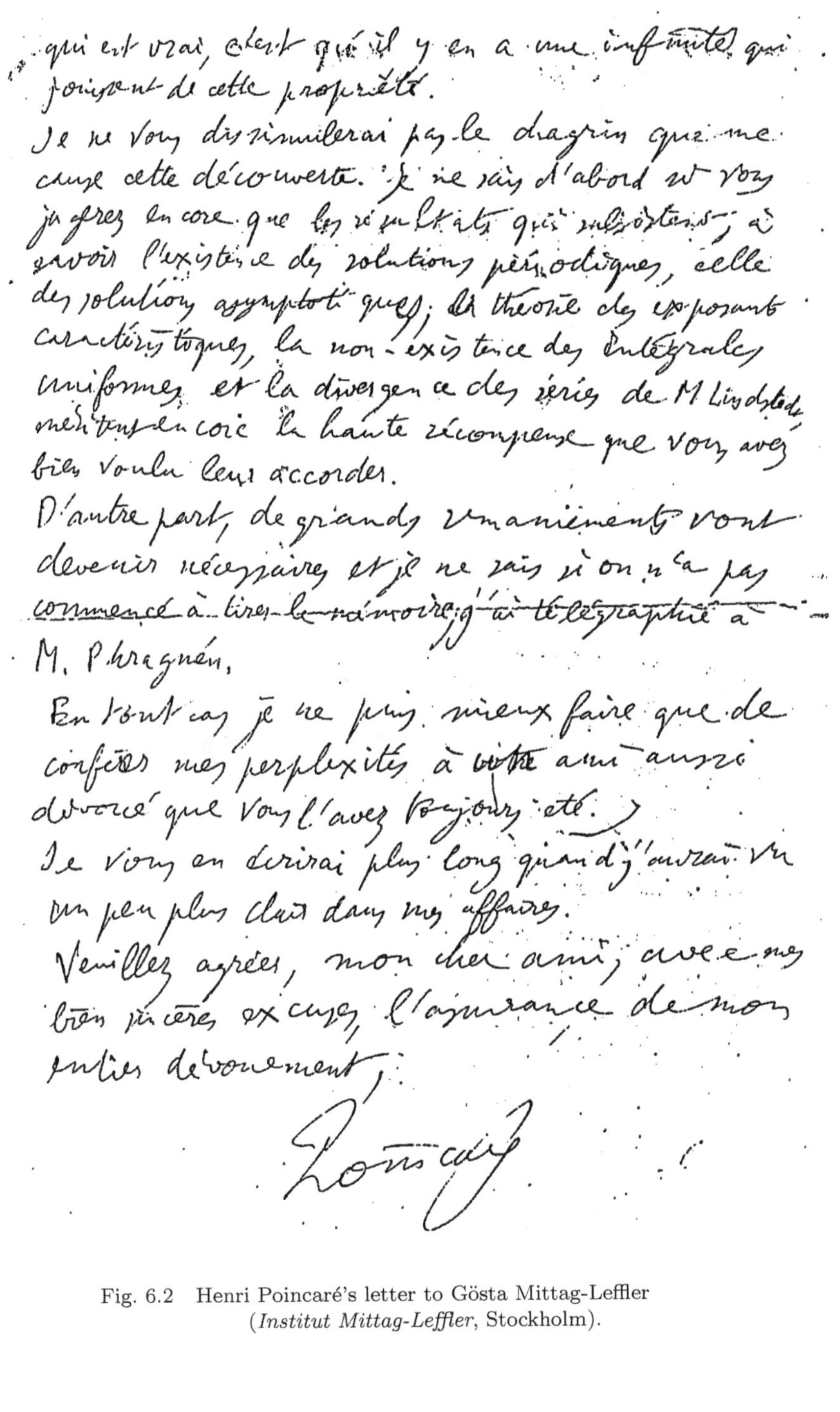

qui est vrai, c'est qu'il y en a une infinité qui jouissent de cette propriété.

Je ne vous dissimulerai pas le chagrin que me cause cette découverte. Je ne sais d'abord si vous jugerez encore que les résultats qui subsistent, à savoir l'existence des solutions périodiques, celle des solutions asymptotiques, la théorie des exposants caractéristiques, la non-existence des intégrales uniformes et la divergence des séries de M Lindstedt méritent encore la haute récompense que vous avez bien voulu leur accorder.

D'autre part, de grands remaniements vont devenir nécessaires et je ne sais si on n'a pas commencé à tirer le mémoire; j'ai télégraphié à M. Phragmén.

En tout cas je ne puis mieux faire que de confier mes perplexités à ~~votre~~ ami aussi dévoué que vous l'avez toujours été.

Je vous en écrirai plus long quand j'aurai vu un peu plus clair dans mes affaires.

Veuillez agréer, mon cher ami, avec mes bien sincères excuses, l'assurance de mon entier dévouement,

Poincaré

Fig. 6.2 Henri Poincaré's letter to Gösta Mittag-Leffler (*Institut Mittag-Leffler*, Stockholm).

"It has been hotly debated in the best backgrounds and not in the most friendly way that in the memoir of Poincaré some significant errors have been discovered, hence the need to revise a paragraph long enough from what has already been written."

Fifteen years later, Gustaf Eneström published in 1904 in the *Bibliotheca Mathematica* an article entitled: "Ist es zweckmäßig, daß mathematische Zeitschriftenartikel datiert werden ?" (Is it appropriate that mathematical journal articles are dated?)

"Ist es zweckmäßig, daß mathematische Zeitschriftenartikel datiert werden ?

Im Jahre 1885 wurde vom König Oscar II. von Schweden ein Preis für die Beantwortung einer Frage über das Problem der drei Körper gestiftet und die Preisschriften sollten vor dem 1. Juni 1888 eingereicht sein, um dann von drei Preissrichtern, darunter K. WEIERSTRASS, geprüft zu werden.

Die eine Hälfte des Preises wurde Herrn H. POINCARÉ zuerkannt, umd im 13. Bande der *Acta Mathematica* erschien im Jahre 1890 eine Arbeit von ihm unter dem Titel: *Sur le problème des trois corps et les équations de la dynamique. Mémoire couronné du prix de S.M. le roi Oscar II le 21 janvier 1889.* Wenn man überhaupt von der Zuverlässigkeit einer Datierung sprechen darf, wäre es wohl erlaubt zu behaupten, daß die im 13. Bande der *Acta Mathematica* veröffentlichte Arbeit des Herrn POINCARÉ am 21. Januar 1889 fertig vorlag – möglicherweise knnte man so weit gehen, daß sie am 1. Juni 1888 fertig gewesen sein mußte.

Aber nach einem kürzlich erschienenen Berichte des Herrn HUGO BUCHOLZ, der mit den betreffenden Verbältnissen sehr vertraut ist, muß die veröffentlichte Arbeit des Herrn POINCARÉ eine wesentlich andere sein als die möglicherweise am 1. Juni 1888 fertige und angeblich am 21. Januar 1889 vorhandene Preisschrift. Nach Herrn BUCHUOLZ verhält es sich nämlich so, daß die wirklich eingereichte Preisschrift im Jahre 1889 (die Bogen sind vom 29 April bis 13 November 1889 gedruckt worden) zusammen mit Zusätzen des Verfassers unter dem Titel: *Sur le problème des trois corps et les équations de la dynamique. Mémoire couronné du prix de S.M. le roi Oscar II le 21 janvier 1889. Avec des Notes par l'auteur* gedruckt wurde, um in den *Acta Mathematica* zu erscheinen, aber ihre Ausgabe im letzten Moment – Sonderabzüge waren schon versandt – vermieden wurde, weil man auf einen Fehler in der Preisarbeit aufmerksam ward, der die Grundlagen der gekrönten Arbeit derart berührte, daß er ihre Ausgabe unmöglich machte. An Stelle dieser verfehlten Arbeit redigierte Herr POINCARÉ eilends nach dem 13. November 1889 eine nudere Abhandlung, nämlich die oben erwähnte im Jahre 1890 veröffentlichte (die Bogen sind vom 28. April bis 21. Oktober 1889 gedruckt).

Aus dem Umstande, daß die Arbeit ausdrücklich als am 21. Januar 1889 gekrönt bezeichnet worden ist, darf man also nicht einmal folgern, daß Herr POINCARÉ vor dem 21. Januar 1889 die darin enthaltenen Resultate gefunden hatte. Wenn aber in einem solchen Falle (mit WEIERSTRASS selbst als offiziell angezeigtem Preisrichter!) die Datierung wesentlich irreleitend ist, so ist es wohl erlaubt zu behaupten, daß man in einigen Kreisen ähnlichen Angaben überhaupt keine Bedeutung zuerkennt[11]."

---

[11] "In 1885, a prize was created by King Oscar II of Sweden to answer the question of the three-body problem and it was thus necessary to get organized so that the memoirs were submitted before June 1, 1888, for being reviewed then by the referees among which was K. Weierstrass. One part of the prize was attributed to M. Poincaré in 1890 and his memoir entitled *Sur le problème des trois corps et les équations de la dynamique. Mémoire couronné du prix de S.M. le roi Oscar II le 21 janvier 1889* was published in Volume 13 of *Acta Mathematica work.* If one really must speak with the reliability of a date it would be possible to argue that the work published by M. Poincaré in vol. 13 of Acta Mathematica was ready on January 21st, 1889, one could potentially go as far as saying it was ready on June 1st, 1888. But according to a recent report by Mr. HUGO BUCHOLZ, who is very familiar with this kind of question, the work published by M. Poincare had to be completely different from that which was delivered on June 1, 1888 and also different from the winning memoir dated from January 21, 1889. According to Bucholz, the prize memoir was published in 1889 (the sheets were printed from 29 April to 13 November 1889) and the additions of the author under the title: *Sur le problème des trois corps et les équations de la dynamique. Mémoire couronné du prix de S.M. le roi Oscar II le 21 janvier 1889* to appear in *Acta Mathematica.* But at the last moment his edition was stopped while offprints have been already sent, to avoid drawing attention to an error in the study which could shake the foundations of the prize and would make it impossible the edition of the winning memoir. In place of this work Mr. Poincaré hastily wrote another memoir, namely the one above-mentioned published in 1890, (the sheets were printed from 28 April 28 to 21 October 1890) edited after November 13, 1889. Because the memoir has been specifically designated as being awarded on January 21, 1889, we can not even conclude that Poincare had found before 21 January, 1889, the results that it contains. If in such a case (even with WEIERSTRASS as official judge! (Weierstrass has later regretted his participation as a referee in the work of Poincaré)) the establishment of a date is extremely misleading, it is possible to affirm that, in some backgrounds, one gives no meaning to this kind of information."

Just after Poincaré's death we could find in some obituaries references to this "mistake". As an example in an article published on October 4, 1912, the mathematician George Abram Miller wrote:

> "Poincaré won great fame in connection with his prize memoir relating to the problem of three bodies. In 1885 King Oscar II. of Sweden offered a prize for the solution of a question in reference to this general problem, and one half of this prize was awarded to Poincare for his article entitled, "Sur le problème des trois corps et les équations de la dynamique," published in the *Acta Mathematica* in 1890. In the *Bibliotheca Mathematica* for 1904, page 198, Eneström (see above) calls attention to the interesting fact that the copy of this memoir for which the prize had been actually awarded contained a serious error, and that the given published article was really prepared for the press after the prize had been awarded."

In December 1912, the astronomer Forest Ray Moulton wrote an article devoted to Henri Poincaré in which he recalled that:

> "It has been remarked a number of times recently[12] that the original memoir of Poincaré on the problem of three bodies, for which the prize of King Oscar II was awarded, contained an error; and that the published paper differed from the one originally submitted. Unfortunately and erroneously the impression has been left in some of these statements that the first investigation was quite wrong and of little value. The original memoir did contain an error which was discovered by Phragmén, of Stockholm, but it affected only the discussion of the existence of the asymptotic solutions; and in correcting this part Poincaré made no attempt to conceal the facts and confessed fully his obligations to Phragmén. While the error was unfortunate, there is not the slightest doubt that in spite of it, and even if it had been known at the time, the prize was correctly bestowed. If all the parts affected by the error are omitted, the memoir still remains one whose equal in originality in results secured, and in extent of valuable field opened, it is difficult to find elsewhere. There are but very few men, even of high reputation, who have produced more in their whole lives that was really new and valuable than that which was correct in the original investigation submitted by Poincaré."

---

[12]Moulton made probably reference to Miller.

6.4 Winning Recognition

The French press[13], which seemed to know nothing about that mistake, continued to devote extensive columns to him, giving thus many accounts of the distinctions and honors he was awarded with.

It is amusing to note that as to the spelling of his name, his celebrity was not yet established, since "Poincaré" was still spelled with two "r".

During the following decade, Poincaré received many honors and decorations. Thus, it could be seen in the newspapers *Le Figaro* and *La Presse* on Friday, May 18, 1894 that he was appointed "officier de la légion d'honneur" (Officer of the Legion of Honour)[14] on the occasion of the centenary of the École Polytechnique. Therefore, the press would talk about Poincaré by using more and more flattering superlatives as his fame grew. In an article entitled "Nos Mathématiciens" (Our Mathematicians), the newspaper *Le Figaro* wrote on January 16, 1895:

> "At the head of the movement is Mr. Poincaré, who is barely thirty-five years old, who in the eyes of all his colleagues, including the venerable Mr. Hermite, is considered as the best mathematician of the time."

The following year, when he submitted, the work of Wilhelm Roentgen (1845-1923) on X-rays, then known as "Photography of the invisible", to the Académie des Sciences, the paper *Le Petit Parisien* of January 24, 1896 wrote:

> "A learned mathematician, Mr. Poincaré, has just made them known to the Académie des Sciences in Paris."

In 1896-97, Dr. Édouard Toulouse (1865-1947), a psychiatrist and journalist, started to take an interest in the scientific and literary figures of his time, in order to conduct a "medical and psychological" study on "intellectual superiority". The study on Henri Poincaré, that would only be completed in 1910 (see below), began with a handwriting analysis. The journalist of the paper *Le Matin* dated February 4, 1897 stated:

---

[13] In the U.S. press it has not been possible to find any reference to the Prize Competition of Oscar II.

[14] Poincaré was made Commander of the Legion of Honour on January 1, 1903. See the paper *Le Temps* of January 16, 1903.

"Maybe, in one of the next volumes[15], will we see more of Mr. Poincaré, the eminent mathematician ...".

At the dawn of the new millennium, Poincaré was asked by the newspaper *Le Figaro* on November 9, 1899, about "L'éternité du monde" ("The eternity of the world") and the following year by the daily paper *Le Temps* on October 3, 1900, about "La mission du vingtième siècle" ("The mission of the twentieth century") (see below). Poincaré was presented in these papers as "our famous mathematician."

On the occasion of wireless telegraphy experiments conducted at the Nice Observatory, many eminent scientists were invited by Bischoffsheim Raphael (1823-1906), the founder of the Observatory, and Poincaré was one of them.

Le Figaro on March 4, 1903, wrote about a dinner with the "prodigious mathematician." Finally, on December 19, 1905, during the last annual session of the Académie des Sciences, the paper *Le Petit Parisien* listed the names of the Académie members and ended as follows:

"Poincaré, the most famous mathematician in the world, and Darboux, the eminent Permanent Secretary."

Regardless of the very obsequious journalistic style towards the world's scientific, political and literary figures of that time, it is interesting to note how Poincaré, in the space of ten years, went from being the "best mathematician of the time" (1895) to the "most famous mathematician in the world" (1905).

---

[15]See E. Toulouse, *Enquête médico-psychologique sur la supériorité intellectuelle : Henri Poincaré*, Paris, Flammarion, 1910, 204 pages.

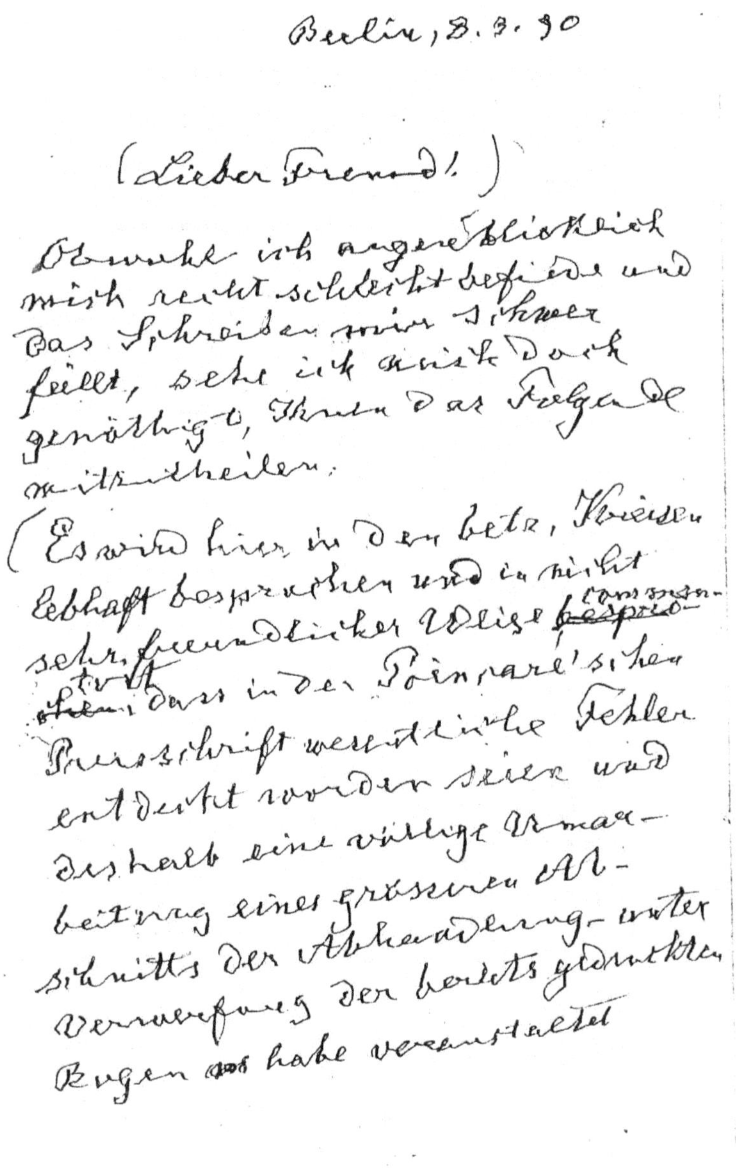

Berlin, 8.3.90

(Lieber Freund!)

Obwohl ich augenblicklich
mich recht schlecht befinde und
das Schreiben mir schwer
fällt, sehe ich mich doch
genöthigt, Ihnen das Folgende
mitzutheilen:

(Es wird hier in den betr. Kreisen
lebhaft besprochen und in nicht
sehr freundlicher Weise ~~besprochen~~ commentirt, dass in der Poincaré'schen
Preisschrift wesentliche Fehler
entdeckt worden seien und
deshalb eine völlige Umar-
beitung eines grösseren Ab-
schnitts der Abhandlung unter
Vernichtung der bereits gedruckten
Bogen habe veranstaltet

Fig. 6.3 Karl Weierstrass's letter to Gösta Mittag-Leffler.

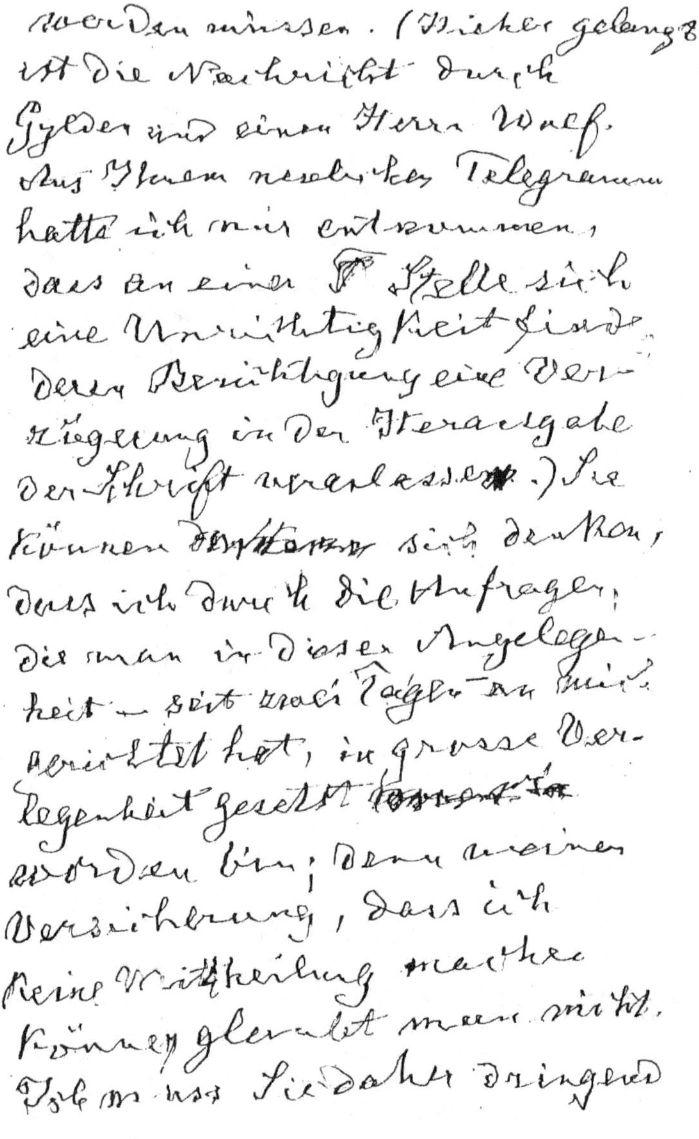
worden müssen. (Bisher gelangt
ist die Nachricht durch
Gyldén und einen Herrn Wolf.
Aus seinem neulichen Telegramm
hatte ich nur entnommen,
dass an einer Stelle sich
eine Unrichtigkeit finde,
deren Berichtigung eine Ver-
zögerung in der Herausgabe
der Schrift veranlasse.) Sie
können sich denken,
dass ich durch die Anfragen,
die man in dieser Angelegenheit – seit zwei Tagen an mich
gerichtet hat, in grosse Ver-
legenheit gesetzt
worden bin; denn meiner
Versicherung, dass ich
keine Mittheilung machen
könne, glaubt man nicht.
Ich muss Sie daher dringend

Fig. 6.4 Karl Weierstrass's letter to Gösta Mittag-Leffler.

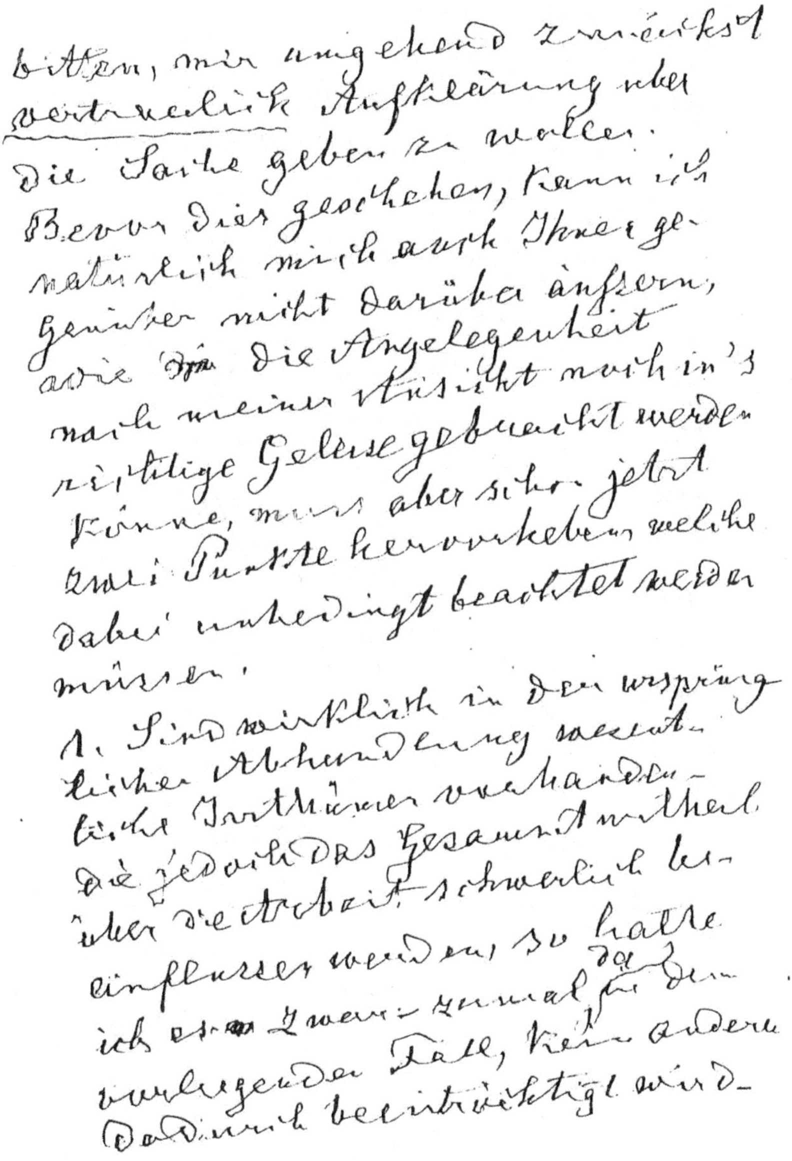

bitten, mir umgehend zunächst
vertrauliche Aufklärung über
die Sache geben zu wollen.
Bevor dies geschehen, kann ich
natürlich mich auch Ihnen ge-
genüber nicht darüber äußern,
wie ... die Angelegenheit
nach meiner Ansicht noch in's
richtige Geleise gebracht werden
könne, muss aber schon jetzt
zwei Punkte hervorheben, welche
dabei unbedingt beachtet werden
müssen.
1. Sind wirklich in der ursprüng-
lichen Abhandlung wesent-
liche Irrthümer vorhanden -
die jedoch das Gesammturtheil
über die Arbeit schwerlich be-
einflussen werden, so hatte
ich es zwar - zumal für den
vorliegenden Fall, kein andere
dadurch beeinträchtigt wird -

Fig. 6.5 Karl Weierstrass's letter to Gösta Mittag-Leffler.

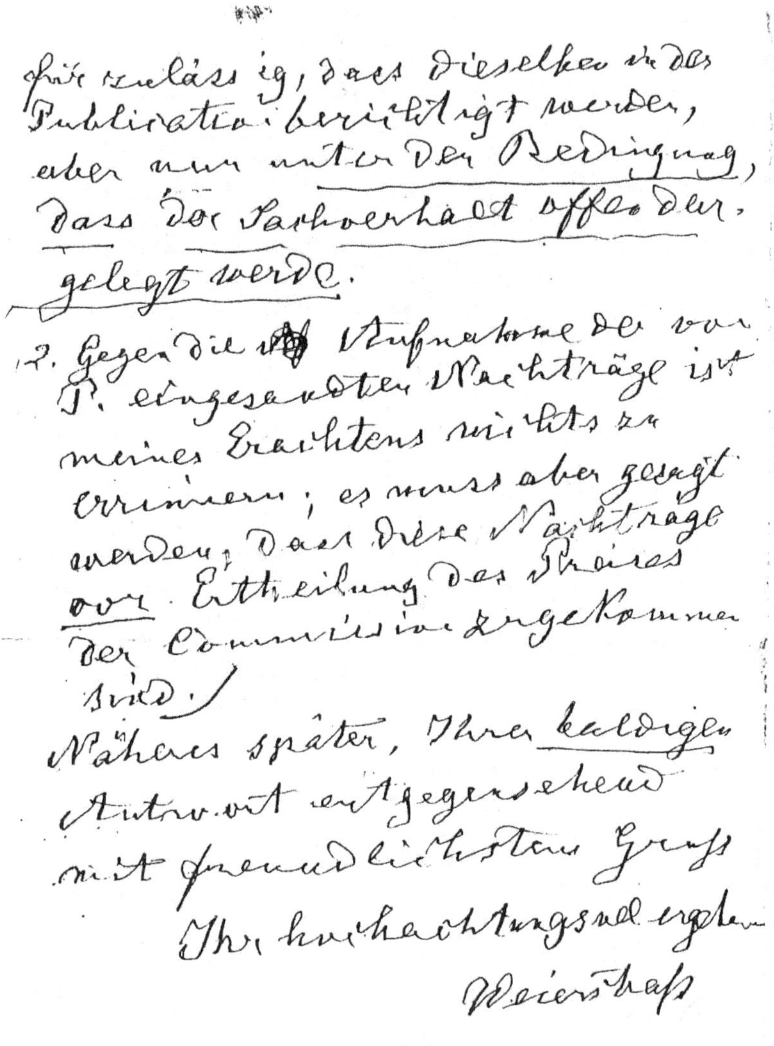

für zulässig, dass dieselben in der
Publication berichtigt werden,
aber nur unter der Bedingung,
dass der Sachverhalt offen dar-
gelegt werde.
2. Gegen die Aufnahme der von
P. eingesandten Nachträge ist
meines Erachtens nichts zu
erinnern; es muss aber gesagt
werden, dass diese Nachträge
nach Ertheilung des Preises
der Commission zugekommen
sind./
Näheres später, Ihrer baldigen
Antwort entgegensehend
mit freundlichstem Gruss
Ihr hochachtungsvoll ergebenster
Weierstrass

Fig. 6.6 Karl Weierstrass's letter to Gösta Mittag-Leffler.

PART 3

The Universal Thinker
and
The Public Figure

To doubt everything or to believe everything are two equally convenient solutions; both dispense with the necessity of reflection.

— H. Poincaré —

Chapter 7

French Geodesy and the Fight over the Meridian

7.1 The Fight over the Meridian

From October 1 to November 1, 1884, an international conference of twenty-five countries including France and Britain took place in Washington and aimed to determine the location of an international reference meridian or prime meridian that would standardize the partition of the earth in twenty-four time zones. They had to choose among the following three proposals:

- The "international" meridian, located on the island of Ferro in the Canaries,
- the meridian of the Paris Observatory and
- the Greenwich meridian on the outskirts of London.

On October 22, 1884, during the seventh session, the following resolution was adopted:

> "That the Conference proposes to the Governments here represented the adoption of the meridian passing through the centre of the transit instrument at the Observatory of Greenwich as the initial meridian for longitude. (Ayes, 22; noes, 1; abstaining, 2.)."

France thus lost the "fight for the meridian" in favor of the British.

On November 2, 1884, the *New York Tribune* reported thus this news:

CLOSE THE MERIDIAN CONFERENCE
WASHINGTON, NOV. 1. – The International Meridian Conference held its final meeting today. The minutes of the proceedings were submitted to the body and were approved. An official copy of these proceedings in pursuance of the resolution will be delivered to the Government of the United States. Upon the resolution adopting the Meridian of Greenwich for a universal initial meridian only one nation voted in the negative – San Domingo. France and Brazil abstained from voting.

On November 3, 1884 one could read in *The Sun*:

The Meridian Conference adjourned on Saturday without marring its good work by the introduction of the extraneous subject which had been subjected to it. The French metric system of weights and measures has strong advocates in this country: it also has opponents. Without discussing either its merits or its drawbacks we may safely say that the Meridian Conference was wise in considering this matter to be outside of its province. Possibly its members might have purchased the French adhesion to the Greenwich prime by recommending the adoption of the metrical system of weights and measures: but this it did not attempt to do and its guarded approval of metric notations had no reference to trade. To reorganize the modes of reckoning of a whole community from the mammoth mill to the handeart huckster would require an assemblage constituted differently from the one which sat in Washington. Not only sailors and scientific men but the world of trade should have representation in such a body. Meanwhile the Meridian Conference has done excellent service in recommending Greenwich as the world's zero longitude and in recommending and defining a universal day. It may be hoped that the various Governments concerned, including France and Brazil, will ratify its work.

However, it seems that britain managed to convince the other delegations to adopt the English meridian, and declared in particular that they were willing to accept the metric system in return which actually only happened in 1965! Though France did not hurry either to recognize the meridian of Greenwich as the international reference. It was actually quite

the opposite, for seven years later, on March 14, 1891, a law was passed to
state that the French legal time would be given by the average time of the
Paris Observatory. A bill was then introduced on March 8, 1897, in order
to adopt the Greenwich "Universal Time", but the Senate was so opposed
to it that the law was only passed fourteen years later, on March 9, 1911.

Poincaré, member of the "Bureau des Longitudes" since January 4,
1893, was directly concerned by this issue, to which he humorously re-
sponded:

> "Nous avons reçu au bureau des longitudes une communica-
> tion du directeur de l'observatoire de Mexico que je me fais un
> plaisir de rappeler ici. "Il existe en France, dit cet astronome,
> une ville qui a précisément le méridien de greenwich, c'est Ar-
> gentan. Adoptez en France l'heure d'Argentan, et l'amour pro-
> pre français sera sauf !" voilà une solution, dit en riant M.
> Poincaré[1]."

In February 1911, in order to study the attachment of the French legal
time to the Greenwich one, an interministerial committee chaired by Henri
Poincaré[2] was formed. The law was passed on March 9, 1911; two days
later (on March 11, 1911), the news spread in *The Washington Herald*.

> Paris. March .10. – Starting exactly at midnight to-night, time
> was annihilated in France for the space of 9 minutes and 21
> seconds. On the stroke of the hour all the clocks in the republic
> were stopped for the time indicated, in order to comply with
> the law making the tune here the same as in all places within
> a radius 15° degrees, and in which the time is regulated from
> Greenwich, England.
> All railway trains, if on time, were held up and those which
> were behind schedule were required to make up the difference.
> Owing to the change in time an interesting question has arisen.
> It is questionable if a child that is born and dies with in the
> lapsed time will really had lived. This point is puzzling the
> legal talent.

---

[1] "We have received here at the "Bureau des Longitudes" a communication from the
director of the Mexico observatory, which I am very pleased to repeat. "There is in
France, said the astronomer, a city through which precisely passes the Greenwich meridian: it is Argentan. France then should adopt the time of Argentan, so that the French
self-esteem can stay intact !" That's a solution, Poincaré said laughingly."

[2] In the meantime Poincaré was President of the "Bureau des Longitudes" three times
in 1899, 1909 and 1910.

FRANCE ADOPTS GREENWICH TIME

All Clocks Stopped for 9 Minutes 21 Seconds.

WEATHER FORECAST.
Fair to-day; generally fair to-morrow; moderate temperature.

THE WASHINGTON HERALD

LARGEST MORNING
CIRCULATION

NO. 1617.   WASHINGTON, D. C., SATURDAY, MARCH 11, 1911.—TWELVE PAGES.   ONE CENT.

The new time will not be used at the wireless station for signaling ships until June 30 next. The present opportunity is taken advantage of, however, to abolish the old custom of keeping the clocks outside railway stations five minutes faster than those inside. It has taken a quarter of a century to overcome the French prejudice against taking time from Greenwich, but now that this has been accomplished, there is a feeling that England in return should adopt the metric system.

The length of 9'21" (nine minutes and twenty seconds) comes from the fact that the Greenwich Observatory is 2°20'14" longitude west of Paris. By dividing the globe (360°) into twenty-four time zones 15° of longitude is obtained for each time zone. It is easy to check that if 15° corresponds to 1 hour, then 2°20'14" corresponds to 9'21".

The Washington Times, on March 11, 1911 also reported this news (See Fig. 7.1).

The Washington Times

Fair and Warmer Tonight; Sunday Cloudy.

LAST EDITION

NUMBER 7016.   Yesterday's Circulation, 50,106   WASHINGTON, SATURDAY EVENING, MARCH 11, 1911.   Sixteen Pages   PRICE ONE CENT.

Stop Clocks in France
So Time Can Catch Up

PARIS, March 11.—In order to be in harmony with Greenwich calculations, all clocks in France were stoppen nine minutes and twenty-one seconds after midnight this morning. The action was according to a new law ordering conformance to Greenwich time. The custom of having clocks at railroad stations five minutes too fast also has been abolished.

Fig. 7.1   *The Washington Times*, of March 11, 1911.

On March 29, 1911, the *Weekly Journal-Miner*, proposed an article entitled: "Dropping out the difference", an overview of the fight over the Meridian:

WEEKLY JOURNAL-MINER

PIONEER PAPER OF ARIZONA.   PRESCOTT, ARIZONA, WEDNESDAY MORNING, MARCH 29, 1911.   FORTY-EIGHTH YEAR.

Fig. 7.2   *Weekly Journal-Miner*, of March 29, 1911.

DROPPING OUT OF DIFFERENCES

A few days ago France brought its time into conformity with that of England by adopting the meridian of the Greenwich Observatory in London as the basic line of computation. Heretofore the meridian of the Paris Observatory was the zero line for France and all her dependencies, but henceforth the reckoning

will be made from Greenwich. This requires a change of a little
less than ten minutes in time, but France is a proud country,
and clung to its own standard, although nearly all the rest of the
countries adopted the British line as a time base long ago. They
did this at a conference held in Washington, in which most of
the countries were represented. For many years United States
time, with its change of an hour for each 15 degrees east or
west, has been based on the Greenwich standard. During many
decades there were wide variations in the calendars of the great
nations. That of Pope Gregory XIII, which, in 1552, superseded
tho Julian calendar, was accepted by most of the Catholic countries promptly, but the Protest ant nations held aloof for a long
time. These divergencies gave rise to the terms "new style"
and "old style," as applied to dates. Protestant Germany did
not adopt the Gregorian scheme until 1700, and England held
out against it until 1753, when it was compelled to drop many
days of its time schedule, and call September 3, September 14.
At that date the new calendar went into operation in all the
British dominions, including, the colonies which, a quarter of
a, century later, became the United States. Russia, the only
great civilized country which was outside of tho scheme until
recently, came in a year ago. She had to drop twelve days from
her almanac. In France's adoption of the Greenwich standard
for her watches and clocks we feel the touch of the vanished
hand. The change is a remit of the entente- with England,
which dates from 1904, and Edward VII, the greatest of the
world's peace makers, was the author of the entente. From the
days of the Norman conquest in 10GG down to the eve of the
Crimean war of 1S54-56, England and France were usually the
Crimean struggle, the distrust between them extended down to
a few years ago. The understanding established between them
by Edward has its most recent manifestation in France's adoption of the Greenwich tune date line.

But this story was not finished as one could read in the *Telegraph*[3] on
January 13, 2012:

> "British scientists preparing to fight to keep meantime at
> Greenwich."

---

[3] *The Daily Telegraph* was a British daily newspaper founded by Arthur B. Sleigh in
June 1855 as *The Daily Telegraph and Courier*. It became the *Telegraph Group* and
then in 2004 the *Telegraph Media Group*.

7.2   The Geodesic Mission and the French Geodesy

In the late XIXth century, the issue of the shape of the earth was still relevant and consisted in calculating the average dimensions of the ellipsoid, including the value of flattening, using highly sophisticated instruments. So in 1898, the members of the International Association of Geodesy decided to resume the operations of mesuring an arc of meridian under two extreme latitudes[4]. After sending the captains Maurain and Lacombe to carry out a reconnaissance mission on May 16, 1898, the "military-scientific" project, which saw the light of day under the name of "revision of the meridian of Quito[5]", was reviewed by an academic committee of the meridian whose rapporteur was no other than Poincaré.

On October 25, Poincaré gave a speech on the French Geodesy during the public session of the five Academies[6].

FRENCH GEODESY[7]

Every one understands what an interest we have in knowing the shape and the dimensions of our globe, but some people would perhaps be astonished at the precision that is sought for. Is this a useless luxury? What is the use of the efforts geodesists devote to it?

If a Member of Parliament were asked this question, I imagine he would answer: "I am led to think that Geodesy is one of the most useful of sciences, for it is one of those that cost us most money." I shall attempt to give a somewhat more precise answer.

The great works of art, those of peace as well as those of war, cannot be undertaken without long studies, which save many gropings, miscalculations, and useless expense. These studies cannot be made without a good map. But a map is nothing but a fanciful picture, of no value whatever if we try to construct it without basing it upon a solid framework. As well might we try to make a human body stand upright with the skeleton removed.

---

[4]For further details see Martina Schiavon, "Les officiers géodésiens du Service géographique de l'armée et la mesure de l'arc de méridien de Quito (1901-1906)," Histoire & mesure, number XXI - 2 (2006), online: http://histoiremesure.revues.org/1746

[5]Quito is located in South America and is the capital of the Republic of Ecuador.

[6]This text entirely reproduced here has been published in Henri Poincaré: *Science & Method*, T. Nelson Publisher, London, 1914, p. 270-283

[7]Throughout this chapter the author is speaking of the work of his own countrymen. In the translation such words as "we" and "our' have been avoided, as far as possible; but where they occur, they must be understood to refer to France and not to England.

Now this framework is obtained by geodetic measurements. Therefore without Geodesy we can have no good map, and without a good map no great public works.

These reasons would no doubt be sufficient to justify much expense, but they are reasons calculated to convince practical men. It is not upon these that we should insist here; there are higher and, upon the whole, more important reasons.

We will therefore state the question differently:

Can Geodesy make us better acquainted with nature?

Does it make us understand its unity and harmony?

An isolated fact indeed is but of little worth, and the conquests of science have a value only if they prepare new ones.

Accordingly, if we happened to discover a little hump upon the terrestrial ellipsoid, this discovery would be of no great interest in itself. It would become precious to the contrary if, in seeking for the cause of the hump, we had the hope of penetrating new secrets.

So when Maupertuis and La Condamine in the eighteenth century braved such diverse climates, it was not only for the sake of knowing the shape of our planet, it was a question of the system of the whole World. If the Earth was flattened, Newton was victorious, and with him the doctrine of gravitation and the whole of the modern celestial mechanics. And to-day, a century and a half since the victory of the Newtonians, are we to suppose that Geodesy has nothing more to teach us? We do not know what there is in the interior of the globe. Mine shafts and borings have given us some knowledge of a stratum one or two miles deep – that is to say, the thousandth part of the total mass; but what is there below that?

Of all the extraordinary voyages dreamt of by Jules Verne, it was perhaps the voyage to the centre of the Earth that led us to the most unexplored regions.

But those deep sunken rocks that we cannot reach, exercise at a distance the attraction that acts upon the pendulum and deforms the terrestrial spheroid. Geodesy can therefore weigh them at a distance, so to speak, and give us information about their disposition. It will thus enable us really to see those mysterious regions which Jules Verne showed us only in imagination.

This is not an empty dream. By comparing all the measurements, M. Faye has reached a result well calculated to cause surprise. In the depths beneath the oceans, there are rocks of very great density, while, on the contrary, beneath the continents there seem to be empty spaces.

New observations will perhaps modify these conclusions in their details, but our revered master has, at any rate, shown us in what direction we must push our researches, and what it is that the geodesist can teach the geologist who is curious about the interior constitution of the Earth, and what material he can supply to the thinker who wishes to reflect upon the past and the origin of this planet.

Now why have I headed this chapter French Geodesy? It is because, in different countries, this science has assumed, more perhaps than any other, a national character; and it is easy so see the reason for this.

There must certainly be rivalries. Scientific rivalries are always courteous, or, at least, almost always. In any case they are necessary, because they are always fruitful.

Well, in these enterprises that demand such long efforts and so many collaborators, the individual is effaced, in spite of himself of course. None has the right to say, this is my work. So the rivalry is not between individuals, but between nations. Thus we are led to ask what share France has taken in the work, and I think we have a right to be proud of what she has done.

At the beginning of the eighteenth century there arose long discussions between the Newtonians, who believed the Earth to be flattened as the theory of gravitation demands, and Cassini, who was misled by inaccurate measurements, and believed the globe to be elongated. Direct observation alone could settle the question. It was the French Academy of Sciences that undertook this task, a gigantic one for that period.

While Maupertuis and Clairaut were measuring a degree of longitude within the Arctic circle, Bouguer and La Condamine turned their faces towards the mountains of the Andes, in regions that were then subject to Spain, and to-day form the Republic of Ecuador. Our emissaries were exposed to great fatigues, for journeys then were not so easy as they are to-day.

It is true that the country in which Maupertuis' operations were conducted was not a desert, and it is even said that he enjoyed among the Lapps those soft creature comforts that are unknown to the true Arctic navigator. It was more or less in the neighbourhood of places to which, in our day, comfortable steamers carry, every summer, crowds of tourists and young English ladies. But at that date Cook's Agency did not exist, and Maupertuis honestly thought that he had made a Polar expedition.

Perhaps he was not altogether wrong. Russians and Swedes are to-day making similar measurements at Spitzbergen, in a country where there are real icepacks. But their resources are far greater, and the difference of date fully compensates for the difference of latitude.

Maupertuis' name has come down to us considerably mauled by the claws of Dr. Akakia, for Maupertuis had the misfortune to displease Voltaire, who was then king of the mind. At first he was extravagantly praised by Voltaire; but the flattery of kings is as much to be dreaded as their disfavour, for it is followed by a terrible day of reckoning. Voltaire himself learnt something of this.

Voltaire called Maupertuis "my kind master of thought," "Marquess of the Arctic Circle," "dear flattener of the world and of Cassini," and even, as supreme flattery, "Sir Isaac Maupertuis"; and he wrote, "There is none but the King of Prussia that I place on a level with you ; his sole defect is that he is not a geometrician." But very soon the scene changes; he no longer speaks of deifying him, like the Argonauts of old, or of bringing down the council of the gods from Olympus to contemplate his work, but of shutting him up in a mad-house. He speaks no more of his sublime mind, but of his despotic pride, backed by very little science and much absurdity.

I do not wish to tell the tale of these mock-heroic conflicts, but I should like to make a few reflections upon two lines of Voltaire's. In his Discours sur la Moderation (there is no question of moderation in praise or blame), the poet wrote:

- Vous avez confirmé dans des lieux pleins d'ennui Ce que Newton connut sans sortir de chez lui[8].

These two lines, which take the place of the hyperbolical praises of earlier date, are most unjust, and without any doubt, Voltaire was too well informed not to realize it.

At that time men valued only the discoveries that can be made without leaving home. To-day it is theory rather that is held in low esteem. But this implies a misconception of the aim of science.

Is nature governed by caprice, or is harmony the reigning influence? That is the question. It is when science reveals this harmony that it becomes beautiful, and for that reason worthy of being cultivated. But whence can this revelation come if not from the accordance of a theory with experience? Our aim then is to find out whether or not this accordance exists. From that moment, these two terms, which must be compared with each

---

[8]You have confirmed, in dreary far-off lands, What Newton knew without ever leaving home.

other, become one as indispensable as the other. To neglect one for the other would be folly. Isolated, theory is empty and experience blind; and both are useless and of no interest alone.

Maupertuis is therefore entitled to his share of the fame. Certainly it is not equal to that of Newton, who had received the divine spark, or even of his collaborator Clairaut. It is not to be despised, however, because his work was necessary; and if France, after being outstripped by England in the seventeenth century, took such full revenge in the following century, it was not only to the genius of the Clairauts, the d'Alemberts, and the Laplaces that she owed it, but also to the long patience of such men as Maupertuis and La Condamine.

We come now to what may be called the second heroic period of Geodesy. France was torn with internal strife, and the whole of Europe was in arms against her. One would suppose that these tremendous struggles must have absorbed all her energies. Far from that, however, she had still some left for the service of science. The men of that day shrank before no enterprise – they were men of faith.

Delambre and Méchain were commissioned to measure an arc running from Dunkirk to Barcelona. This time there is no journey to Lapland or Peru ; the enemy's squadrons would close the roads. But if the expeditions are less distant, the times are so troublous that the obstacles and even the dangers are quite as great.

In France Delambre had to fight against the ill-will of suspicious municipalities. One knows that steeples, which can be seen a long way off, and observed with precision, often serve as signals for geodesists. But in the country Delambre was working through, there were no steeples left. I forget now what proconsul it was who had passed through it and boasted that he had brought down all the steeples that raised their heads arrogantly above the humble dwellings of the common people.

So they erected pyramids of planks covered with white linen to make them more conspicuous. This was taken to mean something quite different. White linen! Who was the foolhardy man who ventured to set up, on our heights so recently liberated, the odious standard of the counter-revolution? The white linen must needs to be edged with blue and red stripes.

Mechain, operating in Spain, met with other but no less serious difficulties. The Spanish country folk were hostile. There was no lack of steeples, but was it not sacrilege to take possession of them with instruments that were mysterious and perhaps diabolical? The revolutionaries were the allies of Spain, but they

were allies who smelt a little of the stake. "We are constantly
threatened," writes Mechain, "with having our throats cut."
Happily, thanks to the exhortations of the priests, and to the
pastoral letters from the bishops, the fiery Spaniards contented
themselves with threats.

Some years later, Mechain made a second expedition to Spain.
He proposed to extend the meridian from Barcelona to the
Balearic Isles. This was the first time that an attempt had
been made to cross a large arm of the sea by triangulation, by
taking observations of signals erected upon some high mountain
in a distant island. The enterprise was well conceived and well
planned, but it failed nevertheless. The French scientist met
with all kinds of difficulties, of which he complains bitterly in
his correspondence. "Hell," he writes, perhaps with some ex-
aggeration, "hell, and all the scourges it vomits upon the earth
– storms, war, pestilence, and dark intrigues – are let loose
against me!"

The fact is that he found among his collaborators more head-
strong arrogance than good-will, and that a thousand incidents
delayed his work. The plague was nothing; fear of the plague
was much more formidable. All the islands mistrusted the
neighboring islands, and were afraid of receiving the scourge
from them. It was only after long weeks that Mechain obtained
permission to land, on condition of having all his papers vine-
gared – such were the antiseptics of those days. Disheartened
and ill, he had just applied for his recall, when he died.

It was Arago and Biot who had the honor of taking up the
unfinished work and bringing it to a happy conclusion. Thanks
to the support of the Spanish Government and the protection
of several bishops, and especially of a celebrated brigand chief,
the operations progressed rapidly enough. They were happily
terminated, and Biot had returned to France, when the storm
burst.

It was the moment when the whole of Spain was taking up
arms to defend her independence against France. Why was this
stranger climbing mountains to make signals? It was evidently
to call the French army. Arago only succeeded in escaping from
the populace by giving himself up as a prisoner. In his prison
his only distraction was reading the account of his own execu-
tion in the Spanish newspapers. The newspapers of those days
sometimes gave premature news. He had at least the consola-
tion of learning that he had died a courageous and a Christian
death.

Prison itself was not safe, and he had to make his escape and
reach Algiers. Thence he sailed for Marseille on an Algerian

ship. This ship was captured by a Spanish privateer, and so Arago was brought back to Spain, and dragged from dungeon to dungeon in the midst of vermin and in the most horrible misery.

If it had only been a question of his subjects and his guests, the Dey would have said nothing. But there were two lions on board, a present the African sovereign was sending to Napoleon. The Dey threatened war.

The vessel and the prisoners were released. The point should have been correctly made, since there was an astronomer on board; but the astronomer was seasick, and the Algerian sailors, who wished to go to Marseille, put in at Bougie. Thence Arago traveled to Algiers, crossing Kabylia on foot through a thousand dangers. He was detained for a long time in Africa and threatened with penal servitude. At last he was able to return to France. His observations, which he had preserved under his shirt, and more extraordinary still, his instruments, had come through these terrible adventures without damage.

Up to this point, France not only occupied the first place, but she held the field almost alone. In the years that followed she did not remain inactive, and the French ordnance map is a model. Yet the new methods of observation and of calculation came principally from Germany and England. It is only during the last forty years that France has regained her position.

She owes it to a scientific officer. General Perrier, who carried out successfully a truly audacious enterprize, the junction of Spain and Africa. Stations were established upon four peaks on the two shores of the Mediterranean. There were long months of waiting for a calm and clear atmosphere. At last there was seen the slender thread of light that had traveled two hundred miles over the sea, and the operation had succeeded.

To-day still more daring projects have been conceived. From a mountain in the vicinity of Nice signals are to be sent to Corsica, no longer with a view to the determination of geodetic questions, but in order to measure the velocity of light. The distance is only one hundred and twenty-five miles, but the ray of light is to make the return journey, after being reflected from a mirror in Corsica. And it must not go astray on the journey, but must return to the exact spot from which it started.

Latterly the activity of French Geodesy has not slackened. We have no more such astonishing adventures to relate, but the scientific work accomplished is enormous. The territory of France beyond the seas, just as that of the mother country, is being covered with triangles measured with precision.

We have become more and more exacting, and what was admired by our fathers does not satisfy us to-day. But as we seek greater exactness, the difficulties increase considerably. We are surrounded by traps, and have to beware of a thousand unsuspected causes of error. It becomes necessary to make more and more infallible instruments.

Here again France has not allowed herself to be outdone. Her apparatus for the measurement of bases and of angles leaves nothing to be desired, and I would also mention Colonel Defforges' pendulum, which makes it possible to determine gravity with a precision unknown till now.

The future of French Geodesy is now in the hands of the geographical department of the army, which has been directed successively by General Bassot and General Berthaut. This has advantages that can hardly be overestimated. For good geodetic work, scientific aptitude alone is not sufficient. A man must be able to endure long fatigues in all climates. The chief must know how to command the obedience of his collaborators and to enforce it upon his native helpers. These are military qualities, and, moreover, it is known that science has always gone hand in hand with courage in the French army.

I would add that a military organization assures the indispensable unity of action. It would be more difficult to reconcile the pretensions of rival scientists, jealous of their independence and anxious about what they call their honour, who would nevertheless have to operate in concert, though separated by great distances. There arose frequent discussions between geodesists of former times, some of which started echoes that were heard long after. The Academy long rang with the quarrel between Bouguer and La Condamine. I do not mean to say that soldiers are free from passions, but discipline imposes silence upon oversensitive vanity.

Several foreign governments have appealed to French officers to organize their geodetic departments. This is a proof that the scientific influence of France abroad has not been weakened.

Her hydrographic engineers also supply a famous contingent to the common work. The chart of her coasts and of her colonies, and the study of tides, offer them a vast field for research. Finally, I would mention the general leveling of France, which is being carried out by M. Lallemand's ingenious and accurate methods.

With such men, we are sure of the future. Work for them to do will not be wanting. The French colonial empire offers them immense tracts imperfectly explored. And that is not all. The International Geodetic Association has recognized the necessity of a new measurement of the arc of Quito, formerly determined by La Condamine. It is the French who have been entrusted with the operation. They had every right, as it was their ancestors who achieved, so to speak, the scientific conquest of the Cordilleras. Moreover, these rights were not contested, and the French Government determined to exercise them.

Captains Maurain and Lacombe made a preliminary survey, and the rapidity with which they accomplished their mission, traveling through difficult countries, and climbing the most precipitous peaks, deserves the highest praise. It excited the admiration of General Alfaro, President of the Republic of Ecuador, who surnamed them *los hombres de hierro, the men of iron.*

The definitive mission started forthwith, under the command of Lieutenant-Colonel (then Commandant) Bourgeois. The results obtained justified the hopes that had been entertained. But the officers met with unexpected difficulties due to the climate. More than once one of them had to remain for several months at an altitude of 13,000 feet, in clouds and snow, without seeing anything of the signals he had to observe, which refused to show themselves. But thanks to their perseverance and courage, the only result was a delay, and an increase in the expenses, and the accuracy of the measurements did not suffer.

Chapter 8

The Controversy over
the Rotation of the Earth

In the early 1890s, Poincaré became interested in philosophical questions; in 1893, he ended up publishing his reflections on "Le continu en
mathématique[1]" and on "Le mécanisme et l'expérience[2]" (Mechanism and
experience) in the journal *Revue de Métaphysique et de Morale*. The reflection on mechanism and experience gave rise to a controversy involving
the French engineer Georges Lechalas (1851-1919) who wrote in an article
entitled: "Sur la réversibilité du monde matériel[3]" (On the reversibility of
the material world), which was published the following year in the same
journal, that "the conclusions of Mr. Poincaré against reversibility are
somehow exaggerated." A few years later, when the controversy over the
rotation of the Earth broke out, Lechalas, who was then a close associate
of the journal *Revue des questions Scientifiques* published by the Scientific
Society of Brussels, intervened in the dispute between the Belgian scientists
Ernest Pasquier (1849-1926) and Lucien Anspach (1857-1915) (see below).

Not ruffled in the slightest, Poincaré continued his philosophical analysis and in 1894, he published a study called "Sur la nature du raisonnement
mathématique[4]" (On the nature of mathematical reasoning) in the journal
Revue de Métaphysique et de Morale. Like the previous publication, the
study was sharply criticized by Lechalas. Three years later, tired of being
systematically attacked by him and the philosopher Louis Couturat (1868-
1914), who had by then also intervened in the controversy, Poincaré reacted

---

[1]See Henri Poincaré, "Le continu mathématique," *Revue de Métaphysique et de Morale*,
vol. 1 (1893), p. 26-34 (On the mathematical continuity)

[2]See Henri Poincaré, "Le mécanisme et l'expérience," *Ibid.*, p. 534-537.)

[3]See Lechalas Georges, "Sur la réversibilité du monde matériel," *Revue de Métaphysique
et de Morale*, vol. 2 (1894), p. 191-197. See also Poincaré's answer on pages 197-198.

[4]See Henri Poincaré, "Sur la nature du raisonnement mathématique," *Revue de
Métaphysique et de Morale*, vol. 2 (1894), p. 371-384.

by writing an article published in the same journal and entitled: "Réponse à quelques critiques[5]" (Responding to a few critics). He then submitted a study called "Les idées de Hertz sur la Mécanique[6]" (Hertz's ideas on Mechanics) to the journal *Revue générale des sciences pures et appliquées*, in which he wrote about the fact that the fundamental principles of Mechanics should be considered as definitions rather than as experimental laws. He then studied "La mesure du temps[7]" (Measure of time) in 1898 and "La logique et l'intuition dans la science mathématique et dans l'enseignement[8]" (Logic and intuition in mathematical science and teaching) in 1899.

Consequently, in spite of having reached a considerable reputation in the fields of mathematics, physics and astronomy, which he gained in particular by winning the first prize in the competition instituted by the King of Sweden and Norway, Poincaré had some trouble making a name for himself as a philosopher at the end of the century. However, even if his vision of the world and his philosophical conceptions sometimes shocked the minds of some of his contemporaries, he did play an important role in the field of the philosophy of science from that time on.

8.1   The Origin of the Controversy

In 1900, from Wednesday the 1st to Sunday the 5th of August, the International Congress of Philosophy chaired by the philosopher Émile Boutroux (1845-1921), Poincaré's brother in law, was held in Paris, at the initiative of the philosopher Xavier Léon[9] (1868-1935). Poincaré was then invited to present the ideas he wrote about in "Sur les principes de la Mécanique[10]" (On the Principles of Mechanics) during the *Logique et Histoire des Sciences session* (Logic and History of Science) which he chaired in the afternoon of Thursday, the 2nd of August. In the talk he gave, Poincaré challenged the existence of an absolute space:

---

[5]See Henri Poincaré, "Réponse à quelques critiques," *Revue de Métaphysique et de Morale*, vol. 5, (1897), p. 59-70.

[6]See Henri Poincaré, "Les idées de Hertz sur la Mécanique," *Revue générale des sciences pures et appliquées*, vol. 8 (1897), p. 734-743.59-70.

[7]See Henri Poincaré, "La mesure du temps," *Revue de Métaphysique et de Morale*, vol. 6 (1898), p. 1-13.

[8]See Henri Poincaré, "La logique et l'intuition dans la science mathématique et dans l'enseignement," *L'Enseignement mathématique*, vol. 1, (1899), p. 157-162.

[9]He was also the founder of the *Revue de Métaphysique et de Morale* in 1893.

[10]See Henri Poincaré, "Sur les principes de la Mécanique," *Bibliothèque du Congrès international de philosophie*, Armand Colin, Paris, (1901), vol. 3, p. 457-494.

"There is no absolute space, and we only conceive of relative motion; and yet in most cases mechanical facts are enunciated as if there is an absolute space to which they can be referred[11]."

He then added:

"Absolute space, that is to say, the mark to which it would be necessary to refer the earth to know whether it really moves, has no objective existence. Hence this affirmation "the earth turns round" has no meaning, since it can be verified by no experiment; since such an experiment not only could not be either realized or dreamed by the boldest Jules Verne but cannot be conceived of without contradiction. Or rather these two propositions: "The earth turns round" and "it is more convenient to suppose the earth turns round" have the same meaning; there is nothing more in the one than in the other[12]."

That sentence generated a very lively debate in the press as well as in the journal *Revue des questions scientifiques*, through which the supporters and opponents of the theory of absolute space and motion conflicted. However, as Poincaré explained himself a little later, the sentence was actually pronounced during a discussion he had with the philosopher Édouard Le Roy (1870-1954), the successor of Henri Bergson at the Collège de France:

"The most often quoted[13] was written in the course of a controversy with Monsieur Le Roy, the principal incident of which was a discussion in the Société Philosophique de France. Mr Le Roy had said: "A scientific fact is created by the savant." And he had been asked: – "Be more exact: what do you mean by a fact?" – "A fact," he had answered, "is, for example, the rotation of the earth." And then the answer came: "No, a fact, by definition, is something that can be proved by a direct experiment; it is the crude result of this experiment. For this reason, the rotation of the earth is not a fact[14]."

The Société française de philosophie (French Philosophical Society) was founded in 1901 by Xavier Léon, Elie Halévy and Léon Brunschvicg among others, following the International Congress of Philosophy. An intervention of Le Roy can be seen in the Congress report, in which he maintained:

---

[11]See Henri Poincaré, *Ibid.*, p. 458.

[12]See Henri Poincaré, *Ibid.*, p. 483.

[13]The most quoted sentence. See above.

[14]See Henri Poincaré, "La Terre tourne-t-elle?" *Bulletin de la Société astronomique de France* (mai 1904), p. 216-217.

"The scientist makes the scientific facts, and is far from receiving them passively[15]."

His talk summarized a very long article entitled: *Science et Philosophie*[16] (Science and Philosophy) which was published in 1899 in the journal *Revue de Métaphysique et de Morale*. In the second part of it, Le Roy wrote:

"In conclusion, far from being received passively by our mind, facts are in a way created by it[17]."

Then he added:

"I will conclude with a more complex example. Let the fact be the rotation of the Earth. It is detected by the experience of Foucault's pendulum[18]."

From that moment on, Poincaré's sentence as an answer to Le Roy was taken up by the newspapers and the controversy was born and grew.

In 1902, and then in 1904, three events that seemed unrelated actually brought the controversy in the public space. The first one was when the Foucault pendulum was moved to the Panthéon, and the second one was the publication of Poincaré's work: *La Science et l'Hypothèse*[19] (Science and Hypothesis), which included a chapter on *Le Mouvement relatif et le Mouvement absolu (Relative and absolute motion)*, which was based on the talk he gave at the International Congress of Philosophy, and in which he repeated the famous sentence about "the Earth that turns round". The last event was when the work of the Austrian physicist and philosopher Ernst Mach (1838-1916) was translated; the first edition of the book, in which he strongly criticizes the notions of absolute space and motion, had first been published in German in 1883.

---

[15]See "Congrès international de philosophie," *Revue de Métaphysique et de Morale*, vol. 8, (1900), p. 503-699.

[16]See Édouard Le Roy, "Science et Philosophie," *Revue de Métaphysique et de Morale*, vol. 7, (1899), p. 375-425, p. 503-562, p. 706-731 and *Revue de Métaphysique et de Morale*, vol. 8, (1900), p. 37-72.

[17]*Ibid.* p. 517.

[18]*Ibid.*

[19]See Henri Poincaré, *La Science et l'Hypothèse*, Flammarion, Paris, 1902.

8.2 Moving the Foucault Pendulum to the Panthéon

It was apparently on February 5, 1902, during a session of the *Société Astronomique de France* chaired by Henri Poincaré, that the project of moving the Foucault pendulum to the Panthéon was approved.

> "The pendulum of the Panthéon. – The SECRETARY GENERAL[20] states that after the last session, during which the Society so warmly joined the wish expressed by Mr. de Fonvielle[21] to see the beautiful and instructive experience of Foucault renewed under the dome of the Panthéon (interrupted by the coup d'État of December 1851 before all the conclusions could be drawn), he has been the spokesman of the Société Astronomique de France to the Director of the Beaux-Arts. "The Director of the Beaux-Arts himself would consider the completion of this project with the greatest interest; he supports it completely, and will support it in front of the Minister of Public Instruction as well. "Besides, the architect of the Panthéon, Mr. Nénot, the learned builder of the Sorbonne – and our colleague in this Society, – will examine the issue in practical terms immediately after the centennial celebrations of Victor Hugo's birth, which must precisely take place at the Panthéon on the 26th of this month. "We can then hope to very soon reinstall this grand and majestic demonstration of the rotation of the Earth[22], so that public education can take the greatest advantage of it."

Indeed, fifty-one years before that event, precisely on February 3, 1851, the French physicist Léon Foucault (1819-1868) presented a memoir entitled: "Démonstration physique du mouvement de rotation de la terre au moyen du pendule[23]" (Physical demonstration of the rotation of the Earth using the pendulum) in front of the members of the Académie des Sciences, which began as follows:

---

[20] It was Camille Flammarion (1842-1925) who was president of the Astronomical Society of France.

[21] The french journalist, science popularizer and aeronaut Wilfrid Fonvielle (1824-1914) gave a conference at the Tour Saint-Jacques on October 14, 1887 on the *Démonstration populaire du mouvement de la terre à l'aide du pendule de Léon Foucault*, Éd. Spectateur Militaire, 1887.

[22] Voir *Bulletin de la Société Astronomique*, (1902), p. 113.

[23] See Léon Foucault, "Démonstration physique du mouvement de rotation de la terre au moyen du pendule," *Comptes rendus hebdomadaire des séances de l'Académie des Sciences*, 3 février 1851, t. 32, p. 135-138.

"The pendulum has been the subject of many important observations, which were mostly related to the duration of the oscillations; those that I intend to inform the Académie of have mainly focused on the oscillation plan's direction which, by moving gradually from east to west, provides a sensitive sign of the diurnal motion of the Earth."

A month later, on March 31, 1851, the experience of the Foucault pendulum was installed in the Panthéon at the request of the President of the Republic Louis-Napoléon Bonaparte, who became Napoléon III after the coup d'État of December 2, 1851. To commemorate the fiftieth anniversary of Foucault's experiment, the pendulum was reinstalled in the Pantheon. The *Houston Daily Post* reported this new on June 15, 1902 (See Fig. 8.1).

(Special to The Post)

Paris June 14 – "You are invited to come to the Pantheon to see the earth turn," is the wording of several hundred invitations sent by Camille Flammarion the famous astronomer to prominent scientists and literatures of Paris this morning Foucault's memorable experiment to prove the rotation of this planet is about to be repeated under the auspices of the French Astronomical society in connection with the celebration of the fiftieth anniversary of the original demonstration.

Attached to a wire more than seventy five yards in length the identical pendulum Foucault used will swing from a point just below the top of the dome of the Pantheon, marking its varying passages across a small circular ring of white and on the floor beneath the dome. After a quarter of an hour the four-inch ring will be wiped out – "if" say the scientific wits "Flammarion arranges the machinery rightly." Foucault's pendulum which weighs sixty pounds has been reposing fifty years in the Museum of Arts and Crafts Flammarion, who gave this information this morning said: "There are still a great many people who do not believe that the earth turns, if indeed they ever heard the fact." President Loubet has also been asked to witness the astronomical experiment, and he will be surprised by a passing in feat in importance anything of that nature seen here for half a century.

The inauguration took place in the early afternoon of October 22, 1902 in the presence of Mr. Chaumié, Minister of Public Instruction, and of many eminent scientists including Henri Poincaré and Camille Flammarion. The sculptors Frédéric Auguste Bartholdi and Auguste Rodin were also

MAILABLE EDITION.

32 PAGES TODAY.

HOUSTON DAILY POST.

XVIIITH YEAR—NO. 72. · HOUSTON, TEXAS, SUNDAY, JUNE 15. 1902. PRICE: 5 CENTS.

TO SEE EARTH TURN.

French Astronomer Invites Many Guests to See Demonstration.

FIFTIETH ANNIVERSARY

Of Foucault's Memorable Experiment to Witness Duplicate.

THE IDENTICAL PENDULUM USED

In Former Exemplifications Will Again Be Utilized.

FROM DOME OF THE PANTHEON

A Wire Seventy-five Yards Long Will
Suspend the Pendulum—Great Interest Among Scientists.

Fig. 8.1 *Houston Daily Post*, June 15, 1902.

present. The Catholic French newspaper *La Croix* proposed in a section entitled *Causerie Scientifique* (Scientific Gossip) a detailed explanation of Foucault's experiment as well as an illustration (See Fig. 8.2).

The article written by the science editor under the pseudonym of Somsoc began as follows:

"Under the action of gravity, the pendulum, away from the vertical, will return to it by a series of successive oscillations occurring in a fixed plane, since no force acts to change this plane, and as the earth rotates below the pendulum, the oscillation plane of the latter would seem to rotate relative to the earth in the opposite direction to that of the earth's rotation, that is to say in the same direction as the celestial sphere and that in twenty-four hours. By targeting a star[24] located in the oscillation plane, the pendulum will then not leave the star for the whole duration of the experiment."

Fig. 8.2   *La Croix* du 26 octobre 1902.

A little later, he added: "The oscillation plane is not a material object ...It belongs to the space, to the absolute space."

Flammarion is familiar with this idea of an absolute space. In his inaugural lecture at the Panthéon, he explained:

> "...Similarly the inhabitant of the Earth can create for himself, by means of the pendulum, a kind of compass arbitrarily oriented in absolute space, and whose apparent motion reveals the actual movement of the earth that supports it[25]."

The notion of absolute space was introduced by Isaac Newton (1642-1727) who believed he had proved its existence thanks to the experiment of

---

[24]Such as the Polar Star or Beta Centauri which are sufficiently distant from the Earth to appear motionless. This is why they are generally called "fixed stars." They form, with the Sun or the Earth, a frame of reference called "solid stellar". The question of the relative and not absolute immobility of these stars was the heart of the controversy and discord. See below.

[25]See "Discours de M. Flammarion," *Bulletin de la Société Astronomique*, (1902), p. 475.

the bucket of water suspended from a rope, whose torsion gave the bucket a circular motion, making the surface of the water go from flat to concave.

But can an absolute space really exist?

The question was raised long before the pendulum was moved to the Panthéon and the experiment was renewed, and had already caused a heated debate. Indeed, right after Foucault had submitted his findings to the Académie des Sciences, the French astronomer and mathematician Jacques Philippe Marie Binet (1786-1856) had submitted a note: "Sur le mouvement du pendule simple en ayant égard au mouvement diurne de la terre[26]" ("On the motion of the simple pendulum regarding the diurnal motion of the earth") on February 17, 1851, in which he had established the differential equations of motion and shown that the period of oscillations was really in inverse proportion to the sine of the latitude of where the experiment took place. According to Stéphane Deligeorges[27]:

> "J.M Binet's paper causes an intense scientific controversy. This quarrel is between two clans: the synthetists and the analysts, of whom Binet is the leader. For him, it is urgent to justify the reasons for this empirical finding by calculation. He has built in only a few days an analytical theory of Foucault's experiment. Need we be reminded that all are outstanding mathematicians, jewels of this French school of mathematical physics of which the country is so proud. The others, the geometricians, like Foucault, content themselves with a simple mechanical or geometrical demonstration. Poinsot is on their side[28]."

Indeed, Binet's paper was immediately followed by a series of remarks[29] by the mathematician Louis Poinsot (1777-1859) who wrote:

> "...This movement is a purely geometrical phenomenon, the explanation of which must be provided by simple geometry, as

---

[26] Jacques Philippe Marie Binet, "Sur le mouvement du pendule simple en ayant égard au mouvement diurne de la terre," *Comptes rendus hebdomadaire des séances de l'Académie des Sciences*, 17 février 1851, t. 32, p. 197-205.

[27] See Stéphane Deligeorges, Foucault et ses pendules, Éditions Carré, 1990, Paris.

[28] *Ibid.*, p. 67.

[29] Louis Poinsot, "Remarques de M. POINSOT sur l'ingénieuse expérience imaginée par M. Léon Foucault pour rendre sensible le mouvement de rotation de la terre," *Comptes rendus hebdomadaire des séances de l'Académie des Sciences*, 17 février 1851, t. 32, p. 206-207.

did Foucault, and not by the principles of dynamics that have nothing to do with it[30]."

But the source of the discord did not lie in the sole opposition between the geometrical and the analytical point of view. Poinsot also highlighted the problem of the relativity of motion and of the existence of an absolute space:

> "The problem is to find some object or plan on earth which we know for sure that it remains fixed in absolute space, or at least that it is not involved in the rotational motion the earth could have around the vertical of the observer's location. For if such plan can be found, and we see him turn around the vertical in a certain direction, it is clear that it will be the earth itself which will be turning in the opposite direction. The difficulty of the question is then to be able to obtain, on earth, a plan which has the property that was just written about[31]."

In U.S.A. one finds echoes of Foucault's experiment in many daily papers such as *The Times* of November 9, 1902 (*Foucault's pendulum again swings in the Panthéon*), *The Saint Louis Republic* of November 23, 1902 (*Earth's movement pictured by pendulum*), The *Houston Daily Post* of December 14, 1902 (*Earth and the Pendulum*) to name but a few (See Figures below).

Fig. 8.3   *The Times*, November 9, 1902.

---

[30] *Ibid.*, p. 206.
[31] *Ibid.*, p. 206.

FOUCAULT'S PENDULUM AGAIN SWINGS IN THE PANTHEON.

(Special Cable Dispatch to The Times, Copyright, 1902.)

PARIS, Nov. 8.—If there are travelers who still doubt that the earth revolves on its axis, to be convinced they need only to visit the Pantheon, where the Astronomical Society of France has revived Foucault's experiments of 1851 with a pendulum swung from the dome, 224 feet above the floor. This pendulum consists of a fine steel wire sustaining at its lower end a copper ball weighing sixty-six pounds.

From the lower surface of the ball a point protrudes, which strikes near the extremities of its swing two little mounds of fine sand, whereby the direction of the plane of oscillation is determined; also there is placed underneath a graduated card, from which the particular angle of swing may be read off. Special precautions are taken in starting the pendulum, for it is absolutely necessary that it should swing straight, and have no sideway movement.

Each complete oscillation takes about sixteen seconds, and it would swing perpetually if not retarded by the resistance of the air. Soon, however, it will be observed that the original plane of swing is being departed from, the point below the ball begins to wear down the molecules of sand along the rim of the mounds, indicating a deviation from east to west. The deviation thus observed, however, is only apparent. The plane of swing really remains immovable, and in truth it is the earth that rotates beneath it from west to east; therefore, the rotation of the earth is rendered perceptible to the eyes of all.

◁EARTH'S MOVEMENT PICTURED BY PENDULUM.▷

CAMILLE FLAMMARION RENEWS INTEREST IN HISTORIC SUBJECT.

CAMILLE FLAMMARION

FIG. I.
—VIEW FROM ABOVE—

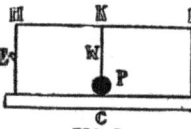

FIG. 2.
—VIEW FROM THE SIDE—

PROF. JOHN K. REES.
HEAD OF THE ASTRONOMICAL DEPT. COLUMBIA UNIVERSITY.

WRITTEN FOR THE SUNDAY REPUBLIC.

It is fifty-one years since Foucault, the French astronomer, gave his famous demonstration of the earth's rotation, in the Paris Pantheon, after which our National Capitol was modeled.

From the great dome he set a pendulum—a wire tipped with a cannon ball—swinging over a table encircled by a ridge of sand. A pin attached to the bottom of the ball marked the path of the pendulum in the sand at each swing across the table.

As a pendulum in motion is not moved a hair's breadth from its course by the revolving earth, the table was seen slowly turning by the pendulum's track on the sand.

Foucault's experiments were stopped by the coup d'etat of Louis Napoleon, December 2, 1851.

Recently, however, Camille Flammarion has renewed interest in the subject. The other day he swung a piano wire pendulum 328 feet long, carrying a fifty-six-pound iron ball, with a stylus attached for marking the earth's movement on the sand.

The exhibition, again in the Pantheon, was of such importance that eminent men delivered addresses to the large assembly of scientists and public officials present. A report of the proceedings was sent by cable over the world.

In view of the popular interest awakened by the subject Professor John K. Rees of Columbia University has consented to further explain the experiment in detail for the readers of The Sunday Republic.

His account of the various astronomical conjectures and demonstrations leading up to Foucault's exhibitions in the Pantheon, together with what has since been achieved in that direction, makes an interesting story.

BY PROFESSOR JOHN K. REES.

The great astronomer and geographer, Ptolemy (130), did not consider that the rotation of the earth on an axis was possible. He thought the velocity would be so great that the air would be left behind. Even if the air was carried around bodies floating in the air would be left behind.

Copernicus (1543), having better knowledge of the distance of the stars, argued that if the stars revolved about the earth in a day their velocities would be almost infinite.

The hypothesis of the daily revolution of the earth be considered much more probable than the daily revolution of the celestial sphere.

The discovery of the telescope enabled Galileo and others to show that the sun,

moon and Jupiter revolved on axes and Jupiter and Saturn had satellites which went around them.

Analogy, therefore, confirmed the idea of a rotating earth.

During the last century experimental proofs have been devised to prove this rotation.

Foucault's pendulum experiment in the Pantheon in Paris is the most striking proof.

His experiment depended on the fact that if a heavy ball is suspended by a wire and then allowed to oscillate like a pendulum, the plane of vibration will not change.

Suppose that over a round table, like that illustrated in the diagram, capable of revolution, without jar, there is suspended vertically above the center (C) a heavy ball (P) by a wire. Gently pull the ball to one side (as P1) and let it go. It will oscillate in a vertical plane, of which X C M is the trace on the table.

Now revolve the table as the arrow indicates.

If in a few seconds of time the point X moves to Z the pendulum will be oscillating in the same vertical plane as before, but the marks on the table will revolve and the line X C M will be in the new position, Z C N. If we are not cognizant of the table's motion the plane of the pendulum's vibration will appear to move the other way.

In one complete revolution of the table to the left the plane of the pendulum swing will appear to make a complete revolution to the right.

If a pendulum then is suspended above the North Pole of the earth in twenty-four sidereal hours the earth will revolve and the pendulum vibrating plane will appear to go round in the opposite direction at the same time.

So also at the South Pole.

If the experiment is tried on the equator, and, for example, the pendulum swings in a north and south direction, as the earth revolves, the same points will be north and south, and the swinging plane will not change, even apparently.

It remains fixed to our eyes.

At the poles the terrestrial plane under the pendulum revolves in twenty-four hours.

At the equator it remains fixed, with reference to the swing of the pendulum.

In any latitude between the equator and the pole the time of a complete revolution of the pendulum's swinging plane, as it appears to the observer, will be somewhere between twenty-four hours and infinity.

The law of change is such that at the Pantheon in Paris, in latitude north 49 deg.

50 min. 49 sec., the time required for a complete change of the plane of swing, apparently to the observer, will be 31 hours 47 minutes and 14.6 seconds of mean or ordinary clock time.

Foucault worked out the theory and tried experiments in his laboratory, which were very satisfactory.

So much interest was taken in the matter that, with the aid of Arago, a plan was devised to swing a pendulum under the dome of the Pantheon that the proof might be made visible to all interested.

The apparatus was mounted in 1851.

The length of the pendulum, from the suspension point to the center of oscillation of the ball, was 67 meters (218 feet), and the ball weight 28 kilograms (61 pounds).

A pin fastened to the under side of the ball scraped a mark in a little ridge of sand placed on a rail fastened in a circular form around the central point.

The time of one swing was 8.2 seconds.

The apparent deviation of the plane in one oscillation of the pendulum was about 1½ minutes of arc.

The air resists the motion of the pendulum ball and would soon bring it to rest.

In order to overcome this resistance Foucault devised an ingenious electric apparatus, which accelerated by magnetic attraction the motion of the iron ball at the center of every swing.

This apparatus made it possible to cause the pendulum to swing for as long a time as was desired.

The circle of the Pantheon was 18 meters in circumference and the deviation apparently of the vibration plane of the pendulum at each return to the same place was about 2.3 millimeters measured on that circle.

The experimental proof was received with great applause, and since that time it has been repeated at a number of places.

In May, 1851, the experiment was tried at the Cathedral in Reims, and again in June, 1868, at the Cathedral in Amiens.

Foucault also devised an experiment proving the earth's rotation, using a gyroscope.

During the summer of 1900 there was exhibited an experiment at the Paris Astronomical Observatory which, with the aid of a lantern, showed the earth's rotation on the screen.

It seems strange that even to-day there are many persons who believe in a flat earth and an earth that does not rotate on an axis.

The Foucault experiment could be suc-

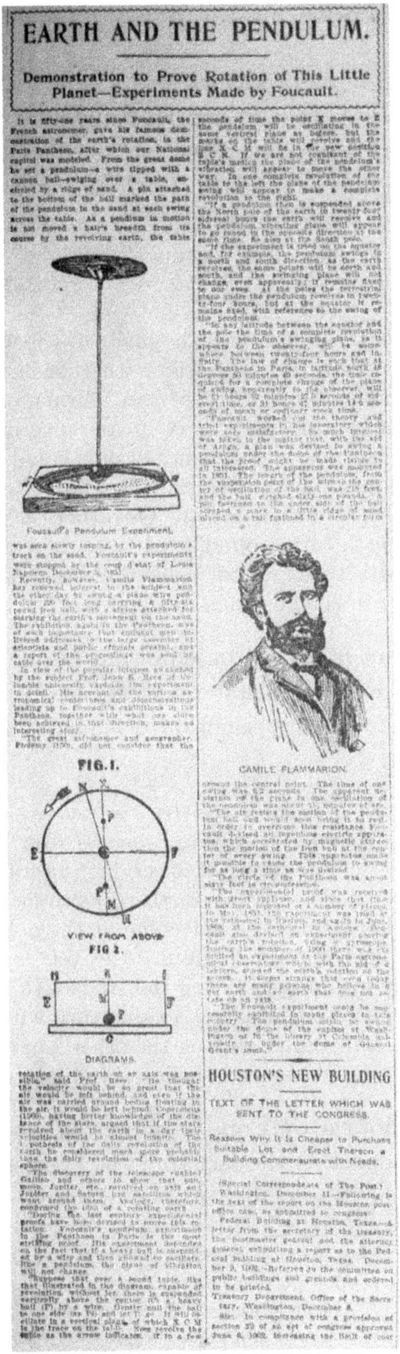

EARTH AND THE PENDULUM.

Demonstration to Prove Rotation of This Little Planet—Experiments Made by Foucault.

Foucault's Pendulum Experiment.

FIG. I.

VIEW FROM ABOVE
FIG 2.

DIAGRAMS

CAMILE FLAMMARION

HOUSTON'S NEW BUILDING

TEXT OF THE LETTER WHICH WAS SENT TO THE CONGRESS.

Reasons Why It Is Cheaper to Purchase Suitable Lot and Erect Thereon a Building Commensurate with Needs.

8.3   Science and Hypothesis

One month after the pendulum was moved to the Panthéon, the first philosophical work of Poincaré: Science and Hypothesis[32] was submitted to the Académie des Sciences[33] on November 10, 1902, and to the *Société Astronomique de France* on December 3, 1902. In Chapter VIII entitled: *Le Mouvement relatif et le Mouvement absolu* (Relative and absolute motion), Poincaré repeated in extenso the sentence that was at the origin of the controversy:

> "Absolute space, that is to say, the mark to which it would be necessary to refer the earth to know whether it really moves, has no objective existence. Hence this affirmation "the earth turns round" has no meaning, since it can be verified by no experiment; since such an experiment not only could not be either realized or dreamed by the boldest Jules Verne but cannot be conceived of without contradiction. Or rather these two propositions: "The earth turns round" and "it is more convenient to suppose the earth turns round" have the same meaning; there is nothing more in the one than in the other[34]."

The latter statement is mainly based on his intimate belief in the non-existence of an absolute space that he wrote about in the preamble of the book. Regarding the relative motion, Poincaré wrote in the few lines preceding this excerpt:

> "I will dwell on the case of relative motion referring to axes which rotate uniformly. If the sky were for ever covered with clouds, and if we had no means of observing the stars, we might, nevertheless, conclude that the earth turns round. We should be warned of this fact by the flattening at the poles, or by the experiment of Foucault's pendulum. And yet, would there in this case be any meaning in saying that the earth turns round? If there is no absolute space, can a thing turn without turning with respect to something; and, on the other hand, how can we admit Newton's conclusion and believe in absolute space?"

But Poincaré was not the only one to refute the existence of an absolute space and to call into question the fact that the experience of the Foucault pendulum provided conclusive evidence of the diurnal rotation of the Earth.

---

[32] See Henri Poincaré, *La Science et l'Hypothèse*, Flammarion, Paris, 1902.

[33] See Ernest Pasquier, "À propos du pendule de Foucault," *Revue des questions scientifiques*, 1903, vol. 53, p. 501-515 et le journal *Le Temps* du 12 novembre 1902.

[34] See Henri Poincaré, *La Science et l'Hypothèse*, Flammarion, Paris, 1902, p. 141.

8.4   The Skeptical Polytechnician

Indeed, on November 29, 1902, the weekly paper *L'Illustration* received a letter from an anonymous student from the École Polytechnique, entitled:

Le pendule de Foucault prouve-t-il quelque chose[35]?

In his letter, the "skeptical student from Polytechnique", (he was called as such in the article), wrote:

> "If we turn to the mechanics, we can see that it is entirely based on fundamental propositions which were accepted as proven by the everyday experience, but which are impossible to prove, because it is impossible to find in the world one completely still body. Only relative movements of a body relative to another which is itself in motion can be observed, and the consequences are applied to the movement of a body relative to another which would be fixed. It can therefore be said that the basis of all mechanics has a lot of shortcomings; but one keeps on accepting it as indisputable until proven otherwise, and anyone who would dare to call it into question would be called a fool."

To see how relevant the reasoning of this supposed student of the École Polytechnique was, (he signed his letter under the initials L.F., which are remarkably similar to those of Léon Foucault) is somehow confusing, to say the least, when compared with Poincaré's conclusion, presented below, on the relative movement and the non-existence of an absolute space. Could the author of the letter be Poincaré?

Following this letter came the response of Camille Flammarion, who said:

> "The experiment of the Foucault pendulum was not necessary to convince us of the movement of the Earth. It does only one thing, which is confirming it, showing a shift of the oscillation plane which is explained by this movement and could not be explained otherwise. If we only had this experiment to prove this movement; if we lived in a world constantly covered with clouds, which would keep us from seeing the Sun, the Moon and the stars; if Astronomy, this celestial revelation, did not

---

[35] Does the Foucault pendulum actually prove something? See "Le pendule de Foucault prouve-t-il quelque chose?" *Bulletin de la Société Astronomique de France*, janvier 1903, p. 29-31, reproduction of a letter and a response extracted from *L'Illustration* of november 29, 1902.

exist, this pendulum movement would certainly not be interpreted, and would prove nothing. This experiment is a simple
confirmation, a material fact which appeals to every eye, a sup-
plement, a way to spell it out."

If Flammarion reached the same conclusion as Poincaré regarding the
impossibility of proving the diurnal rotation of the globe using a Foucault
pendulum in the case of an "isolated" Earth, he however made no reference
to the absolute space in relation to which this motion was supposed to
occur.

8.5   Mach's Mechanics

In his book entitled *La Mécanique : exposé historique et critique de son
développement*[36] (The science of mechanics: a critical and historical account
of its development) whose first edition was published in German in 1883,
the Austrian physicist and philosopher Ernst Mach (1838-1916) was highly
critical of the notions of absolute space and motion. The book was finally
translated in 1904 by the mathematician and physicist Émile Bertrand
(1872-1929)[37]:

"If the earth is affected with an absolute *rotation* about its
axis, centrifugal forces are set up in the earth: it assumes an
oblate form, the acceleration of gravity is diminished at the
equator, the plane of Foucault's pendulum rotates, and so on.
All these phenomena disappear if the earth is at rest and the
other heavenly bodies are affected with absolute motion round
it, such that the same *relative* rotation is produced. This is,
indeed, the case, if we start *ab initio* from the idea of absolute
space. But if we take our stand on the basis of facts, we shall
find we have knowledge only of relative spaces and motions.
Relatively, not considering the unknown and neglected medium
of space, the motions of the universe are the same whether

---

[36] See Ernst Mach, *Die Mechanik in ihrer Entwickelung historisch-kritisch dargestellt*,
Leipzig, F. A. Brockhaus, 1883, 1888, 1897, 1901, 1904, and Ernst Mach, *La Mécanique.
Exposé historique et critique de son développement*, translated from the fourth German
edition, preface by Émile Picard, Paris, A. Hermann, 1904. The French daily paper the
Journal des débats politiques et littéraires of November 25, 1903 tells us that this work
was presented to the Académie des Sciences by Émile Picard. The French daily paper
Le Temps of January 28, 1904 gave a bibliographical review. Thus, it seems that the
book was available as soon as late 1903 and early January 1904.
[37] Poincaré, who could read German very well from his earlier age had probably had
access to this document before it was translated.

we adopt the Ptolemaic or the Copernican mode of view. Both views are, indeed, equally *correct*; only the latter is more simple and more practical. The universe is not twice given, with an earth at rest and an earth in motion; but only once, with its relative motions, alone determinable. It is, accordingly, not permitted us to say how things would be if the earth did not rotate[38]."

He then concluded by writing in favor of a rotation of the Earth relative to the stars called fixed:

"For me, only relative motions exist (*Erhaltung, der Arbeit*, p. 48; *Science of Mechanics*, p. 229) and I can see, in this regard, no distinction between rotation and translation. When a body moves relatively to the fixed stars, centrifugal forces are produced; when it moves relatively to some different body, and not relatively to the fixed stars, no centrifugal forces are produced. I have no objection to calling the first rotation 'absolute' rotation, if it be remembered that nothing is meant by such a designation except relative rotation with respect to the fixed stars[39]."

During this pre-relativist period, the notions of absolute space and motion as well as those of absolute time were bitterly debated by physicists and also by philosophers. Nevertheless, the arguments advanced by Mach and Poincaré seemed to offend the public opinion and the wisest minds.

Consequently, many newspapers would assume that Poincaré had doubts about the diurnal rotation of our globe, and numerous articles entitled: "La Terre tourne-t-elle?" ("Does the Earth rotate?") would regularly appear in newspaper columns.

8.6 Does the Earth Rotate?

In early January 1904, an incident led to a heated controversy between Catholics and Seculars: the case of Father Alfred Loisy (1857-1940). Theologian and exegete cleric, he published in 1902 a book entitled *L'Évangile et l'Église*[40] (The Gospel and the Church, nicknamed "Red Book" because of the color of its cover) in which his historical and philological approach of the *Saintes Écritures* (Holy Scriptures) called into question some of the

---

[38] *Ibid.*, p. 225.
[39] *Ibid.*, p. 231.
[40] See Alfred Loisy, *L'Évangile et l'Église*, Picard, Paris, 1902.

Church's dogmas. The condemnation of this work by order of the Holy Office in December 1903 provoked a great emotion and this anathema inflamed the debate that quickly turned into an opposition between the Church and Science.

And who else than Poincaré could better represent Science?

The newspaper *The Sun* on December 25, 1903, reported on the banishment of Abbé Loisy's books.

PAPAL BAN ON LOISY'S BOOKS.

Pius X. Takes the Action Which Leo XIII. Refused to Take.

Special Cable Despatch to THE SUN.

PARIS, Dec. 24.—Five of the best known works of Abbe Loisy, the Roman Catholic Biblical critic, have been placed upon the Index Expurgatorius. Cardinal Richard has received the damnatory decree from the Vatican.

It was accompanied by a letter from Cardinal Merry del Val, Papal Secretary of State, stating that the Pope was profoundly grieved by the disastrous effects of the volumes, which bristle with the gravest errors. Two of the works are "L'Evangile et l'Eglise" and "Etudes Evangeliques." Cardinal Richard communicated the decree to Abbé Loisy, who has signified his submission.

The decree will cause a sensation among Catholics, and it is predicted that it will have vital consequences upon the future development of Catholicism. It is interesting to recall that Pope Leo refused to condemn Abbé Loisy's works.

The newspaper *The Wichita Daily Eagle* on December 27, 1903, published an article on the put in the index of the works of Abbé Loisy.

PUT IN THE INDEX.

Would Have the Works of Abbe Loisy Disapproved.

Rome, Dec. 26.—It is known that Cardinal Richard has urged the vatican to have the works of Abbe Loisy put in the index expurgatorious, fearing that delay to do so would be interpreted as a rejection of his first condemnation of them.

Archbishop Mignot, of Albi, made a brilliant defense of Abbe Loisy, but is said to have failed in his object.

It is the belief of unprejudiced people that Abbe Loisy's theories of biblical criticism and religious philosophy cannot be repressed, and it has been ascertained that the abbe will not abjure his works.

The French daily newspaper *Le Matin* on December 28, 1903 recalled the reasons of his condemnation:

> "Called by the duties of his office and the desire to refute the negation of Protestant rationalism in-depth study of writing, Abbé Loisy could convince himself that, along with ideal truths adopted by the consciousness of all ages, Holy books contained a childish conception of material contingencies and their teaching on the birth and growth of the worlds, the age of the Earth and the history of humanity went beyond the imagination allowed to the gravity of the eternal."

Paradoxically, it was an article published in the same journal and entitled *Comments of a Parisian*, written by the French journalist Henri Harduin opinion (1844-1908), that triggered the controversy: he used the condemnation of the Abbé in order to put light on a certain immobility of the Church that he opposes to a perpetual questioning of science.

"The time has perhaps come, about radium, to make this point is that the superiority of science over religion is that, for her, the dogma, the intangible dogma does not exist. She admits new facts that religions do not admit. This unknown fact, she is always ready to examine, discuss while religions condemn it because it disturbs what is established. Example: A man stood up, Galileo, and said, "The Earth rotates, it rotates around the Sun."
Immediately, the religious leaders draw up themselves against him:
– The Earth does not rotate, because if she turned she was no longer the center of the world, which has always been taught, what we know from revelation, which, consequently, is true.
– But...
– No, the Earth does not rotate. If such a proposition were accepted or even just discussed, the dogma would be reached, faith would disappear, producing a crack in the building representing our beliefs, everything would collapse.
– But see.
– No, we won't see anything. The question may arise and doubt leads to ungodliness. That is, it is what has always been. That and nothing else. And Galileo is condemned...
But one scientist has found a new element, the radium. All concepts taught, admitted on the properties seem to become totally upset. Immediately, science reacts. Something new! Let see this new fact. It would demolish perhaps, scientific dogma. So much the better if truth succeeds to error, science will burn what she loved and will love what she has burned.
And that is why it is not science that goes bankrupt, but religions, one after the other, disappearing by block, never to return, while science is reborn from its ashes perpetually."

This article then produced a chain reaction in the press. Especially in the journal *La Libre Parole* of January 9, 1904 in which the founder of this anti-semitic French newspaper, Édouard Drumont (1844-1917), answered to Henri Harduin as follows:

"Journalists in search of a theme for a chronicle, as our colleague Harduin, who took the task to amuse the readers of *Le Matin*, do not miss this opportunity to lecture solemnly the Church; they brandish immediately Galileo: "You see, says Mr. Harduin, what a contrast between science and the religion! The religion condemned Galileo while the Science bows down in front of a new fact established and acknowledges his past mistakes. The argument would have some value if Science had reached any degree of certainty, while in reality, it is still made of conjectures and assumptions. There is no evidence at all that the Earth rotates, as claimed by Galileo, and wether it is not the center of the planetary system. Mr. Harduin, who is not more learned than me, asserts imperturbably that the Earth rotates; but Mr. Poincaré, who is, at the moment, the first of the French physicists and geometers and who is probably more educated than Mr. Harduin and me, has by no means this affirmative tone which is that of half-ignorant". He said: "It is argued that the Earth rotates, and I do not see any problem for me. It is a nice and convenient hypothesis to explain the formation and evolution of worlds, but after all, this is a hypothesis that can be neither confirmed nor refuted by any objective evidence."

Then, Drumont quoted the sentences pronounced by Poincaré (see above). A confusion had then settled in the minds. Poincaré was talking about the diurnal rotation of the Earth around its axis and not of the annual revolution of the Earth around the Sun. Nevertheless, the interferometry experiments conducted by Albert Michelson and Edward Morley from 1881 to 1887 had not demonstrated the relative motion of the Earth and the Sun[41].

The answer of Drumont encouraged a journalist of the French newspaper *Le Figaro* to amplify the controversy on the Earth's rotation in an article published on February 2nd, 1904 and entitled: *Do we Turn?*

Tournons-nous ?

∗*∗ M. Drumont soutient présentement, dans la *Libre Parole*, une polémique assez vive sur la question. de savoir, en définitive, si la Terre tourne. C'est un problème qui n'a peut-être pas beaucoup d'actualité ; mais enfin nous voudrions bien savoir à quoi nous en tenir.

M. Drumont citait M. Poincaré ; cet illustre mathématicien, qui est membre de l'Institut, « sans affirmer que la Terre ne tournait pas, affirmait que rien ne prouvait qu'elle tournât ».

---

[41] More precisely, it was about measuring the speed of the Earth relative to ether (hypothetical fluid filling the whole space and whose existence seemed then necessary to the propagation of light), regarded as an absolute reference. See A.A. Michelson and E.W. Morley, "On the relative motion of the earth and the luminiferous ether," *American Journal of Science*, 34 (1887), p. 333-345.

From then on, this questioning of the Earth's rotation unleashed French columnists who pursued the controversy on a humoristic tone. As an example, the article published in the newspaper *Journal des débats politiques et littéraires* of March 23rd, 1904 and entitled: *It turns probably*. The day after, the same journal published an article entitled: *Does the Earth rotate?* in which Poincaré is again involved. In the early spring of 1904, the controversy had reached its climax, and Poincaré had to intervene. He then wrote an open letter to Camille Flammarion entitled "La Terre tourne-t-elle?" (Does the Earth rotate?) which was published in the *Bulletin de la Société Astronomique de France* of May 1904 and preceded by a preamble recalling the facts:

> "A number of newspapers in France and abroad have continued to publish articles under this title, and claimed that Mr. Poincaré had some doubts about the rotation of our planet, despite the article published here by M. Flammarion, and made the best demonstrated truths of modern astronomy be suspiciously considered; so the eminent professor of the Faculty of Science thought he would help to destroy the legend that is sought to be created by writing the following letter to M. Flammarion. As we have said before, (March Bulletin, p. 118), to make the public assume that our great mathematician has doubts – and that he could be doubting for a single moment – regarding the movements of the Earth amounts to exceeding his metaphysical discussion on the "relative and absolute motion" in an eerily way, for he is one of those whose work has best proved these movements."

> "My dear Colleague,

> I am beginning to be rather exasperated by all the noise a section of the press is making about sentences taken from one of my works, – and the ridiculous opinions these newspapers attribute me. The articles from which those sentences were borrowed appeared in a metaphysical review; in them I spoke a language well understood by constant readers of that review. The article most often quoted was written in the course of a controversy with Mr LE ROY, the principal incident of which was a discussion in the Société Philosophique de France. Monsieu LE ROY had said: "A scientific fact is created by the savant." And he had been asked: "Be more exact: what do you mean by a fact?" "A fact," he had answered, "is for example the rotation of the Earth." And then the reply came: "No, a fact, by definition, is something that can be proved by a direct experiment; it is the

crude result of this experiment. For this reason, the rotation of the earth is not a fact."

When I said, "these two sentences: "The earth turns round" and "it is more convenient to suppose the earth turns round have the same meaning", I spoke the language of modern metaphysics[42]. In the same language one says, offhand: The two sentences "The exterior world exists," and "It is convenient to assume that the exterior world exists" have one and the same meaning. Thus, the rotation of the Earth is certain in the same degree as is the existence of external objects. I think there is reassurance in this for those who might have been frightened by unusual words. As for the conclusions that people have wished to draw, it is useless to show how absurd they are. What I have said would not have justified the persecution of Galileo, first, because even error should not be persecuted, next because, even from a metaphysical point of view, it is not false that the Earth rotates; thus Galileo cannot have made a mistake.

This does not mean, either, that one may teach with impunity that the Earth does not rotate, for the reason, if for none other, that a belief in this rotation is a means as indispensable for him who wishes to think learnedly as is the railroad, for example, to him who wishes to travel speedily. As for the proofs of this rotation, they are too well known for me to dwell on them. If the earth did not rotate, we should have to admit that the stars describe in twenty-four hours an immense circumference which light would take centuries to traverse. Now, those who look upon metaphysics as out of date since Auguste Comte will tell me that there can be no modern metaphysics. But the denial of all metaphysics is in itself metaphysical, and it is precisely that view that I call modern metaphysics. Forgive this chatter.

Yours sincerely

POINCARÉ

---

[42]Poincaré's answer is quite disappointing, since he does not come back to the main argument that he had used, which is the non-existence of an absolute space relative to which one was supposed to determine the absolute rotation of the Earth around itself. His letter takes almost the same turn as Galileo's abjuration, since he ends up having to "hide" behind the language of modern metaphysics which would have given him a free hand to say and write these two fateful sentences. Indeed, if modern metaphysics means using timeless and universal concepts that are not submitted to reality, we can consider that the search for an absolute space is a metaphysical approach. However, from a physical point of view, and more specifically from a mechanical point of view, the absence of such space contradicts the assertion according to which the experience of the Foucault pendulum is a demonstration of the diurnal rotation of the Earth.

Unfortunately, despite his intervention, this controversy would haunt Poincaré until the end of his life as evidenced by a chapter of the children book he published in 1911 entitled "Ce que disent les choses[43] (What facts tell us) in which he implicitly came back to the controversy right from the first pages.

> "...When the sky seems to turn around, Is it really the sky that moves, or is it fixed while we are the ones who turn?"

That incident marked Poincaré's life so strongly that several of his biographers mention it. Here is how the science historian Georges Sarton (1884-1956) of Belgian origin recalled that event in the obituary he devoted to Poincaré when he passed away:

> "Henri Poincaré has to thoroughly call into question the classical principles of mechanics, and in particular the principle of relativity. The usual exposition of this principle is as follows: the movement of any system must obey the same laws, whether they are referred to fixed axes or to moving axes drawn into a uniform rectilinear motion. This results from the very form of the fundamental equation of dynamics. But we can give the principle of relativity a much more extensive meaning, which can be summarized as follows: it is impossible to understand absolute space and time, – and yet, how is it that we can demonstrate, by the experiment of Foucault for example, the rotation of a system, – let us say at once, to fix our ideas, the rotation of the Earth? Is not there a glaring inconsistency? But this contradiction only exists when defining relativity in two different ways, without realizing it. If we keep to the physical point of view, that is to say, if we adopt the first definition, it is clear that the rotation of the Earth is real; it is the Earth that rotates, since it is oblate and the Foucault pendulum swings! But it is wrong to conclude, as did Newton, that there is an absolute space, because when we look at things on the broader perspective, we go from the physical concept of relativity – limited by the experimental realities – to the psychological notion[44]."

---

[43]See "Ce que disent les choses," Henri Poincaré, Edmond Perrier, Paul Painlevé, Hachette 1911, p. 6.

[44]See Georges Sarton, "Notice nécrologique de Henri Poincaré," *Ciel et Terre, Bulletin de la Société Belge d'Astronomie*, XXXIVème année, n° 1 & n° 2, 1913, p. 39.

The French astronomer Charles Nordmann (1881-1940) wrote about the controversy in a note on Poincaré:

"However, those men – do they still deserve the name of scientists? – who see in a scientific conquest nothing but the benefit that certain groups can make out of it, those who, in the presence of any new fact exclaim "Ah! I wonder how the clericals will react!" Those who, on the other hand, consider "bias as a moral obligation, as people do when dominated by their concern for apologetics; Poincaré does not spare those men his irony." All of them raised around Poincaré and Poincarism a very unexpected storm, which clamor is not yet forgotten, the day when seizing a sentence of Science et Hypothèse, they claimed that the earth did not rotate, that Poincaré, unexpected auxiliary of the Grand Inquisitor, stood against Galileo, and that the latter had been rightly convicted. That event turned to a serious scandal. Outlining his ideas on the uncertainty of our knowledge, our inability to know anything other than the relative, and in particular, both our logical and experimental inability to understand absolute space, Poincaré had wrote these lines, which have been the source of the whole controversy: "Absolute space, that is to say, the mark to which it would be necessary to refer the earth to know whether it really moves, has no objective existence. Hence this affirmation "the earth turns round" has no meaning; or rather these two propositions: "The earth turns round" and "it is more convenient to suppose the earth turns round" have the same meaning." The error of those who decided to fight about it was to have not understood, probably because they have not sufficiently studied it, the particular aspect of Poincaré's agnosticism. Where we usually say "There are varying degrees of certainty," he would rather say: "There are varying degrees of uncertainty," and although this formula is less common, it is what is most true, since there is no certainty. There is nothing but impossible, possible and probable things. Having not appreciated all of this, some have then eerily mistaken on Poincaré's famous assertion. And if Poincaré had written "These two propositions "the "outside world exists" and: "It is more convenient to suppose it "exists", have the same meaning," who would have dared concluding that Poincaré maintained the non-existence of the outside world? And this alone would settle the issue, since the rotation of the Earth has the same degree of certainty that the very existence of the outside world, and the very existence of the earth. But we can go further: we said that according to Poincarism, a physical theory is even truer if it shows more true connections; on the other hand, common sense knows that between any two explanations of a fact, the truer is the one that contains the fewest hypotheses, and especially the fewest absurd hypotheses. Now the hypothesis of the rotation of the Earth shows some true connections between the diurnal movement of the celestial bodies, the flattening of the poles, the rotation of the Foucault pendulum, the gyration of cyclones, the trade winds, and many other phenomena; only this hypothesis enables the celestial mechanics to exist and to plan some new phenomena in advance, verified as true by experiment. The immobility of the earth is possible, absolutely speaking, but there is then no connection between all these phenomena and it is necessary to accumulate the most improbable hypotheses in order to explain them. The case is heard. "The truth, for which Galileo suffered, remains therefore the truth, although it has not altogether the same meaning as for the vulgar, and its true meaning is much more subtle, more profound and more rich." And thus, Poincaré could answer with humor to a reporter who anxiously came to ask for news of the Copernican system, "You may safely take the risk to repeat it, The earth moves! Galileo was right! E pur si muove." Those who believed they served the religion cause and weaken science at the same time by raising this controversy were mistaken. In fact, science can prove nothing, either for or against religious beliefs, as they are inherently and by definition out of the discussion; science was never able to kill faith, except in men whose faith was as fragile as a dead leaf, ready to fall at the first breath[45]."

Finally, about the open letter that Poincaré had addressed to Camille Flammarion[46], Paul Appell wrote:

"H. Poincaré, always vigorous, and taking the perspective of the description of movements, had asked himself what was the best way to describe the movements of the celestial bodies. He had this idea classical idea when studying elements that, to describe a movement, one must choose a system of rigid comparison considered as immobile. Thus, a wheel rotates in relation to a car considered as immobile, but the car rotates in relation to the wheel; an object that moves along the deck of a running ship moves in relation to the boat in a certain way, but is animated quite differently in relation to the banks. To describe the movements of the celestial bodies, one must then choose a

---

[45]See "Henri Poincaré, son œuvre scientifique, sa philosophie," *Revue des deux Mondes*, vol. 11, p. 331-368, 1912.
[46]See "La Terre tourne-t-elle ?" *Bulletin de la Société Astronomique de France*, 1er mai 1904, p. 216-217.

comparison system. In this purpose, the skull of a given man, who would then be immobile by definition, could be chosen; but this choice would obviously not be convenient; the Earth can be chosen, as it was by the ancients; with Newton, rectangular axes can be chosen, which have the center of gravity of the solar system as their origin and which are turned towards three supposingly fixed stars. This last system that is chosen now, for it is the most convenient. In relation to this system are established the principles of mechanics; if the earth was considered as immobile, the principles of mechanics would be modified; or if a theory dear to Poincaré was followed, according to which the same fact can be mathematically explained in an infinite number of ways, the principles remaining the same, then the forces would be modified[47]."

---

[47]See Appell, p. 84-85 referred to above.

Chapter 9

The Philosophical Work
and its Impact

The previous chapter naturally leads us to consider now the impact of
Poincaré's philosophical work in the press of his time. The controversy
over the rotation of the earth has indeed, as seen above, put forward some
short excerpts from *La science et l'hypothèse* (Science and Hypothesis).
These same extracts were taken up many times and the examples chosen
by Poincaré were taken up by others almost identically. For example, the
image of a land continually covered with clouds can be found in Pasquier
and Flammarion. It can be found as well forty years later in Emile Borel,
when he speaks of "The scientific revolution of the twentieth century" and
more specifically of "The relativity of the Universe" in his book *L'évolution
de la mécanique* (The evolution of mechanics):

> "Supposing that the earth was constantly surrounded by clouds,
> so that the observations of the stars were impossible, and sec-
> ondly, that there was no vast oceans, but only large lakes sep-
> arated by undulating mountainous areas. Men would thus be
> led to consider the earth as flat and to see it as an unlimited
> plan in all directions, until the increased speed of communica-
> tions would make them find it was possible to come back to the
> starting point after going around the Earth[1]."

In France, *Science and Hypothesis* was published in December 1902 as
evidenced by a communication made by Henri Poincaré at the Académie
des Sciences. The English translation was published in 1905.

The ideological appropriation of Poincaré's writings on the famous issue
of the rotation of the earth (reduced to the issue of the conviction of Galileo

---

[1]Émile Borel, *L'évolution de la mécanique*, Flammarion, Bibliothèque de Philosophie
Scientifique, Paris, 1943, p. 199. It is interesting to note about this passage, as about
anything Borel wrote in his book on the "scientific revolution" that relativity created,
that he mentions Poincaré nowhere, not even on the philosophical question.

and even of Giordano Bruno!) in ultra Catholic newspapers and the heated debates that came with it certainly contributed to the quick success of *La science et l'hypothèse*: what better advertising indeed could the collection *Bibliothèque de Philosophie Scientifique* of the Flammarion edition house, in which the book was published, have hoped for?

One must not forget about the social context of the time. In the early XXth century, only a minority of French people had access to this kind of knowledge: those of the upper middle class who theoretically lived in Paris and in major cities. For that matter, an index of this very elitist hierarchy is given by the percentage of students going further than primary school (or high primary school) and entering high school: between 3% and 5% per year on the period going from the Jules Ferry laws of 1882 to the high school reform of 1902. One may therefore be surprised at the success of *La science et l'hypothèse* – as well as the other philosophical works by Henri Poincaré, arduous for the uninitiated. Laurent Rollet actually wondered about it in his thesis:

"If the renown of Poincaré-the-scientist is easily understand-able, one can wonder about the one of Poincaré-the-philosopher. From 1902 to his death, in the *Bibliothèque de Philosophie Sci-entifique* of the Flammarion edition house, Poincaré had in-deed published three books that helped ensure his fame with the general public: *La science et l'hypothèse* (1902), *La valeur de la science* (1905) and *Science et méthode* (1908). In 1913, his heirs finally had to make up from sundries one last posthu-mous volume entitled *Dernières pensées*. The success of these works was resounding (and enduring), the number of impres-sions reached enormous figures: in 1925, his book *La science et l'hypothèse* had already been printed in 40,000 copies, *La valeur de la science* in 32,000, *Science et méthode* in 22,000 and *Dernières pensées* in 16,000. As soon as 1912, the first three books had been translated in most European languages and circulated widely throughout the world; In 1910, *La sci-ence et l'hypothèse* had already been translated into German, English, Spanish, Hungarian, Japanese and Swedish, and *La valeur de la science* into German, English and Spanish." The figures of the books's distribution may seem small as we talked about a "resounding success". But the remarks above explain why such sales are considered that way a posteriori. And one perhaps more significant fact is the number of foreign transla-tions. Some even agree to say that the Poincaré's philosophy has had more impact and has been better appreciated – and on a longer range – abroad than in our own country[2]. This can be explained by the highly compartmentalized organization of knowledge in France, unlike the Anglo-Saxon countries, for example: French philosophers have not always considered Poincaré's writings as part of their discipline, but rather as a form of popularization of a scholar whose scientific recognition could only be won in his specialized fields (mathematics and physics). Besides, as demonstrated by Anne-Françoise Schmid, what makes the originality of Poincaré's epistemology and established his work as a starting point for a new way to practice the philosophy of science lies precisely in two key aspects that could in principle have confused the "true" philosophers. First of all, he was not a philosopher himself: "He worked his way into the philosophical circle thanks to the marriage of his sister Aline to the philosopher Émile Boutroux, with whom he collaborated in several ways. He wrote, for example, a scientific appendix to Boutroux's edition of Leibniz's La Monadologie. Though Poincaré did not study philosophy, he was to become fairly informed through the discussions of the French philosophers of his time[3]." That is how he also got to extensively contribute to the journal *Revue de Métaphysique et de Morale*, founded in 1895, as Boutroux had one of the most active part in it. This is also how he got invited to the first major congress of psychology and philosophy held in Paris in 1900. And entering the philosophical circle enabled him to associate with the founding members of the journal and the French Philosophical Society (founded in 1901), as well as all those who contributed to it. Among the most famous at the time: Bergson, Alain, Durkheim, Milhaud, Couturat, etc.. The second aspect lies in the original philosophical approach of Poincaré. His thinking was indeed part of his scientific practices and therefore of its related disciplines. Anne-Françoise Schmid speaks of a "regional" philosophy: "It is a regional philosophy, for it offers specific forms of philosophical thought for each scientific discipline[4]". It can obviously be clearly noticed simply by reading the highly discipline-structured table of contents of *La science et l'hypothèse* but also *La valeur de la science*. And "the remarkable features of Poincaré's philosophy of science therefore command not to interpret it according to (...) a discipline, but according to the discipline and to how it is related to the

---

[2]See Laurent Rollet, *Henri Poincaré. Des mathématiques à la philosophie*, PhD Thesis, Université de Nancy 2, Advisor: Gerhard Heinzmann, 1999.

[3]Anne-Françoise Schmid, *Henri Poincaré. Les sciences et la philosophie*, L'Harmattan, Paris, 2001, p. 14.

[4]*Ibid.*

other ones[5]". In this sense, Poincaré may appear at the time as not being part of the "innermost circle" of philosophers and, while they continued their quest for a general philosophy of all sciences, Poincaré started from the scientific contents and their forms of development in each discipline, in order to bring out their specific characteristics, and while developing some philosophical patterns, science after science, he unified them into one structure – a "core" one might say – which took into account both the contents of each science, but also the connections between the different fields of scientific knowledge. He was therefore certainly misunderstood, for his work seemed to be "fragmented", but once again, he was also a discoverer: he showed that a philosophy of science cannot be developed without going into the contents, without distinguishing the sciences from one other, and without taking into account both their history and what makes the link between the different fields of knowledge. Content, history, differentiation and links: these were to be the basis of the subsequent epistemological approaches (for example from Popper to Kuhn, then into the theories of complexity and reflexivity, as in Edgar Morin). But let's return to the public success of Poincaré's philosophical works (a success that could make them appear even more suspect in the eyes of "true" philosophers). Anastasios Brenner has lengthily demonstrated the influence of Poincaré's philosophical work in France and abroad. He quotes philosophers, epistemologists, and schools of thought who have read it, taken it up, increased it or at least used it. In a non-exhaustive list, regarding the foreign countries, can be quoted the philosophers of the Vienna Circle but also Popper, Russell, of course, Mach, Quine, Grünbaum, and Hansson, and closer to us, Thomas Kuhn[6]. All schools of thought attempting to exceed or, at least, to revamp the positivism inherited from Auguste Comte (this was actually one of the ambitions of the founders of the journal *Revue de Métaphysique et de Morale*) have read Poincaré, but it was in France that this legacy was the least perceptible at first: his untimely death in 1912 and the beginning of war two years later, then a new generation of philosophers, seem to contribute to the reasons for that situation[7].

---

[5] *Ibid.*

[6] See Anastasios Brenner, *Les origines françaises de la philosophie des sciences*, PUF, Paris, 2003, especially pages 67 and following and pages 109 and following.

[7] *Ibid.*, p. 99-109.

9.1 Science and Hypothesis: "Latin without Crying or Greek without Tears"

The quick popularity and the approximate appropriation of *La science et l'hypothèse* (Science and hypothesis) were in any case confirmed in 1913 by Léon Brunschvicg in the pages devoted to Poincaré's philosophy in the journal *Revue de Métaphysique et de Morale*:

> "In substituting the notion of convenience for that of intuitional verity, Poincaré seems to have overthrown the objectivity of geometry and rational physics, and to have allied himself (sic) with the tradition of nominalist empiricism. He exposed himself to the risk that his incomparable authority as a scholar was invoked in the controversies led in the last years of the XIXth century against the value of intellectual speculation. The trend became invincible in 1902, when his first articles and memoirs of general interest were united under the title *Science et l'Hypothèse* (Science and Hypothesis), in the Library of Scientific Philosophy, which was to become rapidly popular.
>
> Undoubtedly, at the height of theoretical reflection as at the height of moral life, the challenge is less to give than to meet who deserves to receive. The author of la *Science et l'Hypothèse* certainly enjoyed using powerful expressions, seemingly disconcerting, and which can shake the numb mind. Among the mass of his readers, for lack of the attention and intellectual disinterestedness that would have enabled them to understand such a concise and focused thought as his, the paradoxical expressions turned into paradoxes which put the intelligence to flight, and did nothing but arouse some ancient prejudices. Poincaré had wanted to cure people of the illusion that there could be an automatical knowledge that would go on following eternal laws without requiring the intervention of a scrupulous and challenging review. He did not separate the scientific spirit from the spiritual independence, and if I might use a famous expression, I would say he strove for restoring freedom of conscience in the fields of mathematics, mechanics, astronomy and physics."

Although we lack of space here (and it is not the right book to do so) to go into detail about Poincaré's philosophical views, this excerpt from Brunschvicg's text is worth our attention. It indeed gives us several pieces of information. First of all, it reminds us that *La science et l'hypothèse* (Science and Hypothesis) is a compilation of scattered texts (conferences, articles) written earlier by Poincaré. Jules Vuillemin actually tells us about it in the preface to a recent edition of this book[8]: if we refer the reader to this preface, let's just specify that it gives the dates of the writings's original production, and we can thus see that *La science et l'hypothèse* (Science and Hypothesis) was being written ... since 1894! Poincaré simplified texts that were originally written mostly for specialists, in order to make them accessible to a wider readership. This is perhaps one of the reasons for the ostracism Poincaré was subjected to by certain French philosophers: the book was not written as an original work of philosophy: it is a patchwork of texts originally addressed to readerships of very heterogeneous disciplines (mathematicians, physicists, logicians, philosophers ...). But Brunschvicg also tells us that Poincaré's radically original thinking had already raised discussion in the late XIXth century, well before the publication of his book. The subject has already been raised, first regarding the issue of the rotation of the Earth, which had caused the initial reactions at the congress of philosophy in Paris in 1900. It was also the case for issues related to geometry, logic, experimental physics and mathematics. But these exchanges were then held between experts of the issues that had been raised: for example, they had set Poincaré against Russell (on the foundations of geometry and logicism), Le Roy (on conventionalism in science other than geometry), Duhem or even Couturat. Brunschvicg then confirms that "the trend became invincible" when the public took up Poincaré's writings, arousing "ancient prejudices" in the writings of people devoid "of attention and intellectual disinterestedness" needed to be able to understand the work, and only guided by partisan views and thirst for controversy. It happened that way as soon as 1902 and the release of Poincaré's first philosophical book, *La science et l'hypothèse* (Science and Hypothesis). Brunschvicg lastly speaks of Poincaré's "incomparable authority as a scholar" when the book was released. That authority, the aura of this figure, the dissemination of his writings (sometimes unwillingly) in the public on various subjects, have obviously also contributed to the success of his philosophical works, although they remained inaccessible to "the mass of his readers": we shall return to Poincaré as a "public man" in the fourth part of this book.

In 1912, French physicist Gabriel Lippmann (1845-1921) spoke in other words of the gap between the level of Poincaré's philosophical work and the one of his expended readership:

---

[8]Henri Poincaré, *La science et l'hypothèse,* preface by Jules Vuillemin, professor at the Collège de France, Flammarion, 1968.

"Poincaré's philosophy that implies a deep knowledge of mechanics and mathematical physics, which is one of the most abstruse and most inaccessible of disciplines, has moreover become popular: this shows how difficult it is to understand[9]."

And René Dugas summed up the misunderstanding in two well-chosen sentences:

" ... The general public, the press and even the world have felt fascinated by *La science et l'hypothèse*, for they were convinced that they would find something like Latin without crying or Greek without tears, if I might use this old image. It has been a source of incomprehension and misunderstanding[10]."

As Jules Vuillemin reminds us about Poincaré's first philosophical work, "The general purpose of the work is clear. To the systematic and widespread conventionalism of scholars and philosophers such as Le Roy, Poincaré responds with a critical study." In fact, all the philosophical work of Poincaré has been the subject of a far deeper controversy than the issue of the rotation of the earth, which had set him against three major philosophers of his time: Pierre Duhem (1881-1916), founder of the current of thought defined under the appellation of "epistemological holism"; Gaston Milhaud (1858-1918) and Édouard Le Roy (1870-1954), both intuitionists and radical conventionalists.

However, there was no trace of this controversy in the "general public" press: only the specialists were concerned by that affair, and during the previous years, they exchanged their points of view through lively discussions in conferences or articles in more confidential journals. This controversy was based on subjects far too profound for the mainstream press readers, and journalists themselves could not measure its profundity: we shall say more about it with an article by Jehan Sedan that was published in the journal *Revue Illustrée* in 1908. The debate was obviously less appropriable – and less "effective" – ideologically and politically than the one involving Galileo, Copernicus and ... the Church and freethinkers.

---

[9]See Gabriel Lippmann's adress during the session of Monday, December 16, 1912, *Comptes rendus hebdomadaire des séances de l'Académie des Sciences*, December 16, 1912, t. 155, p. 1277-1283.

[10]René Dugas, "Henri Poincaré devant les principes de la mécanique", in *Revue scientifique*, T. XXXIX, 1951, p. on; 81. Quoted by Jean Mawhin, "La terre tourne-t-elle, a propos de la philosophie scientifique d'Henri Poincaré", in Stoffel Jean-François (éd), Le réalisme, Contributions au séminaire d'histoire des sciences 1993-1994, Centre interfacultaire d'étude en histoire des sciences, Louvain-la-Neuve, 1996, p. 215-252.

On February 22nd, 1908, *The New York Times* proposed a review of Poincaré's first philosophical book, *La science et l'hypothèse*:

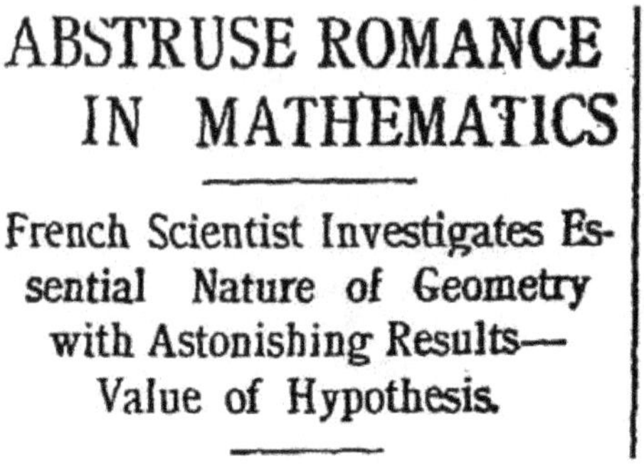

ABSTRUSE ROMANCE IN MATHEMATICS

French Scientist Investigates Essential Nature of Geometry with Astonishing Results— Value of Hypothesis.

Fig. 9.1   *The New York Times* of February 22, 1908.

"Because it is the one thing in a universe or relativities which pretends to "a perfect rigor" – to the absolute – there is to the rigorously scientific mind something suspiciously unscientific about mathematics.

"The very possibility of mathematical science seems an insoluble contradiction," remarks Poincaré (one of the rigorous ones) in his enlivening volume on "Science and Hypothesis" translated from the French by J. Larmor of Cambridge, England, and published in this country by Charles Scribners Sons. M. Poincaré, you are to observe, is rigorous only at logician – and the fascinating series of reflections upon – which he embarks leads you gently to the utmost confines of the imaginable and beyond. His first business is to put mathematics in its place. That is partly accomplished by exposing the science of numbers in its very earliest stages – showing it at work trying to prove that two and two make tour. This process resolves itself into a series of formal definitions, each of which is true because the others are assumed to be true.

You may assume any three of 'em and deduce the fourth beautifully – but you are always driven back upon at least three assumptions. Afterward every additional principle is arrived at by "reasoning by recurrence" – upon a basis of induction. A thing is true of a. It is also true of a plus 1, and so on; therefore it is true of any number. "The essential characteristic of reasoning by recurrence is that it contains condensed, so to speak, in a single formula, an infinite number of syllogisms."

This is why, M. Poincaré pursues, we cannot conceive of a mind powerful enough to see at a glance the whole body of mathematical truth. A chess player can combine for four or five moves ahead; but, however extraordinary player he may be, he cannot prepare for more than a finite number of moves. If he applies his faculties to arithmetic he cannot conceive its general truths by direct intuition alone; to prove even the smallest theorem be must use reasoning by recurrence, for that is the only instrument which enables us to pass from the finite to the infinite."

Obviously, the great deductive science of mathematics, the science of the absolute, derives some of its original data from induction, experience – which is never absolute. The question naturally arises whether (in that case) mathematics is not merely a system of names and definitions which correspond to no reality.

M. Poincaré enters upon that. He tackles the Euclidian geometry, and particularly Euclid's third postulate, the one which asserts that only one line can be drawn through a given point parallel to a given line. This postulate has never been proved. One Lobatchewsky (a rigorous logician) has assumed, therefore, that any number of lines can be so drawn, and constructed upon that assumption a whole system of geometry which does not at any point contradict itself. Similarly one Riemann (another rigorous logician) has supposed that what we call planes only appear so because of their small extent, and so reduced all geometry to the spherical form. He also has rejected the postulate of parallel lines. His substitute premise, naturally, is that no line can be drawn through a given point parallel to a given line. Clearly so; for in spherical geometry a line is an arc of a great circle and no two great circles can ever be parallel.

This geometry also works out without self-contradiction at any point. The effect on individual theorems is, of course diverse. For instance, the sum of the angles of a triangle, In Euclidian geometry, equal to two right angles, is in Lobatchewsky's always less, and in Riemann's always greater than two right angles. It is interesting to observe that for a very small world (a minor moon, say) Riemann's geometry would be more convenient for ordinary surface measurements than Euclid's. The point made by M. Poincaré is that the non-Euclidian geometries, based suppositions contrary to every-day experience, are, when the conditions are suitably approximated, equally true with the Euclidian may, in fact, be reduced to forms of the Euclidian. He infers that geometry is therefore not a mere set of independent definitions. It is based on experience, it corresponds exactly with no known physical facts, but it is true, would be true, in one or other of its conceivable forms, if the set of experiences from which we argue it had to be very deeply modified. In other words, he justifies mathematics with its inductive basis and its deductive form an absolute science.

Such imaginings indicate that the number of geometries which are entirety geometrical and self-consistent is infinite, and hint at vast possibilities in the way of the application of mathematics to any number of actual or imaginable worlds quite outside our present experience. It appears they all fit in as a part of the scheme; that it is impossible to imagine one that will not fit in.

Further on the nature and function of the hypothesis occupies the author's active mind. One is not, to scorn, he makes it plain, even "outworn hypotheses."

It is only by virtue of the hypothesis that we can make experiments of any value. For it is the generalization which enables us to predict. And a hypothesis is useful just so long and, so far as it enables predictions to be made. If the hypothesis serves as a guide to certain relations of the facts it generalizes, it does not matter whether it is in itself true. For the business of science is with relations. It serves, perhaps, until experiment shows the way to introduce its set of facts into a larger set generalized by another hypothesis the tendency being toward simplicity. It was useful, it may still be useful so far as it goes.

For instance, pre-Copernican hypotheses of the arrangement of the universe enabled astronomers to predict heavenly motions of certain kinds with as much accuracy as can be attained under our modern hypotheses. But our hypotheses co-ordinate more phenomena. And successive hypotheses will co-ordinate still more. The point insisted on by M. Poincaré is this: The legitimate scientific sphere of the hypothesis is its sufficiency to co-ordinate the facts – not the actual content of the hypothesis considered as a thing by itself – its objective truth. For there is no final objective truth. Hypothesis builds on dead hypotheses, and science grows by the constant bringing of more particulars under some general, while at the same time new particulars are discovered which eventually fit with the others into a scheme expressed by the same or other generals. Sometimes, as in the case of the discovery of the properties of radium, one set of new particulars enables you to set a whole army of familiar facts in order under a hypothesis which will serve till the like thing happens again.

It is astonishing how, by sticking to the relations at things, by employing all the weapons of the imagination in the service of his rigorous logic, M. Poincaré managed to enlarge the horizon, while he illuminates the whole, territory embraced in that circle. He was a master of language equally with logic, and his admirably lucid French had been rendered into admirably lucid English by Mr. Larmor, the translator. You may find in the book an open door and a practicable and pleasant path leading into all sorts of enticing regions of intellectual adventure. And M. Poincaré was always ready to give you his stimulating company part of the way. It was, without abating one jolt of rigor or pure reason, the romance of the abstruse."

One week later another review of this book was published in *The New York Times* by A.C. Pleydell:

New York Times Saturday Review of Books:

The interesting review of M. Poincaré's volume on "Science and Hypothesis" suggests the question whether the function of the hypothesis in the field of science is not identical with that of "principle" in the domain of ethics? Are not principles really hypotheses and which to base conduct? As the business of science is with relations of things, the business of ethics is the relation or human actions. M. Poincaré is quoted to the effect that "the legitimate scientific sphere of the hypothesis is its sufficiency to coordinate the facts, not the actual content of the hypothesis considered as a thing by itself, its objective truth. For there is no final objective truth. Hypothesis builds on dead hypotheses." It this is true of what we term principles of morals, it explains the difficulties encountered by those who consider accepted principles as final, and it answers those who say that, because a certain principle is not wholly tree (as it does not apply to every case) therefore all the rules of conduct that have been based upon it are necessarily false.

A. C, PLEYDELL. New York, Feb. 26.

9.2 The Value of Science. The "Strangest Interpretations"

La Valeur de la Science (The Value of Science), in which Poincaré took up again his criticism of Édouard Le Roy's conventionalism even more bluntly two years later, does not actually spark off the same media interest: nothing sensational or "accessible" to offer to the readers. There is therefore little trace of this publication in the mainstream press. The French newspaper *Le Figaro* of April 14, 1905, through the writing of the journalist and writer Philippe Emmanuel Glaser (1874-1930), announced the publication of *La Valeur de la Science* (The Value of Science) written by "the eminent scholar H. Poincaré", and which was going to inaugurate the "Scientific Philosophy Library's collection." The last part of the book, entitled *La valeur objective de la Science* (The objective value of science), includes a chapter on *La Science et la Réalité* (Science and Reality) in which Poincaré wrote a paragraph supposed to definitively close the debate on the rotation of the earth. But the debate was apparently no longer at issue in late 1904 and early 1905, and the press did not seem to pick up the controversy again.

Did Poincaré's more argued explanation manage to ease people's minds? Is his thought then better understood and assimilated? His relativism better apprehended? In any case, it is certain that Poincaré did argue in a more educational way:

> " ... Therefore, have I said in *Science and Hypothesis*, this affirmation, the earth turns round, has no meaning ... or rather these two propositions, the earth turns round, and, it is more convenient to suppose that the earth turns round, have one and the same meaning." These words have given rise to the strangest interpretations. Some have thought they saw in them the rehabilitation of Ptolemy's system, and perhaps the justification of Galileo's conviction. Those who had read attentively the whole volume could not, however, delude themselves. This truth, the earth turns round, was put on the same footing as Euclid's postulate[11], for example. Was that to reject it? But after what we have just explained in the fourth part, we may go further. A physical theory, we have said, is by so much the more true, as it puts in evidence more true relations. In the light of this new principle, let us examine the question which occupies us. No, there is no absolute space; these two contradictory propositions: "The earth turns round" and "The earth does not turn round" are, therefore, neither of them more true than the other. To affirm one while denying the other, in the kinematic sense, would be to admit the existence of absolute space[12]. But if the one reveals true relations that the other hides from us, we can nevertheless regard it as physically more true than the other, since it has a richer content. Now in this regard no doubt is possible. The truth for which Galileo suffered remains, therefore, the truth, although it has not altogether the same meaning as for the vulgar, and its true meaning is much more subtle, more profound and more rich[13]."

---

[11]Poincaré implicitly refers to the letter sent by the skeptical student from Polytechnique." See above.

[12]Poincaré returns this time to the field of physics to justify his assertion.

[13]See Henri Poincaré, *La Valeur de la Science*, collection "Bibliothèque de Philosophie scientifique" of Gustave Le Bon, Flammarion, Paris, 1905, p. 271-274.

However, all the efforts that Poincaré made to put an end to the debate on the rotation of the earth, in the last paragraph but one of *La Valeur de la Science* (The Value of Science) were in vain, at least on the long range. Indeed, when the writer Gaston Rageot (1871-1942) published *Les Savants et la Philosophie*[14] (Scholars and Philosophy), a large part of which was devoted to Henri Poincaré, the literary critic Gaston Deschamps (1861-1931), who presented the book in the paper *Le Temps* of November 1, 1908, wrote about it as follows, and not without a certain irony:

> "In his book on the Value of Science, M. Poincaré reassures us fully regarding the rotation of the Earth. He urges us to keep asserting, without fear of error, that the Earth does rotate. That is settled. Let it be said. And thank you for letting us know. But on this spinning ball, swept away into the infinite space by the most dizzying gyrations, what happens to the traditional maxims which mankind had needed so far to live well and die well ? Do we have scientific reasons to distinguish between good and evil, vice and virtue, truth and lie, honor and dishonor? Alas! Poincaré answers us bluntly: Ethics and science have their own domains, which touch but do not interpenetrate. The one shows us to what goal we should aspire, the other, given the goal, teaches us how to attain it. So they can never conflict since they can never meet. There can no more be immoral science than there can be scientific morals[15] Thereupon, Mr. Gaston Rageot, without ceasing to admire the genius of the great mathematician who had the courage to write this depressing statement, murmur under his breath the fatal word "failure". And to find the solution to the moral question, the he will look elsewhere than on the blackboard full of transcendental equations."

Obviously, the question of the relation between science and ethics is used to once again divert the assertions of Poincaré on anything but ethics, and to rely on it to show that, in the end, scientists-philosophers (we are simplifying here), should only use their "blackboard" and "transcendental equations" instead of making "depressing statements" on the "moral question".

But Poincaré does not a priori tackle this question at all when writing about the issue of the rotation of the earth: the relation between science and ethics is discussed in the introduction of *La valeur de la science* (the Value

---

[14]See Gaston Rageot, *Les Savants et la Philosophie*, Felix Alcan, Paris. 1908.
[15]See Henri Poincaré, *La Valeur de la Science*, op cit, p. 4.

of Science), the rotation of the earth is tackled in its last part, and Gaston Deschamps thus took the liberty of cutting the text short, which once again distorted the reading and interpretation of the latter point. That does not mean that Poincaré did not care about ethics in the scholar's practice: we shall see more about it in the excerpts reproduced below.

9.3   Science and Method: The "Granitic Rationalism"

As we already said, we do not claim to study the philosophy of Henri Poincaré in minute detail; we only aim to say a few words about how his work was received in the mainstream press. His third book, *Science et Méthode* (Science and Method), was published in late 1908, and Poincaré, who had then already been a member of the Académie française for six months, offered his own interpretation of the book in a summary of "key ideas" that he agreed to write for the French newspaper *Le matin*, and which was published on the front page on November 25 under the title "Comment se fait la science" (What is science made of). We could not miss this opportunity (Poincaré did not often take part in this type of activities) to offer here a reading of Poincaré by Poincaré himself; furthermore, this reading was widely distributed, for it was published in one of the most read dailies of his time. We therefore offer to our readers the direct reading of the article below, although it will be seen that Henri Poincaré did not entirely play the game regarding the exercise offered by the newspaper: the verb "extract" chosen by the editorial staff in the introductory paragraph of the article was indeed not randomly chosen ... The numbering (from 1 to 3) of certain parts are of our own making: they will be used in the analysis that follows the text.

> "1– Tolstoy explains somewhere in his writings why, in his opinion, "Science for Science's sake" is an absurd conception. We cannot know all the facts, since they are practically infinite in number. We must make a selection; and that being so, can this selection be governed by the mere caprice of our curiosity? Is it not better to be guided by utility, by our practical, and more especially our moral, necessities? Have we not some better occupation than counting the number of lady-birds in existence on this planet? It is clear that for him the word utility has not the meaning assigned to it by business men, and, after them, by the greater number of our contemporaries. He cares but little for the industrial applications of science, for the marvels of electricity or of auto-mobilism, which he regards rather as

hindrances to moral progress. For him the useful is exclusively what is capable of making men better. It is hardly necessary for me to state that, for my part, I could not be satisfied with either of these ideals. I have no liking either for a greedy and narrow plutocracy, or for a virtuous unaspiring democracy, solely occupied in turning the other cheek, in which we should find good people devoid of curiosity, who, avoiding all excesses, would not die of any disease – save boredom. But it is all a matter of taste, and that is not the point I wish to discuss. None the less the question remains, and it claims our attention. If our selection is only determined by caprice or by immediate necessity, there can be no science for science's sake, and consequently no science. Is this true? There is no disputing the fact that a selection must be made: however great our activity, facts outstrip us, and we can never overtake them; while the scientist is discovering one fact, millions and millions are produced in every cubic inch of his body. Trying to make science contain nature is like trying to make the part contain the whole.

Apology for a few fools.

But scientists believe that there is a hierarchy of facts, and that a judicious selection can be made. They are right, for otherwise there would be no science, and science does exist. One has only to open one's eyes to see that the triumphs of industry, which have enriched so many practical men, would never have seen the light if only these practical men had existed, and if they had not been preceded by disinterested fools who died poor, who never thought of the useful, and yet had a guide that was not their own caprice. What these fools did, as Mach has said, was to save their successors the trouble of thinking. If they had worked solely in view of an immediate application, they would have left nothing behind them, and in face of a new requirement, all would have had to be done again. Now the majority of men do not like thinking, and this is perhaps a good thing, since instinct guides them, and very often better than reason would guide a pure intelligence, at least whenever they are pursuing an end that is immediate and always the same. But instinct is routine, and if it were not fertilized by thought, it would advance no further with man than with the bee or the ant. It is necessary, therefore, to think for those who do not like thinking, and as they are many, each one of our thoughts must be useful in as many circumstances as possible. For this reason, the more general a law is, the greater is its value.

Without simple facts, science would be impossible.

This shows us how our selection should be made. The most interesting facts are those which can be used several times,

those which have a chance of recurring. We have been for-
tunate enough to be born in a world where there are such facts.
Suppose that instead of eighty chemical elements we had eighty
millions, and that they were not some common and others rare,
but uniformly distributed. Then each time we picked up a new
pebble there would be a strong probability that it was composed of some unknown substance. Nothing that we knew of
other pebbles would tell us anything about it. Before each new
object we should be like a new-born child; like him we could but
obey our caprices or our necessities. In such a world there would
be no science, perhaps thought and even life would be impossible, since evolution could not have developed the instincts of
self-preservation. Providentially it is not so; but this blessing,
like all those to which we are accustomed, is not appreciated
at its true value. The biologist would be embarrassed if there
were only individuals and no species, and if heredity did not
make children resemble their parents.

2– There is a hierarchy of facts. Some are without any positive
bearing, and teach us nothing but themselves. The scientist
who ascertains them learns nothing but facts, and becomes no
better able to foresee new facts. Such facts, it seems, occur but
once, and are not destined to be repeated. There are, on the
other hand, facts that give a large return, each of which teaches
us a new law. And since he is obliged to make a selection, it is
to these latter facts that the scientist must devote himself. No
doubt this classification is relative, and arises from the frailty
of our mind. The facts that give but a small return are the
complex facts, upon which a multiplicity of circumstances exercise an appreciable influence – circumstances so numerous and
so diverse that we cannot distinguish them all. But I should
say, rather, that they are the facts that we consider complex,
because the entanglement of these circumstances exceeds the
compass of our mind. No doubt a vaster and a keener mind
than ours would judge otherwise. But that matters little; it is
not this superior mind that we have to use, but our own.

What is chance?

The facts that give a large return are those that we consider
simple, whether they are so in reality, because they are only
influenced by a small number of well-defined circumstances, or
whether they take on an appearance of simplicity, because the
multiplicity of circumstances upon which they depend obey the
laws of chance, and so arrive at a mutual compensation. This is
most frequently the case, and is what compelled us to enquire
somewhat closely into the nature of chance. The facts to which
the laws of chance apply become accessible to the scientist, who

would lose heart in face of the extraordinary complication of the problems to which these laws are not applicable.

3– To begin with, what is chance? It is not the absence of all laws, as the ancients believed; it is not the unknown law, as is sometimes said. Chance is something more than the name we give to our ignorance, otherwise there would be no calculation of probabilities; one can not speak of the laws of chance, and insurance companies would go bankrupt. We needed a better definition. The effects we attribute to chance are those due to very small causes, escaping the casual observer but nevertheless considerable, or to multiple and complex causes, which, isolated, would have produced nothing but insignificant results and which become effective only by being accumulated."

For those who have not read *Science et Méthode* (Science and Method), "another" Poincaré seems to appear in these lines. Rather than objectively and neutrally summarizing his book, as might have been expected, he was on the contrary very passionate about the issues he chose to present to the public and seemed to adopt a polemical approach, involving men of science, of letters, of business, and speaking of "greedy and narrow plutocracy", of "virtuous unaspiring democracy" and starting the article by picking on Tolstoy ... Finally, it is the disinterestedness of "a few fools", these men of science "who died poor," that he apparently wants to rehabilitate: they think "for those who do not like thinking" ("as they are many" he says!) and they make their wealth. But if we take a closer look, we can see that parts 1 and 2 are an exact copy of passages from the book. Only the third part was actually written specifically by Poincaré for the occasion; but it can soon be noticed that this passage too can be found in *Science et Méthode* as well: he just simplified the original text for the readers of the French newspaper *Le Matin*. Part 1 is actually the beginning of Chapter I of *Science et Méthode*: "Le choix des faits" ("The Choice of facts", p. 9 in the original edition). As mentioned by Laurent Rollet in the electronic edition of the book, available on the "Archives Henri Poincaré" (website of the University of Nancy), "This chapter takes up the preface to the American edition of *La valeur de la science*: "The Choice of Facts", *The Value of Science*, text translated into English by G. B. Halsted, and published in 1907 in New York. This preface was also published in 1909 in the American philosophical journal *The Monist* (April 1909), p. 231-239. There does not seem to be any significant differences between the two texts[16]."

---

[16]http://www.univ-nancy2.fr/poincare/bhp/hp1908sm.xml.

The second part is extracted from the general conclusion of the book
(p. 307). The titles we have reproduced in bold are not included in the
book: did Poincaré add them himself for the article, or was it the editor's
choice? The question remains. If we now pay attention to the reference to
Tolstoy (1828-1910), we can see that Poincaré does not give the references
of the writing where he criticizes "science for science" and speaks of "usefulness" and particularly of moral usefulness (we would rather write "ethical"
usefulness). Only a few people know that Tolstoy, apart from his brilliant
work, was a highly committed actor at his time: he wrote many essays,
pamphlets, letters to writers of his time, whose titles alone are revealing:
*On the relationship between gender, I can no longer keep silent, Only the
welfare for all, To help those hit by famine, On the courts, Those who are
in need, Reports on the aid to those hit by famine, On Reason and Religion,
On Art*, etc. Poincaré could refer to various writings of Tolstoy, for he often
attacked the "caste" of scientists. But the expressions he chose to repeat in
Science et Méthode seem to refer in particular to a 1887 opuscule translated
into French under the title *Que devons-nous faire ?* (What should we do?),
or to his essay What is Art (1898), or to a letter he addressed to Romain
Rolland on October 4, 1887; the French novelist actually widely spread the
letter, and put it in his memorable biography of Tolstoy, published in 1921
by Hachette[17].

In this letter, the author of War and Peace wrote:

> "How come there is so many fools questioning the usefulness of
> science and art? (...) The false part played in our society by
> science and arts comes from the fact that so-called civilized peo-
> ple, together with the scientists and artists, form a privileged
> caste, like so many priests; and this caste has all the faults of all
> castes. It degrades and lowers the principle in virtue of which
> it was organized. Instead of a true religion, a false one. (...)
> If good had in fact been the criterion of science and art, then
> the positive sciences research, which are completely trivial com-
> pared to the true good of humanity, would never have acquired
> such importance. (...) Human wisdom does not consist in the
> knowledge of things. For there are an infinite number of things
> we can know, and knowing as many things as possible is not
> wisdom. Human wisdom is to know the order of things that is
> worth knowing – it is knowing how to arrange one's knowledge
> based on their importance. But the most important of all sci-

[17]Romain Rolland, *Sur la vie de Tolstoï*, Hachette, Paris, 1921.

ences man can and must learn is the science of living so as to
do the least evil and the greatest possible good."

As can be seen, Tolstoy links science and ethics together, judging in
particular science as unethical, and we find in his writing the idea of the "few
fools" taken up by Poincaré in *Science et Méthode*. In Tolstoy, the fools are
those who, like him, dare to criticize the caste of intellectuals and scientists
who work towards the misfortune of mankind; in Poincaré, conversely, the
disinterested and often poor scientists are the one who sacrifice their lives
for science towards the happiness of mankind.

There is therefore practically no mention of the contents of *Science et
Méthode* in the choices made by Poincaré for the article in the French newspaper *Le Matin*. No mention of the richness of the four "books" that make
up the work: nothing appears on "mathematical reasoning", "new mechanics", "astronomical science"; it only used the highly polemical introduction
to chapter I of Part I on the "scholar and science." Of course, there is
no mention of the chapters of these books, nor of the origin of his texts
which, as in the previous works, were taken up from articles and lectures
that Poincaré held throughout his career. He gave priority to the question
which found an echo in him after reading Tolstoy (and others in his day):
the relation between science and ethics. But his response was extremely
violent, to say the least, as seen above. He however tackled a subject that
was important to him: chance. We know now that his approach had a real
impact on the issue. Reading between the lines, his last paragraph reveals
a program that still keeps the scientists busy one hundred years later, and
they are far from having explored all its implications and applications. This
is therefore a surprising aspect of Henri Poincaré, whose temper appeared
to be quite different so far: a reserved scientist, arguing on the sole basis
of his scientific skills (we shall notice this again when writing about the
Dreyfus Affair), except for a controversy in which he was unwillingly involved by ideologists. The day after this article was published, the French
newspaper *Le matin* announced the publication of the book in the section
"Livres à lire" ("Books to read") On the same page, in another section
on books, entitled "Les livres de la semaine" ("Books of the Week"), the
importance of the book – miswritten "Science and matter," in the newspaper – was highlighted and Poincaré's thought was presented as a "granitic
rationalism."

On December 13th, 1908, the *New York Tribune* published a very short
review of Poincaré's book:

> "The same publishing house[18] brings out "Science et Méthode,"
> by M. Henri Poincaré in which the eminent mathematician ex-
> plains in clear, popular language the methods of mathematical
> reasoning in the solution of problems of every sort, abstruse as
> well as practical. This is the first work written by M. Poincaré
> since he became a member of the French Academy last spring."

The boundary between science and popularization is hard to define,
especially when the writings meant for a lay public come in most cases
from publications and conferences originally written for specialists, as it is
the case in Poincaré. Even if the author did make visible efforts towards
popularization in *Science et Méthode*, there was obviously still a long way
to go. His election to the Academy, recalled by all these articles, and the
fact then that he appeared more frequently in the mainstream press, do
not make it less difficult to understand his thought. We shall return to this
issue in the last part of this book.

Thus, we should not be surprised to see (and we shall end on this example) that the French newspaper *La Croix* of October 11, 1911 (three years
after the publication of the book) offered to its readers a "picturesque problem" taken from the book:

"A picturesque problem

> The most solemn scholars sometimes pleasantly surprise us by
> their unexpected way of asking scientific questions. "Suppose,
> asked Mr. Poincaré, that we have as many pairs of boots as
> there are whole numbers, so that we can number the pairs from
> 1 to infinity, how many boots shall we have? Will the number
> of boots be equal to the number of pairs?" Poincaré presents
> the problem that way in his book *Science et Méthode*. For those
> interested in the problem's solution, you should know that he
> also gives it in the book."

The problem is of course "picturesque" if we simply imagine an infinite
pair of boots row, and if we count 1 for two boots (counting the pairs) or 1
per boot. The example taken by Poincaré to make people understand that
there are there two infinities of the same nature, and that the question of
different kinds of infinities therefore arises, is much more subtle and fundamental; this issue actually changed the very foundations of mathematics,
notably through the seminal work of Cantor (1845-1918) on transfinite set.

---

[18]Bibliothèque de Philosophie Scientifique, Flammarion

But once again, the level of understanding of Poincaré's work is reduced to one anecdote, the text is truncated, and only remains the "picturesque" example used by the mathematician-philosopher to introduce a fundamental reflection on these two fields of knowledge.

9.4   Last Essays: "A Certain Embarrassment"

Science and Method is the last philosophical book by Henri Poincaré that was published while he was still alive. *Dernières pensées* (Last Essays), a posthumous work which Poincaré did not structure himself, followed in early 1913; it was published in the same set led by *Le Bon*: it is then neither a completed work that was not yet published before he died, as often the case in such situation, nor an unfinished work published as it was after his death. The purpose of our book is to look at the life and work of Poincaré through what the press wrote while he was alive, so we will not dwell on the articles that reported the publication of *Dernières pensées*: there were actually only a few of them and consisted mostly in short announcements such as the one published in the French newspaper *Le Figaro* of February 11, 1913.

The editorial project which led to publish these *Last Essays*, gives us part of the content, and reported an editorial context, on, and around Henri Poincaré six months after his disappearance. So we reproduce here:

> "**Thoughts of Henri Poincaré.**
>
> While the Reviews continued about Henri Poincaré's numerous scientific or philosophical studies, friends and editors of the famous mathematician brought together under the title of *Last Essays* various articles that make up a volume. It is the continuation of these works which make a fortune (strike it rich) and which are called *Science and Hypothesis, the Value of Science, Science and Method*. Of the articles contained in this last book, some have especially a scientific object, and though they may interest all readers as a whole, they are not fully intelligible to those who are not familiar with mathematics. Some difficulty will arise to grasp in all their detail, pages devoted to the logic of infinity, or the relationship of matter and ether. Even in the more accessible studies which have for subject Space and Time, or why Space has three dimensions, we will regret not to hear some formulas, and despite the simple appearance, clarity of language, sober firmness of the reasoning, and all the good writer qualities of the author, we will fear, not to be able to

grasp always its thought. The studies the most general and
with an access relatively more easier, have for object the *'Evolution of scientific laws* and *Moral Science*. We know that Henri
Poincaré often returned to this idea. He thought that there can
neither be moral nor immoral science. For him, science was not
able to create a moral, and Science was no more capable of directly destroying the traditional morality. Science can exercise
only indirect action. For the demonstration of his ideas, Henri
Poincaré wrote a very succinct study, with a large apparent
simplicity, with a paradoxical and sometimes mischievous look
that had its charm. There was no scientific morality, he said for
example, for any grammatical reason. Science notices; Science
expresses herself in the indicative, never in the imperative. We
will never draw from Science a proposal that says do this or do
not do that. The moral engine he said again, can only be a feeling. Here, science can help us indirectly, because Science puts
us in touch with something much bigger than us, Science gives
us the habit of disinterest; Science also gives us the habit of considering what is general, that is to say, to put something above
the special interests; finally, Science is a collective work. Hence
Science can have a good influence. But Henri Poincaré did not
deny that science could have a bad impact. Every passion is
exclusive, love for science can be for some a reason of indif-
ference or drought so that to Poincaré the Science has to play
an important role in education, but not an exclusive role, as it
can in some minds have a destructive influence when Science is
elementary, incomplete. "From a science animated of a true experimental spirit, Poincaré wrote, morality has nothing to fear;
such a science is respectful of the past, Science is opposed to this
scientific snobbery so easy to fool by novelty; Science just pro-
gresses step by step, but still in the same direction and always
in the right direction; the best remedy against half-science, it is
more science." As for "science of moral", whose some theorists
have wanted to make a moral, more, the modern and scientific
form of morality, Henri Poincaré did not believe in it. "Science
will, he says, never be a moral; and she cannot replace a moral
as well as a treaty on physiology of digestion cannot replace a
good dinner. Theory in a general way does not seem to the author to have a unique importance: he believed in passions and
instincts. He so believed that if per chance one day morality
should accommodate an absolute determinism, he thought that
the moral forces that lead us would continue to lead us. And
then he was a little bit optimistic. Hopefully, he concluded,
that all would propitiate in absolute, and that in an infinite intelligence that both attitudes, that of the man who acts as if he

were free, and that of the man who thinks as if freedom was nowhere, would seem also legitimate."

The editorial context specified at the beginning of this article ("While the Reviews continued about Henri Poincaré numerous scientific or philosophical studies") can be easily verified by searching the studies in question: and there are indeed more journals and articles from specialists (for example *Revue de Métaphysique et de Morale*) than newspapers of general press. But the article shows that, finally, the ethical question seems to be the only one the profane (*i.e.* the author of the article) can really grasp: therefore it gives a quick list of some of the themes addressed by Poincaré, insists on their "inaccessibility", and only develops the study of this question.

9.5   Poincarism, Opportunism, Commodism, etc.

Poincaré's writings on geometry, taken up in the parts of his four books devoted to mathematics, were unanimously supported by the analysts of his philosophy, which, on this point, is a constructivist philosophy. However, this label is challenged when some applied it to his epistemological readings of the other fields of knowledge. Everyone agreed that Kant's legacy was very present in his work, and people then talked about his Kantianism. In some of his writings, his epistemology resembles empiricism, others resemble idealism. When he spoke about the definition of the objects of science (and especially those of mathematics), some see it as a form of nominalism. As he wondered about how certain theories, certain "visions of the world" are born in the spirits of men, which then make them want to explore a particular way, people would talk about his intuitionism[19]. As he related knowledge to existence, then "one can characterize this as an empirical interpretation. And more, in Poincaré, this empiricism is total; in spite of appearances, it concerns both mathematics and physics[20]."

But people spoke of his psychologism, especially as in *Science et Méthode* (Science and Method), he focused on the separation between language and

---

[19] See for example in Eric Audureau's summary of his article *Le conventionnalisme, conséquence de l'intuitionnisme* (Philosophiques, vol. 31, No. 1, 2004, p. 57-88): "Assuming that the philosophy of Poincaré's knowledge is consistent, I am trying to show that his conventionalism in geometry and physics is only a consequence of his intuitionism."

[20] Anne-Françoise Schmid, *Henri Poincaré. Les sciences et la philosophie*, op. cit., p. 118.

the fact, and the problem of choice: we already saw this aspect in the extract he wrote himself in *Le Matin* of November 25, 1908. Here we deliberately put the emphasis on all these "isms" that were attached to Poincaré's philosophy, and of which he himself complained about. There are certainly more of them that we failed to mention: pragmatism, occasionalism, etc ... but among those that we did not mention, there are also the qualifiers that were specifically created for him (and based on his name) during his lifetime, such as "poincarism" of which the French newspaper *Le Temps* of March 6, 1908 wrote about when Poincaré was elected to the Académie française:

> "Poincarism, by opening new insights into philosophy with a
> very new application of the non-Euclidean geometry hypothe-
> ses, questioned the very principles of scientific certainty."

That was obviously the crisis of physics, the loss of blind faith in science as a vehicle for truth (a faith that obviously resemble scientism, very present in the late XIXth and early XXth century), the emergence of non-Euclidean geometries in the models of mathematics and theoretical physics – so many facts that Poincaré actually developed in his philosophical work which are the source of this cover-all neologism: the "poincarism". Better yet, the same article, evidently to justify the fact that the scientist was elected to the Académie française, linked this "poincarism" to humanism:

> "His findings are no less than what was to be expected of a great
> scholar, who said that human genius is a flash of light between
> two eternities but that this flash of light is everything. There is
> then an obvious connection between this scientific philosophy
> and the humanism of the young literary generation."

About all these qualifiers attributed to Poincaré's philosophy, we cannot help but quote Louis Rougier (1889-1992) from his preface to the edition of *La valeur de la science* (The Value of Science) published in 1946 by the publishing house Editions du Cheval Ailé in Geneva:

> "He is anti-Kantian, he definitely ruins the whole *Esthétique*
> *transcendentale* (Transcendental Aesthetic) (SIC) and however
> sometimes speaks the language of pure criticism. He is anti-
> nominalist and yet evokes a theory of scientific convenience and
> the role of the convention, insufficiently developed, which can
> mislead a mind like Mr. Le Roy's. He is anti-formalist and
> sometimes, when speaking of the pure forms studied by math-
> ematicians, he adopts a language that could make him pass
> for a disciple of Russell or Carnap. The misinterpretation, the

> wrong uses of his thought, were (SIC) one of the reasons that
> led him to write one of his most significant works, *La Valeur
> de la Science* (The Value of Science)*Louis Rougier, preface to
> the edition of La valeur de la science, Editions du Cheval Ailé,
> Geneva, Switzerland, 1946, p. 15..*"

This shows that Poincaré was always in contradiction with himself, according to the points of view of his readers and analysts. Admittedly, Louis Rougier said that "It is only through a certain distance that the meaning of a work can be in the general movement of ideas, of which it was one of the moments," but here, it looks like he is doing a "systematic reconstruction[21]" himself. He was defending and spreading the logical positivism of the Vienna Circle in France, so it is not surprising to see him try to partly situate Poincaré's thought in the tradition of Russell or Carnap[22] On logical positivism, it is today beyond doubt: the philosophers of the Vienna Circle, as we already said, have integrated then exceeded Poincaré's philosophy. On Russell, the connection is much less obvious when reading the letters they exchanged and the disagreements they had. But it was the same with Duhem and Le Roy: like them, Poincaré fit into the scheme of criticizing and questioning the positivism inherited from Auguste Comte, but it did not prevent them from disagreeing on the attempts to develop philosophies that would exceed this positivism.

As for Poincaré's anti-nominalism, Louis Rougier's judgment could be connected to what Anne-Françoise Schmid wrote in the article "Conventionnalisme" ("Conventionalism") from the *Dictionnaire d'histoire et de philosophie des sciences* (Dictionary of History and Philosophy of Science), in which Poincaré actually appears as both nominalist and anti-nominalist: "He [Poincaré] was yet one of the first to criticize Le Roy's doctrine, calling it "absolute nominalism" at the end of *La valeur de la science* (The Value of Science) (1905); he admits nominalism only within narrow limits[23]"; and further: "According to Poincaré, the physicists, because of their "thoughtless nominalism", protect their principles from experimental refutation[24]." This shows that, from the time of Poincaré to the present day, the reading

---

[21] Expression borrowed from Philippe Nabonnand in: "Rougier et l'histoire des sciences", *Philosophia Scientæ*, n° 10-2, 2006, p. 209.

[22] For further details on this point, see the full article by Philippe Nabonnand mentioned in the previous note.

[23] Anne-Françoise Schmid, article "Conventionnalisme" in *Dictionnaire d'histoire et de philosophie des sciences*, Dominique Lecourt (Dir.), PUF, Paris, 2003, p. 244.

[24] *Ibid.*, p. 244-245.

of his philosophy has always been extremely complex and has always re-vealed contradictions, and trying to reduce them is sometimes useless. This is certainly due to the fact that Poincaré could speak different languages depending on whether he was interested in the philosophy of physics, of mathematics, or a more general philosophy of knowledge that we would today classify in the field of epistemology. In this sense we could describe the thought as "pragmatic" – as if Poincaré had adapted it *a posteriori* by writing it for his philosophical works.

But don't forget that these works consist of texts that were written throughout his life, of his work in the various fields of science, and of his exchanges with his contemporaries: he had not written them such as one would have done for a finished work, but as a sum of successive reflec-tions that, according to the circumstances, could have fallen within the province of a certain current of philosophy and epistemology. Poincaré's philosophical work, as well as his scientific work, was then being constantly constructed and merely opened doors and new perspectives: History has shown us over the past century (and it keeps showing us) that both works have led to develop new views and theories that were precisely built on these perspectives.

We will conclude this chapter by referring to an article in the newspaper *La Croix*, of May 21, 1908. In the "Revue des revues" section (Journal among the journals), the newspaper mentioned a delivery of the Journal *Revue de philosophie* of May 1 of the same year. The beginning of the article specifies the context and the subject:

> "**An investigation into the problem of knowledge** The journal of philosophy run by Father E. Peillaube proposes its readers and contributors a programme of study on the problem of knowledge. Here is what would be the actual reasons and purpose of this investigation. Questions regarding the objec-tivity of sensations and ideas, the value of the first principles of reason, the nature of certainty and the definition of truth, in short, the criticism of human knowledge, were at all times, under various names, the most current and troubled issues."

This was a French Catholic newspaper, *La Croix*, which reported a "programme of study", an "investigation" into "the problem of knowledge"; a large project, but which was a bit biased, as we are about to see, by the obviously partisan approach that guides him, at least in the report written by the newspaper. Poincaré was indeed called to agree wholeheartedly with the encyclical "Pascendi Dominici Gregis" of September 8, 1907 in which

Pope Pius X had condemned the "modernism", owing to "principles, spirit and trends common to all writers, speakers and actors, clerical or lay, who work consciously or unconsciously to destroy, and thus recreate in their own way, philosophy, theology, apologetics, history, exegesis, faith, ethics, worship and social action of Catholicism, the religious and Jesus Christ himself[25]"

The article from the newspaper *La Croix* identifies these "modernists": those who claim to follow Kant and criticism, those who claim that "everything is subjective and symbolic in the field of knowledge: scientific laws as metaphysical theories," those "subjectivists" who "asked pragmatism for the certainty that reason could not supply them with," knowing that "pragmatism, which is essentially anti-rational, dissolves the notion of truth that (SIC) it merges with its practical consequences, that is to say, with the useful, and brings us back, despite the noblest efforts, into skepticism."

This is the moment when Poincaré's ideas were taken up. First introduced (associated with Duhem) as a "brilliant representative of the criticism of science in France," his answers to Le Roy and his nominalism in the last part of *La Valeur de la science* (The Value of science) were used as an argument against all these "nominalist", "subjectivist" and "anti-intellectualist" skeptics:

> "Mr. Poincaré fights the nominalist and anti-intellectualist doctrine of Mr. Le Roy, who is not a skeptic, but is yet accused of skepticism, said M Poincaré. He was inevitably a skeptic, although the accusation is probably unfair. Aren't appearances against him? Having a nominalist doctrine, but a realistic heart, he seems to escape the absolute nominalism only by a desperate act of faith. For the anti-intellectualist philosophy, by rejecting the analysis and the discourse, condemns itself by that very fact to be incommunicable; it is one essentially internal philosophy, or at least, only the negations can be communicated; how could one be surprised then that for an outside observer, it takes the face of skepticism?"

Poincaré was then called to help Pius X and his encyclical since, as he alleged, he did not agree that science "could only be a set of recipes or rules of action." Though we do not have enough room here to write further details on the contents of this article from *La Croix*, what is above

---

[25]Expression repeated in a pamphlet written in December 1907 against the *Revue des deux mondes* by brother Gonthier, "des Frères Prêcheurs", and published in La nouvelle France.

allows us once more to show on the one hand that the "isms" were very in vogue at the time, as they were in all subsequent studies of Poincaré's thought, but mostly, on the other hand, that this thought could be taken up in almost every debate that took place within the society of the early twentieth century.

The laws promulgated under the Third Republic on secularism and the separation of Church and State had revived an ideological debate that was recurrent in the history of France since the Revolution, and the scientific backing, the versatility of the work, as well as the aura of a figure such as Henri Poincaré, obviously exposed him more than any other to this kind of appropriation.

PART 4
The Committed Man

Sociology is the science which has the most methods and the least results.

— H. Poincaré —

Chapter 10

The Dreyfus Affair

The Dreyfus Affair, which unfolded from 1894 to 1906, has become the paradigmatic example of the commitment of intellectuals and scientists in a judicial, political, social and ideological debate. It has been recounted and studied so many times that we shall only do a quick review of the major episodes by illustrating them with examples taken from the multitude of newspaper articles (sometimes nauseating) that accompanied it. We will obviously focus on the role of scientists in the second and third part of the affair, that is to say from the famous "J'accuse" by Zola in 1898 and the trial that followed. And we will insist more specifically on the role of Poincaré in this scientific expertise, and how it was conveyed in the press. We deny here trying to plagiarize any serious studies that were produced on the issue before. So we take it upon ourselves to borrow from Laurent Rollet's studies, and we officially and sincerely thank him here for his authorization and support of our undertaking.

We prefer then to name these borrowing right from this introduction. Most of them come from his very valuable contribution to the website; http://images.math.cnrs.fr/; entitled "Des mathématiciens dans l'affaire Dreyfus? Autoforgerie, bertillonnage et calcul des probabilités": to avoid too many cross-references to footnotes, we will simply emphasize what we borrowed from this text with a *. But the borrowing also come from his chapter "L'université et la science" (University and science) from the book "Les évènements fondateurs. L'affaire Dreyfus" (The founding events. The Dreyfus Affair) directed by Vincent Duclert and Perrine Simon-Nahum and published in 2009 by Armand Colin.

10.1   The First Dreyfus Affair: A Brief Overview

This affair essentially unfolded in three stages, although it has been the subject of a significant number of articles and debates in the intervals between these episodes. It started in November 1894 and, among the countless newspaper articles that got hold of it, we chose to refer to the French newspaper *Le Figaro* in an article dated of November 3. Why this choice? The first reason is that it is not the purpose of this book to recount in detail the beginning of this affair, for Poincaré doesn't appear in it until later; besides, we would not have enough space here to put most of the substantial and almost always partisan articles which sustained the debate from the very beginning of the affair. The second reason is that this article has two very instructive points. Firstly, he shows us that right from the beginning, the press condemned Dreyfus without further ado (and way before his trial). Secondly, because this article is very well documented on the functioning of the institutions – of the army in particular, and he tells us already *a priori* what sanction the alleged culprit might be subjected to (for that is precisely what is at stake at the very beginning of the affair). The case had just been divulged to the press and the Figaro started its long article as follows (see Fig. 10.1):

L'AFFAIRE DE TRAHISON

Plusieurs journaux ont donné le nom du coupable, et une note officielle de l'*Agence Havas* ne permet plus aucun doute sur le crime dont nous avons raconté hier les tristes détails. Nous n'avons donc à garder désormais aucune réserve.

C'est le capitaine Alfred Dreyfus, du 14ᵉ régiment d'artillerie, attaché aux bureaux du ministère de la guerre en qualité de stagiaire à l'état-major de l'armée, qui a commis l'action infâme dont nous voulions douter quand même, malgré tous les récits qui nous parvenaient.

Fig. 10.1   *Le Figaro* of November 3, 1894.

THE CASE OF TREASON

"Several newspapers have written the name of the culprit, and after the note of the Agence Havas, there is no doubt as to the crime of which we recounted the sad details yesterday. So we no longer have to keep some reservation. It is Captain Dreyfus, of the 14th Artillery Regiment, attached to the offices of the Ministry of War as an intern at the headquarters of the Army, who committed the infamous action that we still wanted to have doubts about, in spite of all the stories that we have heard."

We can see that Dreyfus was portrayed as guilty right from the start. Let's not forget that he was accused of high treason:

"In late September 1894, the French Intelligence Service, through a maid working at the German Embassy, came into possession of a letter torn into six pieces, and which had no date or signature. Intended for a German military attaché, Colonel Maximilian von Schwarzkoppen, this letter – which was later designated as *the bordereau* (detailed memorandum) – announced the sending of several confidential notes concerning the arming and organization of the French army. Because of the supposed similarity of his handwriting with the one on the bordereau, and because an internship at the Ministry of War had put him in touch with the secret documents mentioned on the bordereau, Captain Alfred Dreyfus, an École Polytechnique student and a Jewish officer of Alsatian origin, was forced to write under dictation then imprisoned at Cherche-Midi in October 1894. Following a closed-door military trial, he was convicted of high treason and sentenced to transportation for life on Devil's Island, a fortified compound in Guyana. The fundamental injustice was committed: denying the French law, Dreyfus was convicted on the basis of documents to which he could not have had access to (a secret file containing false documents had been submitted to the judges without the defense knowing about it)*"

Le Figaro criticized the Ministry of War and the police headquarters which, in his opinion, were too slow to disclose the information, considering that, in the end, the case did not "affect the consideration of our army in any way." But the article was about the "odious crime" committed by Captain Dreyfus, who was "waiting in the Cherche-Midi prison for the members of the court-martial to decide whether or not he committed the abominable crime of high treason". However, for *Le Figaro*, there was absolutely no doubt that he committed it (as it was the case for most of the other newspapers at the time):

> "The odious crime that caused the arrest of Captain Alfred
> Dreyfus is all the more monstrous that we cannot even explain
> it by some pressing needs of money. The French officer, who
> sold abroad some of the secrets of the national defense, owns
> indeed a fine fortune."

This was followed by the long list of the respective fortunes of the Dreyfus family and of his wife, "the daughter of a very wealthy diamond mer-
chant," who lived "in a luxurious apartment in the Avenue du Trocadéro."
And the fact that Dreyfus was a Jew quickly appeared in an almost caricatural portrait: "Captain Dreyfus, who is thirty-five years old, is of size above
the average, has a quite lively complexion, is short-sighted and of a fairly
pronounced Jewish type." Therefore, right from the beginning, Dreyfus
being Jewish was associated with him being necessarily guilty. Let's not
forget the social and political context of that time: Antisemitism was om-
nipresent in all the press, and even elected officials or intellectuals claimed
to follow it; it was well-established in journals (*La Libre Parole* by Édouard
Drumont for instance) and best-selling books (*La France juive*, by the same
Drumont, published in 1888) which were written to spread it. Drumont,
boosted by the impressive success of his book and journal, campaigned
against the Jewish officers of the French army and amplified the hatred of
Jews in France and in the French army. For the authorities, led by the
Minister of War, General Auguste Mercier, it was of utmost importance to
find a culprit – who had to be found among the officers who spent some
time at the headquarters, giving them access to the documents intended
for the German in the famous bordereau, in fact only document in a file
where there was nothing but a presumption of treason, since this document
only announced an upcoming delivery of confidential papers. Dreyfus soon
turned out to be the ideal culprit: he was the only Jew who have had access
to these documents, and he was then only an intern. More importantly, he
came from a Republican family and began a career in an army still bruised
from the fall of 1870, preparing its revenge on Germany, and whose officers
were still essentially ultra-Catholics anti-republicans. In addition, the case
was revealed to the general public by Drumont in *La libre parole* of October
24, 1894 and was thus directly placed under the perspective of the Jewish
responsibility for the misfortunes of the French society: that article marked
the beginning of the "Dreyfus Affair" in the public sphere. At the time,
most of the press was conservative and antisemitic. *Le Figaro* was one of

the more moderate and less biased newspapers on the subject: this is why we chose this newspaper article dated November 3, 1894 to illustrate the first part of the Dreyfus Affair "moderately". Periodicals such as *L'Eclair*, *La Croix*, *L'Intransigeant*, etc.[1] were much more radical. We can see then that the newspapers designated the culprit from the very start and even wrote in advance about the rest of the trial and the coming conviction of Dreyfus, as well as the penalty that he would be subjected to after a rigged and rapid trial. In the same article, *Le Figaro* thus explained the legislation that governed such cases. Taking the example of the Adjutant Chatelain, who in 1883 was sentenced to life imprisonment in a "fortified compound", and who, in 1894, was still in prison in Noumea "where it is very expensive for the State to keep him, being currently the only transported convict that exists in our fortified compounds, and watching him requires a large personnel", the newspaper announced what awaited Dreyfus. The die was then cast and Dreyfus was to be subjected to the penalty announced, as mentioned above: he did not join Chatelain in Noumea, but was deported to Guyana, on an island with a ominous name: *Devil's Island*.

10.2   Three Other Trials

In a predominantly anti-Dreyfusard France, it was difficult to question the judgment pronounced against the captain, and the establishment of a Dreyfusard trend, then a counter-attack by the people who embodied it, was spread over two years and a half, from 1895 to 1897. Among many other protagonists, two of them, one guilty and the other innocent, took part in the case, and were the subject of two other trials which proved the first one innocent and convicted the second one, in order to cover up for the people responsible for the 1894 trial and satisfy the still highly virulent anti-Dreyfusism. These two figures were Commandant Charles Ferdinand Walsin Esterhazy (1847-1923) and Lieutenant-Colonel Georges Picquart (1854-1914). The latter, appointed head of the French intelligence service in July 1895, discovered in documents stolen from the German Embassy some elements showing that Esterhazy was giving information to the Germans. Picquart also discovered a similarity between Esterhazy's handwrit-

---

[1]The literature production on the Dreyfus Affair being very abundant, we refer the readers to the works of Vincent Duclert, a universally recognized specialist of this event, and in particular to the following two books: *Alfred Dreyfus, l'honneur d'un patriote*, Fayard, Paris, 2006; *L'Affaire Dreyfus*, Larousse, Paris, 2009

ing and the handwriting on the bordereau which was used to make Dreyfus found guilty of treason. Without consulting his superiors, Picquart held an investigation which led him to be absolutely certain, with supporting evidence, of Esterhazy's betrayal and guilt in the case for which Dreyfus was convicted. When Picquart reported his findings to the General Staff, they reacted the opposite of what he expected: he became the target of an investigation conducted to prove that, on the contrary, he was the guilty one, and he was taken away and finally posted to Tunisia.

The New York Times reported on November 29th, 1898 this trial:

THE TRIAL OF PICQUART

A Scene in the Chamber of Deputies Created by Discussion.

MINISTER OF WAR IS SILENT

He Refuses to Intervene in the Picquart Affair — A Lively Debate Results, Creating Excitement.

"PARIS. Nov. 28.– The Chamber of Deputies was crowded to-day, much interest being taken in the announced intention of some of the Deputies to interpellate the Government on the Picquart case. M, Paul Deschanel, Republican, announced that he had received a request to interpellate the Government regarding the Picquart proceedings, and the Premier, M. Dupuy, proposed an immediate discussion of the matter. But M. Fournière, Socialist, asked for an adjournment of an hour and a half, in order that the Republican Deputies might be able to consult with their colleagues in the Senate regarding the adoption of a common policy. The Chamber rejected the motion by a vote of 252 to 244. The Minister of War, M. de Freycinet, in the Chamber of Deputies refused to intervene in the Picquart affair, and the House approved the Government's declaration regarding the separation of military and civil powers by a vote of

437 to 73. A Radical Deputy, M. Bos, opened the discussion. He said that while there had been some honesty in the Dreyfus prosecution, there had been nothing but dishonesty in the Picquart affair. These remarks caused uproar. Continuing M. Bos detailed the history of the Picquart "persecution," recalling Col. Picquart's exile to Tunis, and asked the Minister of War, M. de Freycinet, why he had permitted a court-martial to be summoned for Dec. 12. The Deputy also accused Gen. Zurlinden the Military Governor of Paris, who be said, bad promised a revision of the case, with having broken his word. This caused another uproar M. Bos concluded with insisting that the Government ought to postpone the trial of Picquart by court-martial, the charge against him being disclosing the contents of certain military documents to his counsel, for legal purposes growing out of the Dreyfus case, until the decision of the Court of Cassation in the revision of the Dreyfus trial is made known. This brought forth lively applause from the majority of the Deputies. M. Millerand. Radical Socialist, spoke in a similar strain. He said it was absolutely necessary to postpone the Picquart court-martial in order to avoid the scandalous contradictions which otherwise were likely to arise between the verdicts of the court-martial and of the Court of Cassation. The President of the Chamber at this stage of the proceedings was frequently obliged to intervene in order to quiet the uproar on all sides. M. Poincaré[2], Republican, then made an impassioned speech, during the course of which he said it was not necessary to confound the army with a few imprudent men. The members of the court-martial be continued, were above suspicion; but the prosecution of Picquart savored of reprisal. [Applause.] Col. Picquart's secret imprisonment, M. Poincaré further remarked, was beyond all precedent, and there were guilty parties, he claimed, who were enjoying scandalous impunity. [Applause.] "There are other forgers besides Picquart who ought to be prosecuted!" exclaimed the Deputy. "These injustices will end by exasperating the nation." M. Poincaré who was Minister of Public Instruction in 1893-5, created a sensation by adding: "We were attacked for the Dreyfus prosecution in 1894; but I learned of the Dreyfus affair through the newspapers!" Tremendous applause and uproar followed this assertion. M. Barthou, who was Minister of Public Works in 1894, here interjected: "I am ready to indorse the words of M. Poincaré, which are true." This called forth more applause and exclamations of "It is absurd!" "It Is inconceivable!" Thereupon M. Poincaré added: "The only proof of Dreyfus's guilt

---

[2]Raymond Poincaré

in 1894 consisted of the bordereau. No Cabinet Minister, nor
even the President of the Council of Ministers, heard any mention of the confessions Dreyfus is alleged to have made to Capt.
Lebrun-Renault." [Applause.] M. Cavaignac, the former Minister of War, here interjected: "Gen. Mercier secured these confessions." Gen. Mercier was Minister of War at the time of the
Dreyfus trial. M. Poincaré continued: "Capt. Lebrun-Renault,
when he was examined by the President of the Council, did not
mention the Dreyfus confession!" This statement caused applause to break forth from all parts of the house, during which
M. Cavaignac tried to speak, but was howled down although
one Deputy shouted: "Let us hear the hero of the forgery!"
M. Poincaré concluded with saying: "Silence has weighed heav-
ily upon me, and I am now happy to have had the opportunity to tell what I know of the case." [Renewed applause.]
M. Cavignac reasserted that Capt. Lebrun-Renault's evidence
was given to Gen. Mercier. "His report exists," he exclaimed,
amid uproar and cries of "date!" "date!" "but perhaps Capt.
Lebrun-Renault has since retracted his admissions." Shouts of
surprise followed this suggestion. M. de Freycinet said: "The
Government on assuming office found the proceedings pending.
We have only one anxiety and that is to ascertain the truth.
We do not object to furnishing the Court of Cassation with all
the evidence available excepting the evidence involving the national defense. Both the civil and the military courts are fully
equipped to deal with the respective cases, and as all desire to
arrive at the truth it will be reached. The Government asks
the Chamber to respect the independence of the law." After
another appeal from M. Millerand for a postponement of the
Picquart court-martial. M. Dupuy, the Premier, declared that
the Dreyfus affair "must remain purely judicial, as the only
means of reaching the truth, which may now be attained." Referring to the statements of M. Poincaré, M. Dupuy asked why
that Deputy had waited so long "before astonishing the Chamber with his revelations." "We decline to order a postponement
of the court-martial." said the Premier. "To give such an order.
even if we had the right, would be to strike a blow at the principle of separation of the public powers." "It is not within the
province of Parliament or the Government to adjust the connection which may exist between the Dreyfus and Picquart cases.
Our Intervention would be calculated to hamper the work of
the Court of Cassation. We will respect the decisions of the
law. We are a Government of law and refuse to be a Government of arbitrary measures." [Prolonged. cheers,] The order of
the day, approving the statements of the Government respecting the principle of the separation of the judicial and executive

powers, was then adopted by a vote of 437 to 73. The vote in the Chamber enables the anti-Dreyfusites to sing a song of victory, since the Dreyfusite demand was for the Government to order the Picquart court-martial postponed. Nevertheless the whole a debate served to advance the cause of Dreyfus. M. Dupuy's speech is admitted on all hands to have been a master-piece of statesmanship. He did not deny that the Government had power to intervene with Gen. Zurlinden but explained that it would be better for the Court of Cassation to do so. He said that a fortnight ago the Court of Cassation demanded the doc-uments concerning the Picquart affair. At that time, for legal reasons he continued, only copies could be given. Now how-ever, if the originals were demanded by the court they would be placed at its disposal. Perhaps the most significant feature of the debate after M. Poincaré's revelations, which served to draw even closer the bonds of suspicion surrounding Gen. Mercier, is the changing attitude of the Chamber toward M. Cavaignac. The latter's speech before the period of the Henry suicide was accepted and placarded throughout the country as proof of the guilt of Dreyfus. Now he is received with howls at the hands of Deputies when he attempts to justify his attitude. The gen-eral belief is that the Court of Cassation will now demand the Picquart dossier, thus delaying the court-martial. Among the rumors current this evening is one that Gen. Zurlinden, Mil-itary Governor of Paris, has already resigned. There is also a report that Col. Picquart will be released on bail. In the lob-bies of the Chamber M. Dupuy's speech was interpreted as an invitation to the Court of Cassation to ask for the production of the petit bleu and other documents in the Picquart case, which the Government would immediately produce, thus indi-rectly leading to a postponement of the court-martial, which the Government has refused to grant under duress. It was also held that the 'Premier had admitted the right of the Govern-ment to intervene regarding Gen. Zurlinden's action, but had only refrained from fear that intervention would be misinter-preted. An immense mass meeting was held this evening in favor of Col. Picquart. Thousands of people shouting "Con-spuez Rochefort!" and "Conspuez Drummont!" marched to the Cherche-Midl Prison, where Picquart is confined, and cheered and demonstrated there on his behalf. The anti-Picquartites rallied and there were several conflicts between the two bands."

Along with that episode, Mathieu Dreyfus, the brother of the convicted, never ceased to investigate himself on the case where Alfred was the victim. Having become aware of the existence of a secret file undisclosed during the trial, he finally convinced some politicians; an anarchistic journalist, Bernard Lazare (1865-1903), published in November 1896 "A judicial error. The truth about the Dreyfus Affair." The secret file kept by Picquart eventually circulated, in the higher echelons as well, and information filtered in the political milieu and the civil society, fostering the emergence of a Dreyfusard current convinced of the Captain's innocence and requesting a review of the trial. A political figure played in 1897 a key role in that process: it was the Vice President of the Senate, Auguste Scheurer-Kestner, informed of the case by Mathieu Dreyfus's lawyer: Scheurer-Kestner quickly realized that Esterhazy was guilty. Mathieu Dreyfus had meanwhile had the bordereau published in the press, and witnesses were able to testify that the writing on it was very similar to Esterhazy's handwriting. Scheurer-Kestner filed a request for a review of the Dreyfus trial in November 1897 and *Le Figaro*, run at the time by Ferdinand Roday, was then on the Dreyfusard side and was giving more moderate and "diplomatic" information than the anti-Dreyfusard press that did not mince its words. To prove this moderation, here is an extract of the November 14, 1897 edition of this newspaper and of the front-page article entitled "Le dossier de M. Scheurer-Kestner" ("The case of M. Scheurer-Kestner.") We can read there a claim of non-bias by the newspaper:

> "We believe we have, in the midst of information, rumors, gossip and miscellaneous comments which the Dreyfus affair gave rise to, observed the attitude required from a newspaper free from all bias and passion. We have believe we have observed the only attitude that commanded patriotism."

We obviously cannot relate all the ins and outs of this very long affair here. It doesn't come within our subject, and we would anyway only be taking up scattered elements from the countless studies that have been devoted to it almost from the beginning[3]. Let's just not forget that, following the revelations on Picquart's discoveries and the alleged guilt of Esterhazy, the anti-Dreyfusard campaign increased. But the opposite movement, seeking a conviction of Esterhazy and Dreyfus' rehabilitation was expanding rapidly. And Emile Zola, who was part of it, published three consecutive articles in *Le Figaro*: the first one dated 25 November 1897, entitled "M. Scheurer-Kestner." His involvement in the Dreyfusard cause, reported by the new-

---

[3]For example, as soon as 1905, Joseph Reinach dedicated a work in four volumes to the Dreyfus Affair: *Histoire de l'affaire Dreyfus*, Librairie Charpentier et Fasquelle, Paris, 1905. Available in digital format on the website of the bnf : http://gallica.bnf.fr

papers' headlines, thus began two months before his famous "J'accuse": he actually started by supporting Scheurer-Kestner in his request for a review of the trial (See Fig. 10.2).

Fig. 10.2 *L'Aurore* of January 13, 1898.

Picquart, who was suspected of having orchestrated the leaks, was then accused of manipulation and use of false documents by the General Staff who was not afraid to falsify the truth to discredit him and provoke a trial. But at that moment, the case of Esterhazy was known, and not to further tarnish the image of an army which had Dreyfus convicted, the real traitor had to be tried and acquitted. His trial, closed-door and fabricated from beginning to end by the General Staff, took place in January 1898, apparently at his own request so that he could defend himself against the shameful attacks that he was subjected to. Everything was rigged in this judgment, after Esterhazy was cleared of all suspicion and applauded by the anti-Dreyfusards. "Discharged" right after the trial, he left France for England. But enough was enough: politicians reacted to the case; among them was Georges Clémenceau, who was editor of the newspaper *L'Aurore* since 1897, and who published hundreds of Dreyfusard articles in his newspaper as well as in those of his competitors: this figure alone is a way to picture how considerable the journalistic production of both sides of the case was. Besides, Clémenceau is the one to whom we owe the publication (and title) of Zola's famous article on January 13, 1898. The Dreyfus Affair then became the "Zola Affair" and Zola, as we know, was brought to justice as well. At the same time as the Zola affair, and to try to stop those twists and turns and not to lose face, the General Staff wanted to have Picquart convicted for disclosure of confidential documents to Scheurer-Kestner via his friend and lawyer Louis Leblois. Put under arrest on January 13, 1898, he was discharged on February 26. The Ministry of War then lodged a complaint against him, and he was arrested on July 13. This led to the trial called "Picquart-Leblois" before the 8th Criminal Chamber. Picquart also appeared before the court-martial on December 12 because of other (false) accusations. He asked for the "judges settlement" to be applied, which means the designation of a single chamber of indictment, since the two cases were linked. At the end of year 1898, the situation was as follows: Zola, who had been convicted, was in exile in England; Picquart, convicted and not yet cleared, was in prison and guilty Esterhazy was free. It is the Chamber of indictments of the Court of Paris which ultimately dismissed the cases of Picquart and Leblois on June 13, 1899. But both Zola and Picquart cases obviously helped the Dreyfusard cause, for before such denial of the law, many intellectuals committed themselves in the struggle to stand up for Dreyfus, Zola and Picquart (and incidentally to seek the conviction of Esterhazy, although in his case the court decided in his favor). We shall stop here this long introduction, in order to get to the role of scientists – and especially the role of Henri Poincaré – in the judicial review of Dreyfus's trial which was eventually decided and took place in Rennes from August 7, 1899. Indeed, on June 3, 1899, the Court of Cassation rescinded the 1894 judgment and sent the case to be judged before the court-martial in Rennes. Zola came back to France, and Picquart was released. This was the first victory of the judicial institution over the military and political power: this was also to become the paradigmatic example in future debates about the independence of the judiciary. The order by the Chamber of Paris (which we mentioned above) to have Picquart and Leblois's cases dismissed on June 13, was like an echo of the victory (and a form of jurisprudence).

10.3 The Second Dreyfus Affair: The Rennes Trial and the Intervention of Mathematicians

Zola is the one figure remembered by History when it comes to the involvement of intellectuals in the Dreyfus Affair. Although they took some time to be determined to act, there were eventually many of them who positioned themselves in favor of the convicted Captain and who demanded his rehabilitation, as Laurent Rollet reminds us in the study that we mentioned in the introduction:

"A clear idea can be pictured out of this disproportion [in favor of Dreyfusard intellectuals] by comparing the position of academics and learned institutions in the fight between Dreyfusards and anti-Dreyfusards. The Pasteur Institute, the École Normale Superieure, the École Pratique des Hautes Etudes, the School of Anthropology and many provincial faculties of science, being great in number and having quality actors, have constituted some "bastions" of the Dreyfusard engagement. The Academy of Sciences, within the Institut de France which was hesitating between anti-Dreyfusism and neutrality, was mostly Dreyfusard too. The anti-Dreyfusards were far less productive within the university and learned area: although the Ligue de la patrie française ("League of French Patriots") headed by Jules Lemaitre did manage to bring together a significant number of personalities of the intellectual sphere, only a few scientists were part of it in the end*"

The New York Times of September 5, 1899 explained thus the second trial of Rennes:

CERNUSCHI ACCUSES DREYFUS.
"Testifies He Saw Documents Sold by Dreyfus to a Foreign Officer Gonse Contradicted.

RENNES. Sept. 4.– The fifth week of the second trial by court-martial of Capt. Alfred Dreyfus of the artillery, charged with treason in communicating secret papers to a foreign Government, began to-day with the largest attendance yet seen in the Lycee. The interest in the trial grows as the denouement approaches. Six to ten days is given as the outside limit for the further duration of the trial. There was an exceptionally large number of ladies present to-day, their bright costumes giving a gay look to the court-room. The session opened very interestingly with the appearance of the witness M. Cernuschi. He was dressed in a brown lounging suit. His features are unprepossessing, and, in fact, his general appearance did very little credit to the Servian royal house, to which, it is alleged, he belongs. His letter to Col. Jouaust, offering his testimony, stated that having been mixed up in political trouble in Austria-Hungary, he had been obliged to seek refuge in France where he had a friend who was a high official of the Foreign Office of a Central European power. This friend, the witness said, told him that certain foreign agents in France might denounce him, the first name mentioned being that of Dreyfus. Another officer a foreign General of Staff, similarly warned him. One day, the witness said, when he was visiting the latter. He saw him take from his pocket a voluminous packet containing military documents. The officer said that in France one could buy anything, adding: "What is the good of Jews if you don't use them?" Being questioned if he had asked the name of the traitor in this case, M. Cernuschi replied: "No; because the officer had already said Dreyfus was his informant."

AUDIENCE IS INCREDULOUS.

This answer and the tone in which it was delivered evoked a movement of incredulity among the audience. Major Carrière, representing the Government, asked that the court hold further examination of this witness behind closed doors, in view of the diplomatic side of his testimony. M. Labori then arose and announced that since the prosecution had summoned the aid of foreigners, he intended to make formal application to have complete steps taken through foreign channels to ascertain whether the documents mentioned in the bordereau were delivered to a foreign power; and if so, by whom. This announcement which, if Col. Jouaust consented to the application, will have most important consequences. The words of M. Labori created a deep impression, as they made it evident that counsel for the defense is on the war-path today. The second witness called was M. André, clerk to M. Bertulus Judge of the Court of Cassation, who received the confession of Lieut. Col. Henry. M. André deposed that he overheard Lieut. Col. Henry exclaimed: "Don't insist. I beg of you; the honor of the army must be saved before everything." The next important witness was the well-known mathematician. M Painlevé, who began by tearing M. Bertillon's system of argumentation to pieces. M. Painlevé then, entered upon a personal topic, which quickly won him the close attention of the audience and brought on a dramatic scene, which kept the spectators in a state of excitement until he finally left the bar. M. Painlevé referred to his evidence before the Court of Cassation, and protested vehemently against the version given by Gen. Gonse of a conversation with M. Hadamard a cousin of Dreyfus. In which M. Hadamard expressed belief in the guilt of Dreyfus. "Never," exclaimed Painlevé, "did M. Hadamard doubt the innocence of his cousin." Gen. Gonse asked to be heard, and mounted the stage. After declaring that the whole matter was insignificant, he insinuated that the faith of M. Hadamard and M. Painlevé in the innocence of Dreyfus must have been strengthened recently. M. Painlevé replied warmly, insisting that he never had any doubt of Dreyfus's innocence. The two men then went at it hammer and tongs. M. Painlevé facing Gen. Gonse with his arms folded, and thrust home with his questions and retorts until Gen. Gonse became red in the face. Then Gen. Roget joined in the discussion.

LABORI GROWS INDIGNANT.

M. Labori began a cross-examination of Gen. Gonse regarding a certain document in the secret dossier, to which Gen. Gonse had referred, but which had not been submitted to the court. M. Labori, not receiving satisfactory answers and finding that Col. Jouaust declined to allow him to press the matter in the way he wished, became extremely indignant and protested with considerable warmth against Col. Jouaust's veto of his questions. This caused a little scene between Col. Jouaust and M. Labori. Finally the latter asked why a certain dispatch from the French Ambassador at Rome relative to the payment of money to Major Count Esterhazy by an Italian agent had not been included in the secret dossier presented to the court. Gen. Gonse replied that he had not considered the dispatch of sufficient importance to be included in the secret dossier. Col. Jouaust here again refused to allow some of M. Lahori's questions. M. Labori was fuming with indignation, but was obliged to submit. M. Labori asked Gen. Gonse who complied the secret dossier. "I did" shouted Commandant Cuignet from the body of the hall. Commandant Cuignet then came to the bar and declared that be had omitted all documents from abroad, "because foreigners were interested in deceiving us." He added that another dispatch existed, relating to a conversation between a foreign sovereign and a French Military attaché, in the course of which the sovereign said: "What is now occurring in France is proof of the power of the Jews." This dispatch, said Cuignet, although against Dreyfus, was also omitted from the secret dossier. As he made this statement, Commandant Cuignet turned to a brother officer sitting in the place set apart for witnesses and smiled with the self-satisfied air of a man who had made a distinct score.

CAVAIGNAC IN DEMAND.

MM. Demange and Labori immediately arose and expressed surprise that fresh evidence against Dreyfus should be introduced in this way. M. Labori also expressed curiosity respecting documents which were being held back, concerning espionage, which were in the possession of the General Staff, and he insisted that all, these documents should be submitted to the court behind closed doors. The question of the report drawn up by Commandant Cuignet and Officer Wattines dealing exhaustively with the secret dossier, was then introduced, and Gen. Billot arose to explain that the statement was inexact that he took this report away with him. "I gave this report," he said, "to M. Cavaignac, the former Minister of War." "Then," said M. Labori, "let us have M. Cavaignac's explanation of what became of the report." Col. Jouaust called for M. Cavaignac, but the former Minister of War was not in the courtroom, and an Officer was sent to seek him. Meanwhile the testimony of a couple of minor witnesses was heard. The proceedings to this point were very exciting, as at one time, when Gen. Chanoine and M. Paleologue were brought upon the stage to explain Commandant Cuignet's statements, there were five witnesses at the bar, all speaking at once and interrupting one another. The testimony throughout was interspersed with heated scenes between M. Labori and Col. Jouaust. M. Cavaignac could not be found in the precincts of the Lycée, and it was decided to hear him tomorrow. A Commissary of the secret police, named Tomps, was called by the defense, and it was admitted at the end of the day's proceedings that he proved indirectly a strong witness for Dreyfus and a correspondingly damaging witness for the General Staff. His evidence brought out a glaring instance of duplicity on the part or the staff office in suppressing documents which must weaken its own case.

TOMPS AIDS DREYFUS.

Commissary Tomps was called to the General Staff office to investigate a case of espionage, and, naturally, had consultations and close relations with officers of the bureau. The Commissary began his testimony by paying a high tribute to Lieut. Col. Picquart's correct attitude and uprightness in the Dreyfus inquiry, while other officers sought to undermine him by insinuations. Lieut. Col. Henry, the witness asserted, tried to induce him to attribute to Picquart the communication of the bordereau to the Matin, in which journal the bordereau was first published. Then Commissary Tomps came to the most important portion of his testimony, which led to a restricting of his revelations. The witness was asked if he had ever investigated the Paulmier affair which was as follows: Paulmier was the valet of Col. Schwarzkoppen, the German Military Attaché at Paris, and it was alleged that he saw on Schwarzkoppen's desk documents signed by Dreyfus. The General Staff had declared that an effort would be made to get at the truth of this story but Palmier disappeared, and therefore, although the General Staff could not prove the story, it could not be disproved. To a question regarding this case, Commissary Tomps replied that he had not investigated the affair whereupon M. Labori suggested that M. Hennion, Sub-Chief of the Political Police, who is now in Rennes superintending the precautions for the safety of witnesses, may have been intrusted with the inquiry into this case. Col. Jouaust called to Hennion, who was present in the courtroom, "Come here and testify."

LIE TO THE GENERAL STAFF.

M. Hennion ascended the platform and took the oath. He declared that he did investigate the case, and actually found Palmier, who told him there was not a word of truth in the whole story. He never saw any paper bearing the name of Dreyfus. M. Labori immediately called attention to the fact that the General Staff had suppressed Hennion's report in favor of Dreyfus and only declared that the report had been received representing Paulmier as untraceable. Commandant Cuignet and Capt. Junck then arose and insisted that only the report that Paulmier could not be traced had been received at the office of the General Staff. M. Hennion replied, reiterating that he had forwarded a report to the General Staff giving Paulmier's emphatic denial of the whole story. M. Labori asked Commandant Cuignet and Capt. Junck where the report was that they said had been received by the General Staff stating that M. Paulmier could not be found. The officers interrogated were obliged to admit that they were unable to find the report. This practically closed the matter. The Court adjourned after deciding to sit with closed doors tomorrow to investigate M. Cernuschi's testimony.

THE EVIDENCE IN DETAIL.

After a brief session on camera the public sitting of the court-martial was resumed at 7:15 this morning. The first business today was the reading of the letter of resignation written by Lieut. Bruyere of the artillery to M. Cavaignac, then Minister of War resigning his commission and declaring that it was a dishonor to serve in the French Army. Col. Jouaust explained that as a result of this letter Lieut. Bruyere was cashiered. The first witness called to the bar as an Austro-Hungarian refugee named Cernuschi. This witness asked that a letter which he had written to Col. Jouaust be read and it was done. In this letter M. Cernuschi explained that owing to political troubles, he had been obliged to seek refuge in France around September, 1894 till 1897. While he was in France the letter explained, a friend connected with the Foreign Office of another country mentioned to him the names of certain French correspondents of other powers. The first and most important of these names, the writer asserted was that of Dreyfus.

EXPLANATORY. – The name or the Royal House of Servia is Obrenovitch. The "Almanach de Gotha" does not contain the name Cernuschi or that of Cernusky. It is possible that "M. Cernuschi" is one of the sons of the late Prince Miloch, who died in 1860. Two of them are known to be in Austria under names granted them by the courts of Servia.

–Editor THE TIMES.

Another of M. Cernuschi's friends according to this letter showed him the important military papers, such as route maps for mobilization of troops, documents relating to the transport of troops, diagrams of eastern railways, etc., which he declared came from Dreyfus, remarking further that everything was procurable in France by the payment of money, and adding: "What's the good of having Jews if you don't make use of them?" Two days later the letter said, M. Cernuschi's friend precipitately left Paris, and Dreyfus was afterward arrested. The letter concluded with saying that M. Cernuschi told all this to an officer of the War Office who wrote it down. The reading of the letter created a great deal of excitement in court, so it could be easily seen that such hearsay allegations no longer appeal to many in the audience. Col. Jouaust asked the witness if the statements in the letter were all he had to tell the court. M Cernuschi – Yes; certainly. M. Demange wanted the witness to explain his intervention in the case at this late hour but could elicit no reply. M Demange – Has the Government Commissioner made inquiries concerning this witness? Major Carriere replied in the negative and suggested that a secret session be held in order to hear the witness's explanations relative to the diplomatic side of the question.

CERNUSCHI MUST BE SWORN.

M. Labori declared that since the prosecution had applied abroad for evidence which the defense had always carefully abstained from doing, he reserved the right to use every possible diplomatic means to ascertain if documents mentioned in the bordereau had been betrayed, and if so, by whom. [Sensation] M. Labori asked the witness the nationality of the persons mentioned in the letter. M. Cernuschi – I will give them in camera. [Commotion.] M. Labori – As I mean that this witness shall testify under oath, I ask that a secret session be held tomorrow. I intend to notify the other side of his name. He must testify under oath, for I wish the parties against whom his evidence is brought should have all the guarantees the law assures. [Excitement.] M. André, a clerk of M. Bertulus, Judge of the Court of Cassation, testified to hearing Lieut. Col. Henry say to M. Berthulus: "Don't insist, I beg of you. Above all we must save the honor of the army." Witness also heard Lieut. Col. Henry say: "Leave me Esterhazy and let Du Paty de Clam blow out his brains. That's all I ask."

EXPLANATORY. – This refers to the interview that took place between Judge Bertulus and Henry when the latter went to secure from the Judge certain papers of Esterhazy that had been seized at Mlle, Pays's house on July 12, 1898. Henry bore the order of M. Cavaignac. Minister of War to take away any of the impounded papers "which might seem to concern the exterior defense" Judge Bertulus deposed before the Court on this point as follows: "I pointed out to him the principal document. At the sight of them Henry exhibited emotion. He said I could save the honor of the army, and ought to do so. Seeing that my eyes were opened, he did not attempt to discuss but recognized the Basel paper as the account of his journey with Lauth, and ended by acknowledging that the authors of the telegrams, Blanche and Speranza, were Esterhazy and Du Paty de Clam. At this moment, remembering the courteous relations of long standing which I had had with Henry, I felt bound to stop him and say: "This is not all. Esterhazy and Du Paty are guilty. Let Du Paty blow his brains out tonight. and let justice take its course with Esterhazy, forger, and not traitor. But there is still danger, and this danger is you." He said again and again "Save us." Without giving him time to complete his sentence, if indeed he meant to do so, I replied: "Esterhazy is the author of the bordereau." To this Henry said neither yes nor no. He only said again and again to me, "Don't press me, don't press me. Above all the honor of the army."

–Editor THE TIMES.

Dr. Weil came forward to deny that he had ever made statements attributed to him with regard to the guilt of the prisoner, He had always believed Dreyfus innocence and he vigorously protested against such allegations. Dreyfus, the witness said, was a model husband and not a gambler, and therefore it was absolutely untrue, the witness declared, that he had ever made the alleged statements to Rabbi Dreyfus reflecting upon the prisoner.

EXPLANATORY. – Esterhazy first met Dr. Weil, who is a Jew, in 1892, when the former was second for M. Crémieu-Fos, a Jewish Captain of Dragoons, in a duel with M. Drumont. the editor of *La Libre Parole*, Gen. de Boisdeffre reprimanded Esterhazy for being the second of a Jew. With de Boisdeffre's letter in his hand Esterhazy invited the liberality of the Jews until his begging began to assume the proportions of blackmail. For some time, however, M, Weil and M. de Rothschild continued to aid him. Among the last letters that he wrote to M. Weil in 1897 was one in which he announced his intention of killing his wife and children and himself unless something was done for him, Esterhazy has alleged that on one occasion Dr Weil said to him that be believed Dreyfus to be guilty.

–Editor THE TIMES.

M. Demange read a letter from Rabbi Dreyfus denying that he had ever heard a number of scandalous statements which, it has been alleged were made to him. After minor testimony tending to discredit the witness Savignaud and negative the testimony of M. Hadamard, a cousin or Dreyfus, but who did not know the prisoner and therefore could not have made allegations against his private life as asserted, M. Painlevé, a professor in the College of France, followed at the bar.

BERTILLON CRITICIZED.

M. Painlevé exhaustively criticised M. Bertillon's cryptographic system, citing in support of his conclusions the opinion of M. Henri Poincaré, in his opinion the most illustrious mathematician of modern times, who, in a letter the witness read, examined seriatim the deductions of M. Bertillon and demonstrated their fallacy, also pointing out miscalculations made by M. Valerio. Prof. Poincaré's letter fully supported M. Bernard's conclusions. The reading of Prof. Poincaré's letter having been concluded, M. Painlevé repeated his evidence before the Court of Cassation. He vehemently protested against the false versions that had been published of his conversations with M. Hadamard, in which the latter was made to affirm the guilt of Dreyfus. On the contrary, the witness said, M. Hadamard never doubted the prisoner's innocence. Gen. Gonse intervened at this juncture. He was surprised, he said, at the importance attached to the evidence of MM. Hadamard and Painlevé. There had been, Gen. Gonse asserted, at least fluctuations in their views of Dreyfus's character for which Dreyfus's own family were unwilling to give guarantees. M. Painlevé reasserted that both M. Hadamard and himself had always been satisfied that Dreyfus was innocent. As the altercation between Gen. Gonse and M. Painlevé was rapidly becoming heated. M. Labori intervened. A sharp passage at arms followed between M. Labori and Col. Jouaust, leading to considerable excitement.

GONSE ON THE RACK.

M. Labori asked Gen. Gonse why he had incorrectly reported certain information he had collected. Col, Jouaust refused to put the question, and invited M. Labor to study moderation. M. Labori retorted: "The defense is using its rights with the utmost moderation." Col. Jouaust – No. you are not. I beg you not to drawn my voice when I am speaking. Your very tone is wanting in moderation. Moreover, I consider the question unimportant. There were prolonged murmurs of assent and dissent among the audience at this declaration by Col. Jouaust. M. Labori said he was surprised that Gen. Gonse had included incorrect information in the secret dossier, and asked Gen. Gonse who made up the secret dossier. Gen. Gonse – I composed one of the secret dossiers by means of annexed documents communicated too the Ministry; but the minds of all the War Ministers were made up before they had any cognizance of these documents. M. Labori – Does Gen. Gonse assume responsibility for these secret dossiers to July, 1898? Gen. Gonse – Yes. I had charge of It.

EXPLANATORY. – Prior to July, 1898, when Commandant (then Captain) Cuignet was ordered by Minister of War Cavaignac to "investigate" the secret dossier, this mystery had grown from the tour documents that Picquart found in 1896 (in 1894 it had contained more) to nearly 400. In the War once the envelope containing the documents was secured in an iron safe, of which Gribelin, the archivist, kept the key; and the envelope was sealed and endorsed, with directions of Henry's, written as he swore, by the order of Sandherr, that it was not to be opened by any one except in the presence of Gonse or de Boisdeffre or himself. (Henry.) Sandherr,

when he retired, told Picquart, describing it as the secret dossier which
had been shown to the Judges, and as something not to be lightly spoken
of Commandant Cuignet, after he had completed his examination of the
file a year ago, told the Cour de Cassation that, convinced as he was
of the guilt at Dreyfus his conviction was founded principally upon the
confession alleged to have been made to Lebrun-Renault and the contents
of the bordereau. He accorded these the first two lines of proof, as they
fixed the guilt individually upon Dreyfus. The secret dossier he placed in
the third line as yielding only a general corroboration "by a sort of deductions presumptions in conformity with the other two." Ex-Ministers
of War, in giving their evidence before the Cour de Cassation, mysteri-
ously intimated that the secret dossier would be found conclusive against
Dreyfus.

–Editor THE TIMES.

M, Labori – Why, then, that telegram from the French Ambassador at Rome sent by the Foreign Office to the War
Office, referring to payments to Esterhazy by an Italian
agent, was not added to the secret dossier? Gen. Gonse
– There were plenty of others. All were not included, but
only the most important. M. Labori – Was the information
of the French Ambassador at Rome of less importance than
the garbled conversation of M. Painlevé? Col. Jouaust –
I will not put the question. M. Laborl – Why was information against Dreyfus always included in the dossier, and
never any discriminating Esterhazy? Col. Jouaust – I also
refuse to put that question.

FOREIGN PAPERS DEMANDED.

M. Labori – All right, I think the question itself fully answered the purpose.

EXPLANATORY. – The most important piece missing from the secret
dossier is, of course, the original text, together with the correct construction of the Panizzardi dispatch of Nov. 2, 1894, which practically
proved the innocence of Dreyfus. Capt. Freystaetter, one of the judges
of the 1894 court-martial, deposed before the Court in Rennes the other
day that the garbled version of this dispatch, which tended to implicate
Dreyfus, was actually presented to him and his colleagues in 1894. Another missing document is the translation made by Picquart of the cipher
dispatch of January, 1894. It was a message sent by Schwarzkoppen to his
chief in Berlin in reply to a telegram casting doubt on the authenticity of
the documents that the attaché bad been able to send his Government.
Picquart's translation reads: "You doubt? My proof is that my informant
(Esterhazy) is an officer. I have seen his brevet, (lettre de service.) True,
only a regimental officer; but I assure you he brings his information, every bit of it, straight from the Intelligence Bureau. I cannot communicate
directly with Henry.

–Editor THE TIMES.

Commandant Cuignet, who made up the secret dossier, replying to Col. Jouaust, explained that he omitted everything emanating from foreigners as interested and misleading to France. Several documents of this kind had been omitted, particularly one reciting a conversation between a foreign sovereign and a French Attachlé, in the course of which the sovereign was represented as saying that what was occurring in France was proof of the power of the Jews. "That," added Commandant Cuignet, "might be regarded as against Dreyfus; but nevertheless it was not included in the dossier." M. Demange expressed surprise that the document in question had not appeared in the War Office dossier. Commandant Cuignet – It does not appear there because it was received at the Foreign Office. M. Paleologue, intervening, said that the Foreign Office only acted as an intermediary in that matter. M. Labori commented in a surprised way upon the fact that alleged fresh proofs against Dreyfus were still spoken of and demanded that all proofs be produced once for all. Gen. Chanoine was asked by Col. Jouaust if he had any explanations to offer, and replied that his duty was merely to produce the secret dossier, and that he could not say anything regarding documents outside the dossier. Replying to M. Labori, Commandant Cuignet declared that there were documents relating to Dreyfus in a dossier connected with espionage in the Intelligence Department. M. Labori said he must insist that all these documents be produced at the secret session of the court-martial at which M. Cernuschi is to be examined. Gen. Billot, formerly Minister of War, here mounted the platform and said he was glad that reference had been made to the secret dossier, as it enabled him to protest against the insinuation that he had handed Commandant Cuignet a document from the secret dossier. He had banded the document in question to M. Cavaignac.

EXPLANATORY. – The document here referred to is a commentary am the pieces of the secret dossier prepared in 1898 for Gen. Billot by Wattine his son-in-law, and substitute for the Procureur General. This Gen. Billot is understood to have claimed as his private property. As a matter of fact, it was prepared especially for Commandant Cuignet in the hope that he would use it in his report on the secret dossier made to Minister

of War Cavaignac and later to the Cour de Cassation. The Commandant,
however, refused to avail himself of it. It was then given to M, Cavaignac
as an "independent and supplementary" report.

–Editor THE TIMES.

M. Demange begged Col. Jouaust ask M. Cavaignac to produce the document, but as M. Cavaignac was not present
the incident was temporarily dropped. M, Mayet, who is
on the staff of *Le Temps*, testified that the spy Guénée informed him that the War Office had indisputable proof of
the guilt of Dreyfus, and mentioned a snapshot photograph
representing Dreyfus conversing with a Military Attaché at
Brussels.

EXPLANATORY. – Guénée is the police spy who furnished information
concerning Dreyfus alleged immorality. Then *Le Siècle* printed the famous "Un Diplomate" letter, March 25, 1898. Guénée was ordered to
investigate the matter. This letter, which showed all the details of Esterhazy's relations with the German Military Attaché Schwarzkoppen was
actually inspired by Panizzardi, the Italian Attaché, then accredited in
Berne. When Guénée returned from a journey to that city, *Le Petit Journal* published a story that he had secured a photograph of Picquart and
Panizzardi seated together in the Fountain Park. No further mention,
however, has ever been made of the photograph.

–Editor THE TIMES.

After a brief recess of the court-martial, Dr. Peyrot deposed that he met M. Bertulus, Judge of the Court of
Cassation, at Dieppe after the arrest of Lieut. Col. Henry,
and that M. Bertulus narrated to him the dramatic scene in
his office with Henry. M. Bertulus was very jubilant over
Henry's arrest, and said he was convinced that if Henry
were detained, everything would be known in due time.
M. Tomps, a special commissary of the Railway Police,
deposed that he photographed the bordereau by order of
Col. Sandherr. He had not manipulated the plate with a
view to concealing marks upon the document. When the
facsimile of the bordereau was published Lieut. Col. Picquart ordered the witness to discover who had supplied the
photographic copy.

HENRY ACCUSED PICQUART.

While engaged in the investigation of this matter, Lieut. Col. Henry upon one occasion approached the witness and clearly evinced great uneasiness at the successive revelations in the Dreyfus matter. Henry told the witness that the revelations could only have emanated from an individual who had the documents in his hand. Henry, the witness testified, added: "They can only emanate from our office, where only Picquart, Lauth, Gribelin, or myself could have revealed them. I am sure that neither Lauth, Gribelin, nor myself have been so indiscreet. You would do well to discover who is responsible." M. Tomps detailed successive steps in his investigations, showing how Lieut. Col. Henry and Commandant Lauth had brought pressure to bear to make him implicate Lieut. Col. Picquart, and their angry threats when the witness's report did not suit them. They accused the witness of being influenced by some one. Replying to M. Demange, M. Tomps said that he had only once mixed up Esterhazy in connection with the report. Esterhazy had been seen at a foreign agent's residence, which had two exits, and had other suspicious relations. Witness had found corroboration of this. Replying to M. Labori, M. Tomps further detailed Lieut. Col. Henry's pressure upon him with a view to have the communication of the bordereau to the *Matin* ascribed to Lieut. Col. Picquart. Witness did not know if the leakages at the War Office continued after Dreyfus left.

EXPLANATORY. – As a matter of fact the facsimile of the bordereau, which was published in *Le Matin* Nov. 10, 1896 (see Fig. 10.3), was furnished in photographic copy by M. Teyssonieres, an expert employed at the Dreyfus court-martial of December, 1894. A copy had been furnished him, but he had failed to return it at the end of the trial. Besides giving graphologists all over the world an opportunity to compare the writing ill the bordereau with the authentic handwriting of Dreyfus, *Le Matin*'s publication frightened Esterhazy, who was seen in Paris pale and agitated. The facsimile also led to the exposure of Esterhazy through his stock broker De Castro, who recognized his client's writing in a published fac simile of the document.

–Editor THE TIMES.

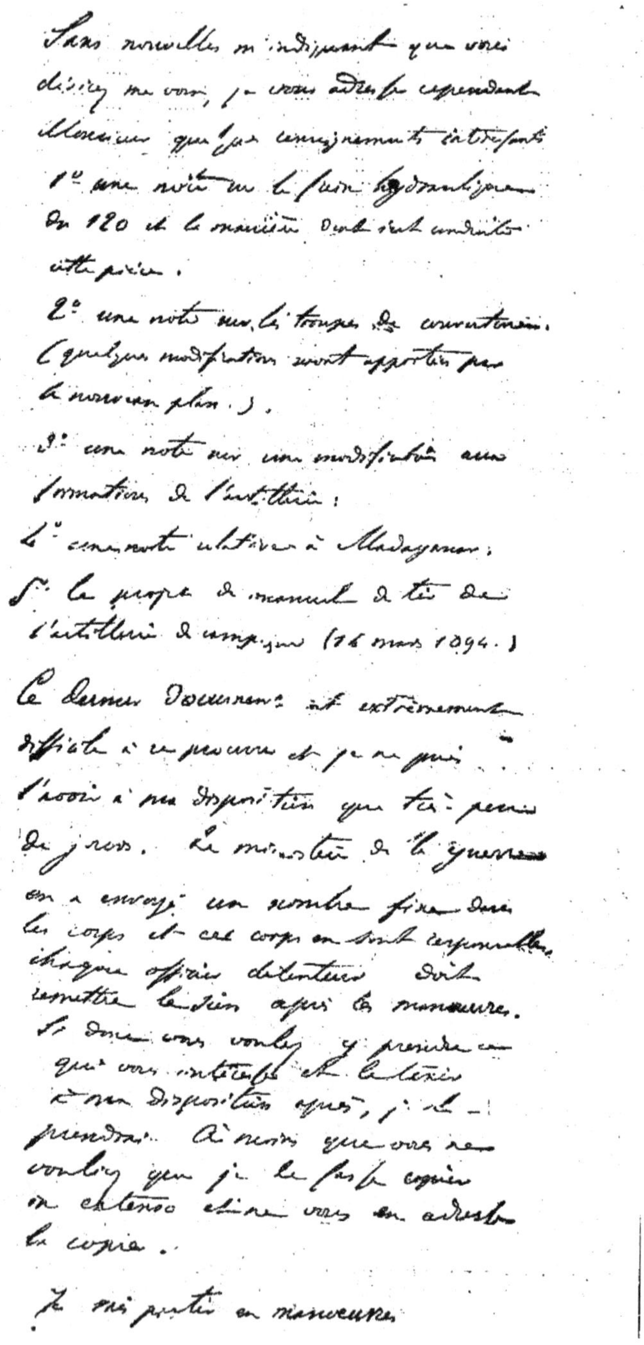

Sans nouvelles m'indiquant que vous
désirez me voir, je vous adresse cependant
Monsieur quelques renseignements intéressants
1° une note sur le frein hydraulique
du 120 et la manière dont s'est conduite
cette pièce.
2° une note sur les troupes de couverture.
(quelques modifications seront apportées par
le nouveau plan.).
3° une note sur une modification aux
formations de l'artillerie;
4° une note relative à Madagascar;
5° le projet de manuel de tir de
l'artillerie de campagne (16 mars 1894.)
Ce dernier document est extrêmement
difficile à se procurer et je ne puis
l'avoir à ma disposition que très peu
de jours. Le ministère de la guerre
en a envoyé un nombre fixe dans
les corps et ces corps en sont responsables,
chaque officier détenteur doit
remettre le sien après les manœuvres.
Si donc vous voulez y prendre ce
qui vous intéresse et le tenir
à ma disposition après, je le
prendrai. À moins que vous ne
vouliez que je le fasse copier
in extenso et ne vous en adresse
la copie.

Je vais partir en manœuvres

Fig. 10.3 *Le Matin* of November 10, 1896.

PAULMIER STORY DENIED.

Detective Hennion testified regarding the assertion to the effect that Paulmier, the valet of Col. Schwarzkoppen, the German Military Attaché, had seen plans of fortresses signed by Dreyfus on his master's table. M. Hennion furnished a typewritten report on the subject, showing that Paulmier never saw or said he had seen such documents. M. Labori pointed out that the Headquarters Staff had alleged that the detective only reported that Paulmier had disappeared, and that his address was unknown. Probably, M. Labori suggested, the gentleman at headquarters merely misunderstood the report of the detective. Commandant Cuignet attempted to explain that the police report indicated that Paulmier had disappeared, but that afterward it was discovered that the police were wrong. Capt. Junck corroborated the statements of Commandant Cuignet, and said that the police had furnished a written report. M. Labori much regretted that this report could not be found and added, amidst much excitement: "But this is always the case. It is always impossible to get at the bottom of interesting incidents owing to documents being missing." Commandant Lauth reappeared with the view of refuting the evidence of M. Tomps. Lauth declared that no one in the Statistical Section dreamed of suspecting Picquart when the inquiry was ordered as to how the *Matin* secured the bordereau. Suspicion attached rather to a civilian clerk who was on friendly terms with Tomps. After Commissary Tomps had replied the court retired to deliberation the subject of holding another secret session. When the members of the court returned Col. Jouaust announced that there would be a sitting in camera to-morrow morning. The name of Seige Bassett was then called. Mr. Bassett is the London correspondent of the *Matin*, who furnished the Esterhazy interviews, and MM. Lahori and Demange pointed out that Esterhazy's confessions were too important to be discussed at the fag end of the day's session. Upon suggestion of counsel for the defense, the court-martial therefore adjourned for the day at 11:40 o'clock A.M.[4]

We can see in this "vow" that the entire intellectual community is represented. And we notice there, for example, Paul Appell and Paul Painlevé. Universities, various academies, the community of lawyers, of engineers, senior officials: the mobilization affected all circles, and politicians remained the least involved. The name of Henri Poincaré does not appear. And it was not added to the supplementary list published in the same newspaper the following day either. Paul Painlevé was the one who stood for Dreyfus and Picquart almost from the beginning and who strove to make other mathematicians and scientists do the same thing: Paul Appell was one of them, as well as Gaston Darboux. Let's note in passing, although we cannot go into details, that petition after petition was written to defend Picquart, Zola and Dreyfus, and thereby a review of the case of Esterhazy was demanded. The petitions of January 14 and 15, 1898 published in the newspaper *Le siècle* et *L'aurore* are two examples. On the present-day site of the Assemblée nationale, we can find the following historical detail:

---

[4]See also http://www.nytimes.com/ref/membercenter/nytarchive.html

"Georges Clémenceau, in *L'Aurore* of January 23, 1898, spoke
of intellectuals to designate the signers of the petitions: Isn't
it a good sign that all these intellectuals who come from varied
backgrounds, gather around one idea and stick to it, unshake-
able? Without the threats that were spread in the confusion
of their conscience! How many of them would also come, if it
were not for the timidity of those who once claimed to guide
the youth, and who, when they should show their faces, choose
to hide? Personally, I would like to see in this the origin of
a movement of opinion which would go beyond all the various
interests, and it is in this peaceful revolt of the French spirit
that I would put my hopes for the future, at a time when we
miss everything[5]."

Henri Poincaré was staying in the background. His first intervention was
an indirect one at the Rennes trial, within the strictly scientific field (and
therefore neutral at the beginning) of scientific expertise, but without him
getting physically involved (for example by testifying): it is the analysis
of the study carried by Bertillon on the famous bordereau that caused the
conviction of Dreyfus that provided him the opportunity to do so. We may
quote Laurent Rollet again. The following lines taken from his study give
us information both on the importance and number of examinations carried
out on the bordereau and on the often impartial approaches of the scientists
who carried them:

"One of the interventions of science and scientists in the case
was that of expert examination. (...). At the heart of these
examinations, that of the bordereau gathered many talents.
From the beginning of the Affair, the issue was to determine the
identity of the author of the bordereau by analyzing his handwriting or the material characteristics of the document. From
1894 to 1906, no less than forty experts were officially designated by justice, to which number can be added the examinations carried out outside any judicial framework (through the
press, pamphlets published at the authors' expense, informal
interventions). From the Zola trial, the Dreyfus Affair turned
into a huge dispute between experts. The examinations and
analysis of the bordereau were carried out with charging or ex-
culpating purposes, under the protective supervision of scientific knowledge and its good methodological practices. Among
the anti-Dreyfusards was developed some interpretation systems largely based on using technical processes to recreate the

---

[5]For a chronology of the Dreyfus Affair (in French) see the website:
http://www.assemblee-nationale.fr/histoire/dreyfus/dreyfus-chrono.asp

bordereau and mathematical analysis tools. It was the case
of Alphonse Bertillon (1853-1914) who defended the theory of
Dreyfus's guilt, relying on photographic reconstructions of the
bordereau and on the (late) use of probability. (...) His keynote
was thus that the bordereau was a complete fabrication; Dreyfus had geometrically created it by mixing his handwriting with
his brother's*."

Hence was developed the term "autoforgery" which made Bertillon's
method successful. "Bertillon was led to intervene in most trials related
to the Affair: he was thus heard not only in the first trial of Dreyfus in
December 1894, but also during the Zola trial in February 1898 and during
the Rennes trial in August 1899 (an interminable several hours testimony,
during which he reconstructed the bordereau with a ruler and a five-cent
coin)." In spite of the audience's smiles and the amused press reports, these
multiple interventions did exert a significant influence. Constantly revised
and remodeled by its author during each of his testimonies, the theory of
autoforgery was then constantly taken up and adapted until 1904: various
contributors tried to give it a mathematical dimension which it lacked at the
start: Captain Valerio was one of them, as well as Commandant Charles
Corps and an anonymous "former student of the École Polytechnique",
author in 1904 of a pamphlet entitled Le Bordereau de M. Bertillon et du
Capitaine Valério (The Bordereau of Mr. Bertillon and Captain Valerio)*."
This anonymous "former student of the École Polytechnique" reminds us
of the "skeptical student from Polytechnique" of the controversy over the
rotation of the Earth: anonymity was often necessary when, being from
the École Polytechnique, the students ventured to publish articles or books
that could be badly received or judged.

Laurent Rollet tells us that "in this dispute between experts the role
of the mathematician Paul Painlevé was essential. Painlevé took a very
active part in the Dreyfusard movement, and the Dreyfus Affair marked
the time when he entered politics*." Consequently we do find his name in
"A vow", the article from Le Temps quoted above. And he was the one
who asked Poincaré, at the Rennes trial, to re-examine the bordereau and
the so-called scientific analysis of Bertillon and Valerio. And he was also
the one that alluded to this work done by Poincaré during the XXth public
hearing of the Rennes trial, as stated by the Journal des débats politiques
et littéraires of September 5, 1899 in a long article devoted to the second
trial of Dreyfus.

During that trial the "The Hadamard-Painlevé incident" occurred: indeed, the mathematician Jacques Hadamard (1865-1963) was then Dreyfus's cousin by marriage, his wife being the daughter of one of his father's cousins. In addition, without having fully committed himself in the Dreyfusard movement, he was convinced of the Captain's innocence. His relationship with Dreyfus was an obstacle to his career, as Painlevé explained at the trial (the testimony was reported by the author of the article, hence the "he said" to designate Painlevé). Paul Painlevé was summoned about the conversation he had with Hadamard at the time of the trial of Zola and whose text had been changed by word of mouth. (Once again the role of the press is put forward): but regardless of this episode, Paul Painlevé was mostly presented in the article as "a high-quality mathematician" who "explains that he scientifically examined Bertillon demonstrations". And the author of the article wrote as follows:

> "He was amazed by the numerous errors made by Bertillon, by how pretentious he was in affecting such certainty, and he was worried at the thought that this demonstration, because of its pseudoscientific nature, could influence the council's decisions."

It is interesting to notice the intellectual honesty of the newspaper that transcribed the words of Painlevé. There was indeed accurate transcripts of the trial, and therefore of what was said there[6]. Painlevé's comments were quite faithfully transcribed, for he actually declared:

> "I was amazed [...] of Bertillon's tone of absolute self-confidence and his claim to introduce mathematical certainty in issues which could not include it in any degree. Seeing this, I was a little worried at the thought that this system, thanks to its pseudoscientific complication, to its seeming ingenuity, thanks also to Bertillon's tone of absolute, imperturbable affirmation [...] could, though quite wrong, in any way affect the council's point of view*."

The account of this testimony was obviously not as impartial in the anti-Dreyfusard newspapers: we shall see an example a little further, still about the Paul Painlevé's testimony.

But let's come back to Bertillon. During the 12th and 13th hearings (on August 25 and 26), he had had full scope to state the "evidence" of Drey-

---

[6] *Le procés Dreyfus devant le Conseil de Guerre de Rennes (7 août - 9 septembre 1899)* (The Dreyfus trial before the Rennes court-martial - August 7-September 9, 1899) - shorthand account in-extenso, Paris, P.-V. Stock, 3 volumes, 1899.

fus's guilt again, and to defend the scientific nature of his investigations, calculations and demonstrations around the famous bordereau. During the August 25 hearing, his testimony lasted part of the morning and the president, as well as the council members got impatient, so when Bertillon told them at 11:40 that he needed another two hours to complete his demonstration, they ended up adjourning the session. He therefore came back the following day, but the doubts about his system (autoforgery and anthropometry) as well as on his demonstration (the previous day, he had written with his own hand a fake bordereau for the jury, as Dreyfus supposedly had) were such that two other "experts" were summoned:

> "The practical experience that concluded the first part of the witness's explanation, as we said yesterday, does not seem to have been a complete success. Bertillon's statement must be completed or rather popularized by Captain Valerio, military cryptographer. But on the other hand, the Council will also hear Mr. Paraf-Javal who intends to refute Bertillon's system[7]."

Of all the experts who, after analyzing the bordereau, had declared Dreyfus guilty, the only ones that were remembered from that date on are Bertillon and captain Valerio: the criticisms and second opinions were thus aimed at them. Painlevé's statement during the 21st hearing offered a fundamental (but not decisive as we shall see) element in that debate between experts. Claude Maurice Bernard's examination (1864-1923) destroyed the Bertillon "system". He was also a signatory to the petition of the intellectuals in January 1898 and intervened again in 1904 on the occasion of the "last Dreyfus trial." Henri Poincaré followed his example first, at the time of the Rennes trial and the letter read by Painlevé. In the article from the *Petit journal*, Paul Painlevé was portrayed as follows:

> "This young academic, summoned to repeat the conversations he had with Mr. Hadamard about Dreyfus, first launched into a criticism of M. Bertillon's calculations, that no one had instructed him to check. M. Painlevé, who was once anti-Dreyfusard, seemed to be driven by a strange zeal, but he is completely wrong if he believes that he has established his scientific superiority over the inventor of anthropometry before the council."

---

[7] *Journal des débats politiques et littéraires* of August 27, 1899.

Once again the newspaper is clearly biased. And this can go as far as to falsify truth. Indeed, Painlevé was never anti-Dreyfusard. It was only a rumor, especially about the distorted conversation he had with Hadamard and the reason he was summoned to Rennes as a witness. Hundreds of articles could be used to illustrate these biases on this particular subject (Painlevé's testimony and Poincaré's indirect intervention), of one side or the other: most newspapers reported on a daily basis the unfolding of the trial which was often on the front pages of their editions. But the example is enough to see how the same fact and the same figures could be portrayed according to the position of the paper that passed (or should we say "conveyed") the information.

Nevertheless, Poincaré finally entered the arena, initially through his friend Paul Painlevé to whom he sent a letter. Neither the *Journal des Débats* nor the *Petit Journal* reproduced this document; however, the same day (September 5), the newspaper *Le Temps* published it in full, and started by merely academically and neutrally present Paul Painlevé: "an examiner at the École Polytechnique, a lecturer at the École Normale." And his words were not interpreted or summarized, but reproduced as they were. Poincaré's letter enlighten us as to the position of Painlevé (he does not want to get involved in the case itself) and his intellectual honesty (note once again in passing the "y" in the Poincaré's name):

> Letter from Mr. Henry Poincaré
> My dear friend,
>
> You have asked for my opinion on the Bertillon system. As for the case itself, I must declare myself incompetent, for I have no knowledge of the subject and I can only rely on those who have some. I am no graphologist either and I do not have time to check the measurements. That said, if you just want to know if this application is correct in the reasoning where Bertillon used probabilistic calculation, then I can give you my opinion. Consider the first of his reasoning, the most understandable of all. But after very technical and specific explanations, his conclusion is final: in summary, Mr. Bernard's calculations are correct. Mr. Bertillon's are not. Even if these calculations were accurate, no conclusion could be valid because the application of probabilistic calculation to the moral sciences are, as said I-don't-remember-who, a scandal for mathematics; because Laplace and Condorcet, who knew how to calculate, found some results lacking in common sense. Nothing in that has any scientific character, and I cannot understand why you are so worried.

I do not know if the defendant will be sentenced, but if he is, it must be on other evidences. It is impossible that such an argument makes any impression on free-minded people having received a solid scientific education.

Yours faithfully.
Poincaré

This was his only involvement – necessarily important, and necessarily heard, whatever the outcome of the trial was – in the Rennes court-martial. Let's wait for the next episode and see his role and position become more apparent. Many people were surprised by the judgment pronounced by the court-martial of the Rennes trial on September 9, 1899: Dreyfus was declared guilty again, although the bordereau may have been written by Esterhazy. The captain therefore benefited from "extenuating circumstances" and his sentence was reduced to 10 years imprisonment. Exhausted by his detention and the two trials, he resolved to ask for pardon, which was granted to him soon after the judgement and allowed him to be released. An amnesty law relating to this case was passed in November 1899: it absolved all the persons involved in the affair, including Esterhazy. The Dreyfusards could not be satisfied with this fact: although pardoned, Dreyfus was still guilty, and what was needed was a trial with a view to clearing him, in order to close this sad chapter in the history of the Third Republic for good.

10.4 The Third Trial: "Wise Men in a Shed"

We will recount here neither the political and institutional developments, nor the doubts about the evidence against Dreyfus other than the famous bordereau, which helped lead to a review of the trial and clearing of Dreyfus by the Court of Cassation through a survey and some other long examinations: from 1904 to 1906. Jean Jaurès, political director of the newspaper *L'Humanité*, was elected in 1902 with what is called the "Cartel des Gauches" ("Left-wing Coalition") and he is the one who reopened the debate on the Dreyfus Affair as soon as 1903, by giving a speech where he expressed his doubts about some of the incriminating evidences. The paper *Le Temps* just published a short news in brief article on its last page:

The Criminal Division of the Court of Cassation decided to entrust Mr. Appell, Dean of the Faculty of Science, Mr. Darboux, permanent secretary of the Academy of Sciences, and Mr. H.

Poincaré, Member of the Institute with scientifically examining
Mr Bertillon's work on the bordereau."

On May 11, 1904 and the following day, *La Presse*, then the *Journal des
débats*, published the same news in brief article, down to the last comma,
which suggests that the information was copied directly from a news agency.
(The paper *L'Humanité* returned to the case in an article published on the
front page of its September 14 edition. They gave the article a humorous
title: "Wise men in a shed".) The pre-trial investigation took two years, the
evidence against Dreyfus were removed one after the other, and obviously
the press of both sides got back into its old ways: we will not give here
more excerpts of the many articles that used the reports of the three mathematicians either as a guarantee of the impartiality of the judiciary, which
was clearing Dreyfus, or as an example of the dishonesty and supposed bias
of the scientists that had been summoned for the review. The trial finally
occurred and reached its verdict in 1906. Of course, the anti-Dreyfusard
press did not stop reacting: it was the case of the paper *La Croix* on June
22, 1906 about the previous day's hearing:

> "Mr. Moras carries on with the reading of his report by reading
> the conclusions of Messrs. Darboux, Appell and Poincaré, the
> experts who contradicted the Bertillon system. They concluded
> with these kind words: "The absurdity of the Bertillon system
> is so obvious that it is hard to believe that this discussion was
> so long, and one might not understand the need for it, if not
> for the whole history of the case." In their report, Messrs.
> Darboux, Appell and Poincaré replaced their arguments with
> insults against the creator of anthropometry. They accused him
> of "reasoning poorly on false documents.""

We shall borrow from the *Journal des débats* of July 14, 1906 the conclusion of this long case and the role of mathematicians in its last two
parts:

> "After a thorough investigation, after long debates, the Court
> of Cassation quashed the judgment of the Rennes court-martial;
> then, trying the former prisoner itself, declared him absolved.
> Any sensible man will consider that nothing remains of the
> Dreyfus affair. Poincaré, Darboux and Appell were one last
> time listed under the name of "the leading mathematicians of
> France and around the world." This slightly excessive qualifi-
> cation confirms in any case how important were the voices of
> scientists in the society of that time, and how crucial was their

role in the examinations that did not come within their sole scientific activities. Once again, Poincaré participated to a true cultural revolution in the relations between science and society: even if he had not personally committed himself in the very controversial issue of Dreyfus's guilt, his scientific impartiality served his image as well as that of science."

LE PROCÈS DE RENNES : Dreyfus devant le Conseil de guerre.

Fig. 10.4 *Le Petit Journal* of 1899.

Chapter 11

The Role Model – The Immortal

In the early twentieth century, Henri Poincaré's work in Mathematics, Analytical Mechanics, Celestial Mechanics and Physics-Mathematics was then universally recognized by the entire international scientific community. His reputation was such that his advice was highly sought-after by many specialists of these fields, but also by journalists who consulted him on diverse and varied issues and for whom he was necessarily an authority. In this regard, the mathematician Eric Temple Bell (1883-1960) wrote in his book entitled on *Men of Mathematics*:

> "During the first decade of the twentieth century, Poincaré's fame increased rapidly and he came to be looked upon, especially in France, as an oracle in all things mathematical. His pronouncements on all manner of questions, from politics to ethics, were usually direct and brief, and were accepted as final by the majority[1]"

11.1 Poincaré and the End of the World

Shortly before the beginning of the twentieth century[2], some traces of these appeals could already be found in the press. Indeed, on November 9, 1899, Charles Chincholle (1845-1902), a journalist of *Le Figaro* had questioned Maurice Loewy (1833-1907) and Henri Poincaré about the end of the world. This question, which may seem surprising at first, was justified by a piece of information published two years before, on September 2, 1897, in the Swiss newspaper *La Liberté* and taken over by the daily *La Presse*:

---

[1]See Eric Temple Bell, *Men of Mathematics*, New York, Simon and Schuster.
[2]The twentieth century only started on January 1, 1901 and ended on December 31, 2000.

THE END OF THE WORLD

La liberté tells us that an Austrian scientist, Mr. Rudolph
Falb, predicted the end of the world on November 13, 1899, at
9 minutes past 3 in the evening. "We could not possibly feel
concerned about this, said our colleague. Ever since year 1000
it has been so often predicted!"

Rudolf Falb (1838-1903) was an Austrian science popularizer who was
interested in many fields such as seismology, meteorology and astronomy.
According to *The New York Times* of June 26, 1887, he was the author of
a theory of earthquakes: "The Falb Earthquake Theory" that is supposed
to have allowed him to predict the one which occurred in Northern Italy in
Belluno, on June 29, 1873.

THE FALB EARTHQUAKE THEORY.

– To Rudolf Falb, of Vienna, belongs the honor of predicting
earthquakes. His first success was in 1873, when he foretold the
Belluno earthquake of June 29, which shook almost all Northern Italy, and resulted in the destruction of some 50 lives. Since
then he has constantly issued seismic predictions, some of which
have been fulfilled and some not. His warning of the recent Riv-
iera disaster was a conspicuous success, and has served to give
him a reputation which it is the lot of few modern prophets to
enjoy. Some days before the catastrophe he wrote to the Austrian papers pointing out that according to his theory (of which
more presently) a critical period would be reached shortly after
midnight on the morning of Feb. 23, and true enough, almost
at the hour stated, the first and most destructive shock took
place. It is not necessary to dwell on the particulars of that
memorable event. Probably no earthquake in history ever produced so much nervous disturbance in proportion to the actual
damage done, and certainly none can equal it in wealth of humorous incident. As an example of a prophecy unfullfilled it
is worth noting that Falb is said to have also predicted that
an earthquake would take place in the South of England on
March 21; no seismic disturbance was felt on that day, but an
amusing illustration of the inconvenience arising from the previous fulfilment of his forecasts was afforded by a lady of our
acquaintance, who upon hearing of the prediction of a fresh
earthquake for March 21, dismantled her drawing room, and
carefully packed up china and other ornaments in anticipation
of the event! The idea that the moon should have something
to do with the production of earthquakes is a very natural one.
The body whose attractive power raises the ocean tides ex-
ercises its influence on the dry land just as much as on the

sea, and the only reason why the land does not respond to the attraction is because of its immobility. But a force so resisted means internal strain, and we have every reason to believe that, corresponding to the tide of movement on the ocean, there is a tide of strain on the land. How may this strain make itself apparent? A breath of Autumn air brings down the leaves that have withstood a Summer's gales, a snapping twig has loosed the Alpine avalanche. The crust of our earth is not solid. There are cavities and fissures in its mass, frail places, where only a touch, as it were may cause collapse; and the series of changes so begun may involve a continent in ruin before it is ended. And the tidal train, as it passes regularly round the globe may one day supply just the needed touch, thus becoming an agent of destruction none the less potent because it only plays the part of trigger-puller. The theory is plausible, and to a certain extent the researches of Prof. Perrey bear it out. He found that earthquakes are rather more frequent when the tidal pull is strong – that is, when the sun and moon are pulling in line, (at new or full moon,) and when the moon is in the part of her orbit nearest to the earth, (perigee.) The difference, however, was only small, and as other investigators have arrived at contradictory results, the lunar theory in this form has not held its ground."

– Murray's Magazine

Nevertheless, it seems that he was regarded as a hoaxer, especially by Camille Flammarion who wrote in his book entitled *La fin du monde* (The End of the World):

> "As soon as the first edition of this book was published (December 1, 1893), another prophet, a Viennese scholar, Dr. Rudolf Falb, predicted the end of the world again, this time on November 13, 1899, because of the collision of a comet with the Earth. And yet, we do not expect any comet on this date, only a meteor shower[3]."

On November 9, 1899, Poincaré and Loewy were asked by *Le Figaro* to give their opinion on "the eternity of the world":

> "We met yesterday Mr. Loewy, director of the observatory of Paris, and Mr. Poincaré, President of the *Bureau des Longitudes*. We also saw at the Institute many of their distinguished colleagues. In exquisite smile they had, from the wording of

---

[3] See Camille Flammarion, *La fin du monde*, Librairie Ernest Flammarion, Paris, 1894, p. 215.

the question, it was clear that we had nothing to fear. The world is solid and does not provide an observation end. No comet threatens us. Both of which could have approach us, those of Biela and of Dunlop are disaggregated so that we may not see them again ever. In any case, nothing indicates, for this year, their return. Where then was this strange noise coming and continuing to the end of the world? Perhaps some mysterious preparations required because science, especially, like discretion."

A few weeks later, Henri de Parville returned this information in the *Revue des Sciences* section in the *Journal des débats politiques et littéraires* of November 23, 1899.

"After the end of the world! ...

Émile de Girardin[4] was quite wrong to deny the power of the press. Wasn't a short "news item" borrowed from a newspaper enough to sow terror among people? A piece of information cut with scissors in some sheet, annotated, enlarged, properly decorated, and here is the "end of the world" is noted, predicted with certainty on November 13 at 9 minutes past 3. Then comes the autosuggestion, and, after having smiled, the most impressionable tell each other "But, what if it was true, in the end?" Gradually, people thought about it and weak brains got forged with chimeras. In short, the short news item has gone around the globe and has turned many minds upside down. In the countryside, we saw women go to church, as the final hour approached. Even in Paris, in some neighborhoods, people felt worried. "Tomorrow is the end of the world," repeated the good people: astronomers have told so. And in the streets where the cards are told, an astronomer is even more reliable than an astrologer. It was abroad, especially in Italy, that the prophecy frightened people the most[5]. We saw women faint. It is clear that one does not expect the end of the world without emotion. By chance, a few shocks of earthquakes precisely occurred on the date that had been set. The hour approaches, people moaned, here are the first convulsions, and they crossed themselves in the streets. In Spain, South Africa, the short news item has caused casualties. Unfortunately in the late nineteenth century, these prophecies of other times can still reach us[6]. Who

---

[4]Émile de Girardin (1806-1881) was the founder of the French daily *La Presse* which Parville alludes to here.

[5]Parville reminds us of Falb's prediction concerning the earthquake of Belluno.

[6]It was still the case in the late twentieth century with the prediction of Paco Rabanne

would have thought? However, the end of the world has been announced many times, both in the past and in modern times. And the earth still rotates with the same placidity. Every time a fanciful astronomer fails his career, he predicts the end of the world. His name goes from mouth to mouth and soon becomes popular. This is a sure way to get out of the darkness. And it is used for this purpose. So we will always, from time to time, be hearing of "ends of the world." All of them will be as benign and silent as it was on November 13, 1899 at 9 minutes past 3 in the afternoon. Where did this last prophecy come from? Let's not mention any names – It had its origin in our next collision, which is today over, with the November ring of shooting stars."

And to reassure the public about the fact that the end of the world, supposedly imminent, was impossible, Henri de Parville used Science, and more particularly the solution that Henri Poincaré found to the three body problem, corresponding to his research on the stability of the solar system. Thus, he adds:

"Mr. Poincaré, who studied the problem of the final state of our solar system, said with great authority (3): "The solar system therefore would tend to a condition in which the sun, all the planets and their satellites, would move with the same velocity round the same axis, as if they were parts of one solid invariable body. The final angular velocity would, on the other hand, differ little from the velocity of revolution of Jupiter. This would be the final state of the solar system if there were not a resisting medium; but the action of this medium, if it exists, would not allow such a condition to be assumed, and would end by precipitating all the planets into the sun." And further: "Thus the celestial bodies do not escape Carnot's law, according to which the world tends to a state of final repose. They would not escape it, even if they were separated by an absolute vacuum. Their energy is dissipated; and although this dissipation only takes place extremely slowly, it is sufficiently rapid that one need not consider terms neglected in the actual demonstrations of the stability of the solar system." It is quite clear. The future appears as if it were to happen tomorrow. The end of our world is clearly not the one that the general public think of. The inhabitants of the earth will fatally be disappearing, killed by the lack of water and the lack of air, killed by the cold. Our world will slowly become uninhabitable."

---

or with the famous prediction of the Mayas for 2012.

(3) yearbook of the 1898 *Bureau des Longitudes*[7]

It is surprising to see that Parville refutes the hypothesis of the end of the world by relying on the stability of the solar system, which we know today to be limited in time[8].

A few years later, Poincaré returned to this issue on the occasion of the publication of his *Leçons sur les hypothèses cosmogoniques*[9] (Lectures on the cosmogonic hypotheses) but from another angle. Indeed, he envisaged the theory of a "heat death" of the Universe based on the principle of energy conservation and the principle of Carnot-Clausius, that is to say, the first and second principle of Thermodynamics[10]. When his book was published, astronomer Charles Nordmann, who regularly ran a popular science column in the newspaper *Le Matin*, wrote on January 27, 1912 an article entitled: *La Mort de l'Univers* (The Death of the Universe) in which he analyzed Poincaré's book.

11.2   Poincaré and Science in the Twentieth Century

On October 3, 1900, Edmond Fazy (1870-1910), columnist for the newspaper *Le Temps*, addressed a letter to Poincaré, in which he asked him what science was going to be in the twentieth century, in his opinion. Poincaré replied with great humor and reserve:

> What we can say about our famous mathematician Poincaré is that, apparently, only a very small number of his peers can fully understand his work. But at least everyone can enjoy this letter he addressed me:

---

[7]Parville refers to Henri Poincaré, "Sur la stabilité du système solaire," *Annuaire du bureau des longitudes*, p. B1-B16, 1898.

[8]The work of Jacques Laskar, "A numerical experiment on the chaotic behavior of the Solar System," *Nature*, 338, p. 237-238, 1989, have shown that the evolution of the orbits of the solar system's planets on a scale of 5 billion years are unpredictable, which could lead, in some cases, to collisions. The stability of the solar system would then no longer be guaranteed.

[9]See Henri Poincaré, *Leçons sur les hypothèses cosmogoniques*, Paris, Librairie Scientifique Hermann, 1911.

[10]*Ibid.* §189, p. 251: "This second principle is sometimes incorrectly stated when saying that a material system tends to homogeneity both in terms of distribution of matter and of temperatures."

September 7, 1900.

Sir,

Your letter arrived today after having traveled a lot. If in 1800, someone had asked any scholar what he thought that science would be in the nineteenth century, such stupidities he would have said, good Lord! That thought keeps me from answering you. I think we will obtain surprising results. This is precisely why I cannot tell you anything about it, for if I could plan them, then how could they still be surprising? Please excuse my silence and accept the assurance of my highest consideration.

POINCARÉ.

11.3 Poincaré and the Martingale Strategy

As everyone knows a martingale is a more or less exact "method" perfected by observing the frequency of gambling gains and losses, and thanks to which the player hopes to secure or increase his gains. On March 10, 1907, through an article entitled *Le Hasard* (Chance) published in the journal *Revue du Mois*, Poincaré analyzed, among other things, the case of the roulette in terms of probabilities. The following year, on October 3, 1908, he sent a letter to the newspaper *Le Matin* in which he strongly criticized the "inventors of infallible martingales." The newspaper reproduced the letter on the front page with a photograph of Poincaré (See Fig. 11.1).

Poincaré returned to "chance" in an article entitled: *Comment se fait la Science?* (What is Science made of?) also published in *Le Matin* of November 25, 1908.

"The facts that give a large return are those that we consider simple, whether they are so in reality, because they are only influenced by a small number of well-defined circumstances, or whether they take on an appearance of simplicity, because the multiplicity of circumstances upon which they depend obey the laws of chance, and so arrive at a mutual compensation. This is most frequently the case, and is what compelled us to enquire somewhat closely into the nature of chance. The facts to which the laws of chance apply become accessible to the scientist, who would lose heart in face of the extraordinary complication of the problems to which these laws are not applicable. To begin with, what is chance? It is not the absence of all laws, as the ancients believed; it is not the unknown law, as is sometimes

Fig. 11.1   *Le Matin* of October 3, 1908.

said. Chance is something more than the name we give to our ignorance, otherwise there would be no calculation of probabilities; one cannot speak of the laws of chance, and insurance companies would go bankrupt. We needed a better definition. The effects we attribute to chance are those due to very small causes, escaping the casual observer but nevertheless considerable, or to multiple and complex causes, which, isolated, would have produced nothing but insignificant results and which become effective only by being accumulated."

Henri Poincaré

In U.S.A. two daily papers reported on this issue. The first was the *Hartford Republican* of July 23, 1909 (See Fig. 11.2) and then, the *McCook Tribune* of June 1, 1911 (See Fig. 11.3).

Chances In Gambling.

Henri Poincare, the leading mathematician of France, declares that there is no infallible martingale or method of doubling one's stakes after every loss. "All one can do," says M. Poincare, "is to combine one's play so as to have a great chance of winning a little and a little chance of losing much or a few chances of gaining much and many chances of losing little. One can arrange his play so as to have one chance of winning a million francs and a million chances of losing a franc or a million chances of winning a franc and one chance of losing a million francs—and that's all."

Fig. 11.2   *Hartford Republican* of July 23, 1909.

Lottery Chances.

M. Henri Poincare, the mathematician, told us a few years ago that if every one who buys a lottery ticket knew how little chance there was of any one winning a prize there could be no successful lottery. The chance of each was about equal to the danger of being killed in a railway accident.— London Truth.

Fig. 11.3   The *McCook Tribune* of June 01, 1911.

In addition to these direct interventions in the press, Poincaré is also cited in many articles on the most diverse subjects, as if adding his name was enough to guarantee the accuracy or truthfulness of the facts alleged by the authors of these articles. Some concepts that he developed in his works of scientific philosophy were also taken up by philosophers and novelists to illustrate their points, then by journalists who did not hesitate then to report them to their readers.

11.4   Poincaré Cited as a Role Model

On April 21, 1907, Gaston Deschamps presented a book by the French-speaking Belgian writer Maurice Maeterlinck (1862-1911) in *Le Temps*'s section *La Vie Littéraire* (Literary Life), entitled *L'intelligence des Fleurs* (The Intelligence of Flowers), and wrote:

> "I firmly believe that poetry always agrees with the truth, and that the science of great scholars get along quite well with the literature of good writers. Mr. Henri Poincaré's fine books on *Science and Hypothesis*, and also on *The Value of Science* could easily bring us evidence to support this reassuring conviction."

The following year, the French essayist Jean Bourdeau (1848-1928) who specialized in German philosophy[11], regularly ran a column in the *Journal des débats politiques et littéraires* in which he analyzed the latest published philosophical works. It is interesting to note that in many of his articles, he systematically referred to Poincaré. For example, he wrote in the edition of April 21, 1908:

> "Pragmatism begins by drawing limits to the scope of science, and those limits are recognized by the scholars themselves and were popularized in France by Mr. Poincaré."

In the edition of May 26, 1908 which follows, he wrote:

> "Poincaré carefully distinguishes science from hypothesis. Hypotheses are always subject to revision. Science entirely lies in the rigor of its methods and would never venture beyond experience[12]."

---

[11]He translated the works of Henri Heine (Mémoires, 1884) and Arthur Schopenhauer (Douleurs du monde, pensées et fragments, 1885).
[12]Bourdeau quote Poincaré again in the same section of the *Journal des débats politiques et littéraires* of July 28, 1908, October 26, 1909, July 26, 1911, November 29, 1911 and December 31, 1911.

With regards to literature, the journalist André Chaumeix (1874-1955), in his *Revue Littéraire* (Literary journal) of the *Journal des débats politiques et littéraires* of March 28, 1909, noted that Claude Farrère (1876-1957), author of *La Bataille* (The Battle) reproduced the last sentence of Poincaré's *The Value of Science in his novel.*

> "All at once, in Mr. Farrère's book, we read this sentence by Mr. Henri Poincaré" – geological history teaches that life is but a short episode between two eternities of death, and that within this very episode conscious thought did not and will not last but an instant. Thought is just a flash of lightning in the middle of a long night. And this flash is everything. "It's a beautiful sentence, which would not have displeased Tchéo-Pe-I[13]. But I regret to say that this book is read in the cabin of a yacht by a reader resembling an American woman, who is lying on a bed dressed in her rings and a black surah shirt. Ah! how Mr. Poincaré would be surprised to know in what costume he is read! and how this approach of metaphysics would seem strange to him."

In 1908, the publication of his three books of scientific philosophy, which largely contributed to make him known in the literary and philosophical world, helped clear the way to the Académie française.

11.5 Poincaré at the Académie Française

The Académie française was founded by Cardinal Richelieu under the reign of Louis XIII. Its main role consisted in watching over the French language to maintain its qualities and follow the necessary evolutions. This mission is carried out every year through the development of the academy's Dictionary, in which the *immortels*[14] (immortal) participate. The Academy consists of forty members, among whom are poets, novelists, theater people, philosophers, doctors, scientists[15], ethnologists, art critics, soldiers,

---

[13] One of the characters of Farrère's novel.

[14] This nickname was given to the Academicians firstly because of the motto "A l'immortalité" ("To immortality") that appears on the seal given to the Academy by its founder, Cardinal Richelieu, and secondly because the position of Academician is an irremovable dignity. No one can resign from the Académie française.

[15] It is important to remember that since it was created, the Académie française elected many members of the Académie des sciences such as Jean le Rond de d'Alembert, Pierre Simon de Laplace, Georges Cuvier, Jean-Baptiste Fourier, Claude Bernard, Joseph Bertrand, Louis Pasteur or Marcellin Berthelot whose scientific skills have been made the most of to develop the Dictionary, for they were able to throw light on the meaning

statesmen, churchmen having particularly rendered the French language illustrious. Their election, often seen by the public as a supreme consecration, alas occurs when one of the members dies.

The death of the chemist, essayist, historian of science and French politician Marcellin Berthelot occurred on March 18, 1907 and allowed Henri Poincaré to submit his application to the Académie française. A few days later, on March 22, *Le Figaro* announced:

> "Even if out of conventions, we are careful not to name any of those who applied for Mr. Berthelot's chair, we actually think that the Academy has decided to reserve his chair for a scholar, and we know for certain that people talk a lot about Mr. Poincaré of the Académie des Sciences."

But Marcellin Berthelot was not only a member of the Académie des Sciences (1873) and of the Académie française (1900), he was also permanent secretary of the Académie des sciences[16] for physical sciences since 1889. A coveted position for which Poincaré also thought of applying. The newspaper *Le Temps* gave an account of this election throughout April and the beginning of May 1907. Thus, on April 4, 1907, it announced:

> "What seems to prevail in most people's opinion in the session room and the waiting hall, where this question is discussed by many academicians, is that this election will not be taking place for another month. No applications have yet been officially submitted. However, some members would consider already, as we are told, to give their vote to Mr. Henri Poincaré, others to Mr. de Lapparent or M. Edmond Perrier, if one of those scholars were willing to apply."

On April 10, 1907 people could read:

> "The only almost certain application that is known so far is that of Mr. Henri Poincaré."

---

of the new words that science and industry were introducing in the French language. François Jacob, for example, is a member of the Académie des sciences since 1977 and of the Académie française since 1996.

[16]The Académie des sciences consists of Members, foreign Associates and Correspondents. The members are divided into sections, but there are two divisions (first division: mathematics, physics and their applications; second division: chemical, natural, biological and medical sciences and their applications), each with its own permanent secretary.

But on May 1, 1907, the first development occurred:

> "The only two applicants known so far are (alphabetically) M.
> de Lapparent and Mr. Henri Poincaré."

Then a second one occurred on May 12, 1907 reported by the same newspaper and also by *Le Figaro*:

> "Mr. Henri Poincaré has just sent a letter to his colleagues of
> the Académie des Sciences, in which he declared that he is will-
> ing to withdraw his application he had submitted for the post
> of permanent secretary for the department of physical sciences,
> as a replacement for Mr. Berthelot. M. de Lapparent remains
> then the only applicant. We know that the election will be held
> next Monday."

According to Laurent Rollet[17], who based his point of view on the correspondence between Poincaré and Lapparent, there was an agreement between them. The first was withdrawing in favor of the latter for the Académie des sciences and the latter was giving the first an unfailing support for the Académie française.

Regarding his application for the Académie française, *Le Temps* announced on April 27, 1907:

> "The Académie received yesterday a letter yesterday, in which
> Henri Poincaré, member of the Académie des Sciences, declares
> to apply for the vacant chair, consequently to the death of Mr.
> Berthelot."

However, another development soon took place. Indeed, in Le Figaro of July 5, 1907 people learned that:

> "Mr. Francis Charmes[18] has also applied for the Mr. Berth-
> elot's chair, competing with M. Henri Poincaré."

Finally, it is the untimely death of Sully-Prudhomme on September 6, 1907 that put an end to this strange saga and encouraged Poincaré to transfer his application for the Académie française to his chair, as indicated by the newspaper *La Croix* on December 7, 1907:

---

[17]See Laurent Rollet, Henri Poincaré (1854-1912): *Des Mathématiques à la Philosophie*,
PhD Thesis, Université de Nancy 2, 1999, p. 296.
[18]Francis Charmes (1848-1916) was a French journalist, diplomat, senior civil servant
and politician.

> "During its yesterday's session, the Académie française was in-
> formed that Mr. Henri Poincaré has transferred his application
> from Berthelot's chair to Sully-Prudhomme's."

Le Figaro of January 20, 1908 allowed no doubt to remain about the
result of those elections.

> "...The chairs of Berthelot and Sully Prudhomme being re-
> served for Messrs. Francis Charmes and Henri Poincaré."

Nevertheless, on the election day, March 5, 1908, most of the daily papers
maintained the suspense. It was the case of the *Petit Parisien*, who wrote:

> "The applicants for the various seats are: To that of Mr. Berth-
> elot, M. Francis Charmes, who has no competitor and who is
> sure to be elected. However, the fight is probably going to
> be strong for the other two seats, as there are many opposing
> competitors. Thus Messrs.. Bergerat, Dorchain, Poincaré of
> the Académie des Sciences; Jean Aicard and Charles Pomairols
> will be competing for the succession of Sully-Prudhomme."

The same day, *Le Figaro* seems more confident about the election of
Poincaré:

> "As for the other two, they are considered done. About the
> succession of Berthelot, no doubt at all: the chair has been
> reserved for Mr. Francis Charmes, single applicant, for a long
> time. Mr. Henri Poincaré, for the chair of Sully Prudhomme,
> is competing with Messrs. Jean Aicard, Pomairols and Emile
> Bergerat. Mr. Augustus Dorchain, who had been an applicant,
> is no longer applying since yesterday. It seems that Mr. Henri
> Poincaré is sure to be elected."

On March 5, 1908, Francis Charmes and Henri Poincaré were indeed
elected to the Académie française, one in the chair 40 of Marcellin Berthelot,
the other in the chair 24 of Sully Prudhomme.

The following day, most newspapers announced the news. *Le Petit
Parisien* published the photo of the three new immortals:

Le Figaro indicated the election results as follows:

> "The academy must choose the next immortal by designating
> the successor of Sully Prudhomme. The applicants are Messrs.
> Henri Poincaré, John Aicard, Emile Bergerat and Charles de
> Pomairols, a close friend of the deceased, charming poet and
> too little known, who has written some admirable pages on
> Lamartine. Poincaré had to wait for the second to win, by 17

MM. Charmes, Poincaré et Richepin entrent à l'Académie française

Cl. Branger.   Cl. Manuel.

Cl. Manuel.

M. Francis Charmes   M. Henri Poincaré   M. Jean Richepin

Fig. 11.4 *Le Petit Parisien* of March 6, 1908.

votes to 10 for Mr. Pomairols, 4 for Mr. Jean Aicard and 2 for Mr. Emile Bergerat."

Then, Alphonse Berget[19], the author of this article, recounted the biography of Poincaré by recalling his main scientific and philosophical contributions.

> "This is a very old custom of the Académie française to always have a scholar among its members. Jean-Baptiste Dumas and Berthelot are, among the modern ones, those we all remember. So this is the continuation of a tradition revived by the forty members of the Académie (or thirty-seven, since there are currently three empty seats), by calling on the famous mathematician they just elected today to be a member of this Académie. Henri Poincaré's lungs are actually already somewhat familiar with the air of the Mazarin Palace: indeed, for twenty-one years

---

[19] Alphonse Berget (1860-1934) was a professor at the Sorbonne and at the Oceanographic Institute of Paris. In 1902, he was commissioned by Camille Flammarion to move the Foucault pendulum to the Pantheon (see above). Also recognized for his popularizing talents, his writings were published many times in newspapers such as *Le Figaro*. He wrote in particular the obituary of Henri Poincaré in this newspaper on July 22, 1912 (see below).

he has been a member of the Académie des sciences, which certainly established its pedigree as well as its fellow institution, the Académie française. It is then as a regular visitor that he will be sitting twice a week instead of once in these classic chairs which are luxurious places in the train of immortality. He was thirty-three when he was appointed member of the Académie des sciences, where he stood out because of his work which was not only remarkable, but also sparkling with mathematical elegance, dazzling with originality. For originality is the dominant characteristic of Poincaré's science. He was always himself, ever since high school, where his mathematical value overflowed the mold into which secondary education wanted to keep him, until his later work, where even when interpreting and analyzing the discoveries made by other scholars, he could make it his eminent personal work. Henri Poincaré was born in Nancy in 1854. Admitted to the École Polytechnique when he was nineteen, he came out in 1875 as an engineer student at the Corps des Mines. But higher mathematics attracted him imperatively; he was got his degree to become Doctor of Mathematical Sciences, and in 1879, he was in charge of a course of infinitesimal analysis at the Faculty of Science of Caen. Then he was called to the Sorbonne, where he was in charge of conferences on differential and integral calculus at the Faculty of Science. I had the pleasure of following his teachings, being then a student at this Faculty that I have never left, and where I have the honor to teach myself. We all, we can say it, had some "enthusiasm" for our master, for he embodies one of these values that shine and do not need to be reasoned to be understood. Such was that of Poincaré, of Appell and Lippmann! Lessons like these are an indelible memory in a scientific career, and often it is the word of a man of genius which directs many vocations. In 1886 he succeeded Lippmann in the chair of mathematical physics, as Lippmann was succeeding Jamin in the chair of general physics. Today, his lectures at the Sorbonne are about celestial mechanics. From 1883 to 1897 he was tutor of analysis at the École Polytechnique. Poincaré's name earlier became popular thanks to some exceptional circumstance. King Oscar of Sweden, the friend and enlightened patron of mathematics, had put a question on the three body problem and the dynamics equations in the contest between all the mathematicians of the world. Each competitor had to send his memoir in a sealed envelope. When they had read the submissions, the jury kept two that they thought should to be rewarded. The envelopes were opened, and people discovered that the two signatories were French mathematicians: Henri Poincaré and Paul Appell. They are now colleagues at the Institute and colleagues at the Sorbonne, where they were the youngest teachers for a long time. Poincaré's work led him to be the best geometrician of our time. He introduced a category of "functions" that are more general than elliptic functions, and which he called "Fuchsian functions", in honor of the famous mathematician Fuchs. He applied these functions to the study of non-Euclidean geometry initiated by Lobatchewski. In astronomy he provided the conclusive argument to those who believe that Saturn's ring is actually formed by a great multitude of small solid satellites very close to each other. He established that if the ring was fluid, its density should not fall below a certain lower limit, which happens to be larger than the upper limit assigned to this density by the English physicist Maxwell, who relied on considerations of a different nature. In mathematical physics, he promoted new ideas in France, developed by foreign scientists, like Maxwell's theories. He was the enthusiastic demonstrator of the Hertzian waves, so much so that thanks to his prodigious mathematical virtuosity, he always made the theories he stated progress; his personal originality appears every time he tackles a subject. And this original way of viewing things, this very personal way of thinking, which surprises those who do not know him inside out, he has embodied it in his books, remarkable Science and Hypothesis and the Value of Science, sometimes disturbing books, but where he managed the feat of presenting the most audacious conceptions of modern science under an accessible form. He concludes there that human genius "is a flash of light between two eternities," but that "this flash is everything." Without doubt, this cannot be read like a novel, and one must come back often to the pages. But isn't this return the mark of admiration, as is the return of the traveler to the shores that charmed him the most? Our scientific assemblies have all asked for the benefit of the great scholar's wisdom: he is a board member of the Observatory, a member of the Bureau des Longitudes. But all these scientific occupations do not keep his mind from being open to all accomplished scholar; he is also an amateur musician, and looking for the purest and highest form of this art, which is that of chamber music, he is one of the most diligent listeners of "the Trumpet" sessions. He is barely fifty years old, and he is being highly productive; and certainly the French mathematicians will certainly be thanking him for adding another few bright jewels to their already rich crown."

Alphonse Berget

The newspaper *La Croix* published this news on the front page with a photo of Poincaré:

Fig. 11.5   *La Croix* of March 6, 1908.

On March 6, 1908, *The New York Times* reports the news:

New French Academicians.

PARIS, March 5.—Francis Charmes, Jean Richepin, and Henri Poincare have been elected members of the French Academy, filling the seats vacated by the deaths of MM. Berthelot, Theuriet, and Sully-Prudhomme.

Fig. 11.6   *The New York Times* of March 6, 1908.

On Sunday, March 8, *Le Figaro* explained to its readers that:

> "Mr. Henri Poincaré, last elected to the Académie française, happens to be the 509th immortal of this Company since it was founded by Richelieu. The first academician was, as we know, Conrart, who created the Académie française along with the Cardinal. The 100th was La Fontaine, the 200th, the Duke of Nivernais, the 300th, Fontanes, the 400th, Ernest Legouvé, and the 500th, Mr. Etienne Lamy."

According to custom, the next step before officially joining the Academy is the introduction to the President of the Republic. The newspaper *Le Temps* of March 19 wrote about this event:

> "The president yesterday received Mr. René Bazin, who came to officially announce the election of Messrs. Francis Charmes, Jean Richepin and Henri Poincaré to the Académie, and, as usual, ask for the Head of State's approbation. Mr. Fallières responded to Mr. Bazin that he was nothing but very pleased about this triple election."

However, Henri Poincaré and Jean Richepin could not be received to the Académie française before "the first weeks of 1909" as indicated by *Le Figaro* of September 2 and *La Croix* and *Le Petit Parisien* of September 3. On Saturday, September 19, *Le Figaro* explained the reasons for this delay[20]:

> "Mr. Thureau-Dangin[21] began to call to arms the welcoming speeches of the last elected to the Academy. To date, only, Poincaré gave the Secretariat of the Institute the eulogy he wrote for his predecessor Sully Prudhomme, Messrs, Francis Charmes and Jean Richepin will have their respects to Berthelot and André Theuriet printed next week. But the three members of the Academy who are to receive these new colleagues have naturally not yet written a single line of their speech. In these conditions, we expect to receive in December only Mr. Francis Charmes. The reception of Messrs, Richepin and Poincaré, which, properly, will only take place after that of Mr. Charmes, are adjourned to the first weeks of 1909."

---

[20] See also *Le Petit Parisien* of September 20.

[21] Paul Thureau-Dangin (1837-1913) was a historian and publicist. He was elected to the Académie Française in 1893 then became permanent secretary.

During the fall, newspapers were maintaining the suspense about the date of Poincaré and Richepin's reception to the Academy[22]. Then a few days before the beginning of winter, *Le Matin* of December 18 announced the news.

In U.S.A., *The New York Times* reports the news on March 22, 1908:

"PARIS, March 5. – M. François Charmes, Mr. Jean Rlchepin and M. Henri Poincaré have been elected members of the French Academy to fill the there vacant places made in the ranks of the Forty Immortals by the deaths of MM. Marcelin Berthelot, André Theuriet and Sully Prudhomme. There were thirty-three members of the famous association present (...) For the armchair of the late Sully Prudhomme the foremost candidate was M. Henri Poincaré the eminent mathematician. An article devoted to Poincaré's work recently appeared in THE NEW YORK TIMES REVIEW OF BOOKS, so there is no necessity for writing of him at length here. He belongs to the ranks of those philosophical mathematicians who like Newton and Lagrange, use literature to vivify their dry science and to bring it into touch with humanity in general. Poincaré, who is still in his early fifties, has long been regarded as one of the most authoritative and eloquent professors of the Paris Faculty of Sciences. His lessons in physics have all been published by his principal students. For example, his "Calculs des Probabilités" was published by M. Albert Quiquet actuary at an important life Insurance company. The new Academician, under the auspices or the Paris Observatory, directs the "Bulletins Astronomiques." He is also a collaborator on the Journal de Mathématiques Pures et Appliquées. As already pointed out in THE NEW YORK TIMES REVIEW OF BOOKS, Poincaré, by his original application of geometrical hypotheses, brings into question the principles – of Euclid himself. He points out that even in mathematics which by many of us has always been considered the most exact of sciences, there is nothing exact after all."

---

[22]See also *Le Figaro* of September 30, October 28, November 4, November 17, November 24 and November 29 and *La Croix* of October 1.

11.6   The Price of Immortality

In the early year 1909, *Le Figaro* of January 3, at the same time as writing
about the date of Messrs. Charmes, Poincaré and Richepin's reception,
reminded people of the price of an habit vert (green habit):

> "The green habit is right for the season, since a reception will be
> taking place on Thursday under the Dome, that of Mr. Francis
> Charmes, followed, on January 28 and February 18, by those
> of Messrs. Henri Poincaré and Jean Richepin. The Institute
> of France's tailor has established the price of this habit, whose
> bars are so ardently coveted, at a rate that has not changed for
> twenty years. He charges exactly 460 francs for it. With the
> official vest, made of "white casimir", the embroidered trousers,
> the ostrich-feather hat, the sword and the sword sheath, the
> "immortality suit" just comes to 659 francs[23]."

It is probably because of this very high price that Tristan Bernard (1866-
1947) once said:

> "The suit worn by the Academicians is expensive, too expen-
> sive! I'll wait for someone my size to die."

11.7   The Reception at the Academy

On Thursday, January 28, 1909, the newspaper *Le Figaro* announced:

> "Henri Poincaré will be ushered in by Messrs. Alfred Mézières[24]
> and Freycinet[25], whom he asked to be his mentors. The ses-
> sion supposedly starting at one, the doors will open at exactly
> noon."

The newspaper *La Croix* published a photograph of Frédéric Masson on
its front page, followed by a summary of his speech he gave as a response
to Poincaré.

---

[23] In 1889, the annual salary of Mittag-Leffler was 840 francs. According to INSEE, 659
francs now account for about 2400 euros. The current price of an academician suit is
almost twelve times this price.

[24] Alfred Mézières (1826-1915) was a French literature historian, journalist and politician, member of the Académie française (1874). He participated in the founding of the
newspaper *Le Temps* in 1864 and chaired the Parisian journalists association.

[25] Charles Louis de Freycinet Saulces (1828-1923) was a French engineer and politician
(X 1846, Mines 1848), member of the Académie des Sciences (1882) and of the Académie
Française (1890).

"The ranks of the Academicians having been stricken by death many times for the past two years, the formal sessions to receive new members have become more frequent at the Académie. Just yesterday, the fortunates of the world of literature, art and politics were invited to attend the "prise de séance" (installation ceremony) of Poincaré, the famous mathematician. And the speech given by the member elect, although serious, seems to have interested the audience just as much as the one given by Mr. Frédéric Masson, the illustrious historian, who was responding to Mr. Henri Poincaré.

CHOSEN IMMORTAL, RICHEPIN OVERJOYED

Kisses Messenger Who Brings Him the News of the Academy's Action.

M. POINCARE ALSO NAMED

Thirty-three Members Present, Including the Aged Francois Coppee— Rostand Among the Absentees.

Foreign Correspondence THE NEW YORK TIMES

Fig. 11.7 *The New York Times* of March 22, 1908.

Fig. 11.8   Henri Poincaré at the Académie française.

Chapter 12

Last Commitments, Last Works

We have seen above that Henri Poincaré repeatedly committed himself in debates of the society of his time, sometimes unwillingly (the controversy over the rotation of the earth), sometimes in response to some friends' requests, (the second trial of Dreyfus), more rarely voluntarily. As long as things remained from a purely scientific point of view, he did not hesitate to highlight his skills and acted as an expert, the man modestly withdrawing before the specialist. We will see that his position changed in his later years.

The press also emphasized his generous and what could be called today "humanitarian" actions. Thus we learn in *Le Temps* of January 10, 1906 that: "The welfare office of the 5th arrondissement has received from Mr. Henri Poincaré, Member of the Institute, 63 rue Claude Bernard, the sum of 500 francs for the poor". He was also part of the initiative committee for the creation of a cancer research institute and he thus appeared in an invitation to subscribe to this institute in *Le Figaro* of November 21, the same year. We then learn in *Le Temps* of April 25, 1910 that he was elected (or reelected) to the board of directors of the Société générale de protection pour l'enfance abandonnée ou coupable (General society for protection of abandoned children). The position of the scholar in relation to politics as well as the uselessness of scientists contributions in the press are two things that Poincaré wrote about quite clearly in 1904:

> "Politics is nowadays a profession which entirely absorbs a man; any scientist who wants to dedicate himself to politics must give up his vocation; if he really wants to be useful to the country, he must give half of his time to the affairs of the Republic; if he wants to keep his seat, he must give the other half to the affairs of his electors; nothing will be left for science. [...] It would therefore be inopportune that all scientists would aim

at the Parliament, because, then, there would be no scientists anymore. One can be resigned, or even rejoice not only for the country, but for science itself, to sacrifice from time to time one of us, more able to be understood by the multitude or the assemblies. After all science needs somebody to defend its interests. But most will have to content themselves with newspaper and journal articles. I doubt that their voices are heard, amidst the clamor of daily struggles[1]."

But his election to the Académie Française in 1908, at the evolution of his own convictions, essentially regarding the content of school programmes, and his well established reputation in all fields of knowledge in France and abroad, led him, at the end of his life, to personally commit himself to ideological issues, mostly related to education. Let us beware of the expression "at the end of his life": it can be written only retrospectively, when the date of death is known. But in 1908, he was only 54 years: it was not because he knew about his close end that he decided to commit himself, but because of his personal convictions that his aura then allowed him to show without fear of being punished by anyone.

Admittedly, Poincaré did not become an elected politician or a minister like some of his friends (for example Paul Painlevé), but would it have been so if he had not died of his illness at the age of 58? Couldn't we say that his commitment within the Comité Républicain de la Représentation Proportionnelle (Republican Committee of Proportional Representation), and his stances on this issue from 1911 showed a possible evolution in this direction? Of course, we cannot answer these questions, but it is a recognized fact that Henri Poincaré seemed to gradually contradict what he had said in 1904 in the text above.

In any case, there is a field in which Poincaré was present in the last ten years of his life, and in which his ideas were evolving and becoming more radical: it is that of education and its organization. From his comments on mathematics meant for high school teachers in 1904 to his joining of the Ligue Française d'Education Morale (French League of Moral Education) one month before he died, and the publication of his opuscule *Les sciences et les humanités* (Sciences and the humanities) published in 1911 under the auspices of the Ligue pour la Culture Française (League for French

---

[1] Extract from Henri Poincaré's contribution to "Sur la participation des savants à la politique ", *Revue politique et littéraire (Revue bleue)* 1, 5th series, 1904, p. 708. Quoted by Laurent Rollet: Henri Poincaré (1854-1912): *Des mathématiques à la philsophie, op. cit.*, p. 246.

Culture), we can clearly see this evolution and the fact that he adopted a more and more radical position. The press obviously gave an account of these different stages, especially from 1908.

12.1 The Press and Poincaré's Lectures at the Faculty of Science

First, it is interesting to notice how faithfully and regularly the *Journal des débats politiques et littéraires* published the programme of Poincaré's lectures at the Faculty of Sciences in Paris. Thus, we learn in the edition of November 12, 1894 that Poincaré teached "the theory of Newtonian potential"; one year later (November 1, 1895) the newspaper published the programme of its teaching on electricity, and then, for example, some details of his lectures on "the theory of electrodynamics" (November 15, 1898) and "the disturbance of the planets" (December 28, 1905), his fundamental teachings in "celestial mechanics and mathematics" (January 15, 1906) which will become "mathematical astronomy and celestial mechanics" in the same newspaper in 1911, etc.

On this school programme subject, Poincaré also appeared in a polemical article of the newspaper *Le Temps* on May 17, 1901. The "private correspondent" of the newspaper in the United States, who signed the article with his initials only (H.B), already spoke about issues that may fuel many debates today, in this text entitled "Les relations universitaires de la France et des États-Unis" (The University relations between France and the United States). Firstly, he wrote about the issue of a lack of visibility, for foreign researchers, of French scientific teachings and of the institutions where they are given (grandes écoles, universities). The author suggested the creation of "a great synoptic, synthetic and systematic table of all the teaching existing in Paris" which "should be spread around the world, with the teachers' names and the subjects of their lectures." On this last point (the lectures subject), he insisted by taking the example of what is done in the United States:

> "There is one other necessary measure, which is the publication of each year school programs six months in advance. Every year in May, American universities print the titles, professors, times and contents of all courses that begin in October. It was around the month of May that American students decide of how to use their time for the next year. They are too calculating to let things become unpredictable, they only make up their mind when they have all information in hand."

Poincaré then appears in a quite spicy anecdote:

> "One day I asked a teacher why there were so few students
> going to France. I have a son, he replied, when he had finished
> his mathematical studies at Harvard, he wanted to listen to
> Poincaré; he was all the more willing to spend a year in France
> as I am French, and thus he is almost French by birth; he wrote
> to the Faculty of Paris to ask them the subject of Poincaré's
> lecture; he was told they did not know; he asked again: same
> answer; on the date of the beginning of classes, it was not known
> yet; my son went to Leipzig, where he knew who he would have
> the opportunity to hear, and on what."

The article is instructive on the (true or false?) shortcomings that it
points out, but also on how appealing Poincaré's lectures were to foreign
students at the time (even if the one mentioned in the example is apparently
half French). And the illustrious professor of the Sorbonne is obviously one
of the scholars the author of the article wrote about at the end of this final
excerpt:

> "We complain of the centralization; we should better see the
> benefits and take advantage of it. Paris is a center unrivaled in
> the world but foreigners cannot even suspect that such a mass
> of resources exists. The Sorbonne has its own programme, the
> College de France, the École des Hautes Études have theirs,
> the Ecole du Louvre has its own, each of the Écoles libres have
> theirs, but nowhere can people find a table of all the courses
> offered by all these institutions; Parisian students attend sev-
> eral schools at once, but that is a combination which foreign-
> ers cannot even imagine. There are many illustrious scholars
> whose lectures and places of lecture are absolutely unknown by
> foreigners."

Poincaré did not respond to this call, or at least no trace of such a
response has been found so far. But he however got involved in mathematical teaching issues, particularly during the introduction of the high schools'
programmes reform due to Minister Georges Leygues in 1902.

12.2 Defense of the Humanities

In the late nineteenth century, and despite the establishment in 1891, in
secondary education, of a modern course of study that did not include dead
languages, science is still too insufficiently present in programmes. After

four years of inquiries and seeking of advice from specialists of all categories (teachers, scholars, politicians, etc ...), Science teaching is reduced to the same level as that of classics in the law proposed by the Minister of public Instruction Georges Leygues.

In the committee for revision of the scientific programmes that was formed in this preliminary phase, the famous Appell and Darboux were here to represent the mathematical field, but Poincaré was not part of it: his cousin Lucien yet committed himself a great deal in this reform and was present in the committee, as representative of the physical sciences field[2].

The empiricist, even sensualist orientation of what is expected of mathematical teaching is part of a movement of ideas already in vogue since the Ferry and Buisson laws of 1882. Hélène Gispert, Nicole Hulin and Marie-Claire Robic summarized this reform in the preface of the book devoted to it, entitled Science et enseignement. L'exemple de la grande réforme des programmes du lycéée au déébut du XXe siècle (INRP - Vuibert, 2007) (Science and Teaching: An example of the great reform of the high schools' programmes in the early twentieth century):

> "The reform will thus profoundly reorganize secondary education, both structurally and in terms of contents. It creates its unity (by removing the distinction between classical secondary education and modern secondary education) ... and ends the monopoly of the humanities by developing language teaching and increasing the emphasis on science teaching, the missions, contents and methods of which are deeply renewed. It seeks a new audience, a diversification of functions of the high schools responsible for educating not only the boys of the liberal bourgeoisie destined for "the high speculations" but also those of the economic and industrial bourgeoisie, the future "General Staff" of the "army of work".[3]"

Although this law had literature and science teachings reduced to the same level, the science teachings were oriented towards a bigger "empiricism": students, helped by their teachers, had to make the most abstract knowledge emerge from the concrete and the intuitive, and particularly mathematical knowledge: geometry, for example, must present each new mathematical object through its construction from a concrete representa-

---

[2]Student at the École Normale Supérieure, Lucien Poincaré (1862-1920), Henri's cousin and Raymond Poincaré's brother, was Inspector General of Public Instruction at the time of the passage of the law in 1902. He later became director of secondary education (1910) then of higher education.

[3]Introduction, p. 22.

tion. This vision of a realistic and inductive pedagogy are reminiscent of the sensualists visions of the beginning of the last century, which were themselves inspired by the philosophies of the 18th century and particularly that of Condillac: in the end, the positivism of Auguste Comte did not have that much resonance on these education choices and on this approach to science that the debate on the reform of 1902 has eventually institutionalized.

Imagined from the last years of the 19th century, this reform involved the Parisian university notables, first informally and individually in the years that precede it, then institutionally after the law was passed. Indeed, its implementation was encouraged and publicized by the organization of series of conferences at the Musée pédagogique (Educational Museum) in 1904 and 1905. Louis Mangin, the director of the museum at that time, invited some renowned academics to come to defend it before an audience consisting largely of secondary school teachers[4]. This Educational Museum was founded by Jules Ferry in Paris in 1879, in order to provide teachers and institutions involved in education a place where political will of reforming primary education could be seen and express itself: it gradually integrated the other levels of education, and almost a century later, it eventually became the National Museum of Education.

It is not surprising therefore that Henri Poincaré was among the speakers of 1904. Invited to speak in the name of science of "General Definitions in mathematics," he took up some of the ideas that he had already defended five years earlier in the first edition of the journal "L'enseignement des mathématiques" (Mathematics teaching), under the title "La logique et l'intuition dans la science mathématique et dans l'enseignement" (Logic and intuition in mathematical science and teaching). He gave up the strictly epistemological and theoretical reflection and qualified it with considerations that were more focused on education. Pragmatic and concerned with the student's success – that is to say their understanding of the science they were taught – he knew that mathematical abstraction was not accessible to all minds, and he was therefore in favor of the teaching vision of his own science as defined by the law. He expressed it several times, and especially in certain passages of Science and Method. The following passage from the article he published in 1899 in the journal "mathematics education" summarizes this aspect of his thought quite well:

---

[4]See "La mobilisation des notables parisiens," in *Science et enseignement, op. cit.* p. 149 and following.

> "The principal aim of mathematical education is to develop cer-
> tain faculties of the mind, and among these intuition is not the
> least precious. It is through it that the mathematical world
> remains in touch with the real world, and even if pure mathe-
> matics could do without it, we should still have to have recourse
> to it to fill up the gulf that separates the symbol from reality.
> The practioner will always need it, and for every pure geome-
> trician there must be a hundred practitioners[5]."

Poincaré was pragmatic. Science was one thing, his teaching was another: intuition, experience and sensualism could be used pedagogically
to make students find their way to some science they would practice completely differently if they made it their job, which was something he constantly defended, especially in *Les sciences et les humanités* (sciences and
the humanities) which we will be talking about below.

Secondary school programmes were entirely reviewed with those elements in mind. But teachers directly concerned by this law and its new
directions also had to be convinced and formed. A series of conferences was
then organized at the Educational Museum in 1904; Poincaré opened it on
January 22 as announced by the *Journal des débats politiques et littéraires*
the following day.

At first, on this issue of balance between the classic and modern teachings, Poincaré's contribution ended there. But the society of the time was,
as often in the course of History, always dealing with recurring debate
between public and private school: the Ferry laws twenty years before,
the separation of church and state, the incessant fights between the ultra
Catholic French newspapers and the "free thinkers", and the more empiricist direction given to teachings fueled those debates. And Henri Poincaré's
ideas were once again taken up without him wanting it in some virulent exchanges which he had a priori nothing to do with. One example is an
exchange that took place in 1906 in the *Journal des débats* on the issue of
Catholic Institutes, which were higher education schools that partly com-
peted with the public ones. In an unsigned article entitled "The Reform of
Catholic Institutes" dated June 18, 1906, the paper explained the problem
as follows:

> "Since 1876, Catholics have forced themselves to make great
> sacrifices in order to form a higher education system compet-
> ing with that of the State. The Catholic Institutes were sup-

---

[5] "La logique et l'intuition dans la science mathématique et dans l'enseignement,"
L'enseignement mathématique 1, pp. 157-162; Œuvres, tome XI, pp. 129-133.

posed to give the clergy and the faithful a solid scientific culture
while protecting them from contacts detrimental to faith. This
goal was at least partly achieved. The intellectual horizon of
the clergy was broadened; and he made a habit of practicing
some new method and criticism, so much so that, apparently,
all the books of its private bookstore had to be changed these
last twenty years. And as everyone agrees on the fact that the
clergy has and will have to keep aware of the evolution of minds,
if he wants to maintain its influence in the contemporary society, no one denies how helpful the Catholic Institutes have
been. However, good Catholics are wondering if these institutes could not be even more helpful by limiting their subject.
And this is what a professor of free higher education is studying
on very good terms in the Lyon journal *Demain* (Tomorrow).
The idea is not removing the Catholic Institutes, even for eco-
nomic reasons. The idea is for them to specialize. Why try to
fight against the faculty teaching in all fields? It is a ruinous
and useless fight. It is ruinous because official education has
resources of men, materials and subsidies that free education
cannot match. It is useless because there are not two sciences
or even two ways of teaching science[6]."

The last sentence goes widely beyond the issue of competition between
the two types of higher education institutions. The Church indeed claimed
its authority over science and how to transmit it, as it repeatedly did since
the French Revolution, and wanted to block the advances that contradicted
its doctrine: we have seen that aspect when talking about the controversy
over the rotation of the earth, but there were much discussion at the time
(like today with the "intelligent design") on the question of the theory of
evolution and Darwinism.

What did Henri Poincaré have to do with the debate on the Catholic
Institutes? He was only wrong (or maybe right) in being part of these men
"that free education cannot match" and he then appeared as such:

"Where would be the harm if the young priests, and even more
so the young laymen learnt Greek in the school of a Croiset,
medicine in the school of a Brouardel, mathematics in the school
of a Poincaré? Of course, one can find, in the ranks of public
higher education, teachers who are neither believers nor even
always respectful of the beliefs of others. But few of them could
fail to do their professional duty, which is not to argue against

---

[6] *Journal des débats politiques et littéraires*, June 18, 1906. Article entitled: "La réforme
des Instituts catholiques" (Catholic Institute Reform)

religion, but to teach what they believe is true and proven. Moreover, the clergy must get used to hearing other bells that the seminar ones. Their beliefs must be tested, and it is not bad for them undergo this test. It would be beneficial for the Catholics not to live out of time. One of the reasons why they are inferior is precisely that they isolate themselves, that they lose contact with the world they live in, and as a result that they find themselves being disoriented when they try to speak to the people."

Mathematician Poincaré was then used as an alibi. We will not give further details about this example, and we refer the reader to the response wrote by Péchenart, Rector of the Catholic Institute of Paris, published three days later in the same newspaper. We just wanted to show here, and this is not an isolated case, that Poincaré often appeared in debates about school, university, teachings, programmes, etc. This was obviously the price of his authority in science.

But when he finally got involved in 1910-1911, it was in a totally different issue: the defence of classics, and therefore of dead languages. This fact may seem contradictory with his commitment in favor of the 1902 law and his 1904 conference. But in the end, it is not as contradictory as it seems.

It is once again in the *Journal des débats* (November 17, 1911) that the detailed information on Poincaré's involvement, voluntary this time, are given to us. The article is a report of a text by Alfred Croiset[7] published in the journal *Revue politique et littéraire*, better known as the *Revue bleue* (as opposed to the *Revue rose*, which is the *Revue scientifique*). Strangely, this text by Croiset does not exist in the *Revue bleue*. There must have been wrong information about the source of the document, for Croiset was then Dean of the Faculty of Arts at the Sorbonne, and was indeed very involved in the debate that inflamed the "New Sorbonne": we have not found any trace of it in the other journals of the time so far, but what matters in the report of the *Journal des débats* is more about the subject itself ("what is the use of Latin?") and the context that it summarizes than about what

---

[7] Alfred Croiset (1845-1923), former student at the École Normale Supérieure, and a specialist in ancient Greek literature, was dean of the Faculty of Letters at the Sorbonne in 1910. He was also dean of the School of Higher Studies in Social Sciences and academician. See the tribute Ferdinand Lot paid him at the Académie française on November 2, 1928: "Notice sur la vie et les travaux de M. Alfred Croiset (1845-1923)" in: *Comptes-rendus des séances de l'Académie des inscriptions et belles-lettres*, vol. 79 (4), 1929, p. 362-384.)

Croiset did actually write. Let's then recount this context before looking at the article itself and the appearance of Henri Poincaré.

On April 28, 1910, the Government published decrees granting to people owning diplomas that did not include Latin the equivalence of the baccalaureate to register at faculties of arts and sciences. Many intellectuals that initially included Classics teachers at the Sorbonne for most of them, reacted "on the loss of the literary vocation of the Sorbonne", "on the harmful effects of abolishing barriers based on Latin, which can only aggravate the involution of higher education now focused on mechanical scholarship and specialization, as the students will come out of courses of study that do not include Latin[8]". The controversy, which attests to both the so-called "crisis of Latin" and "crisis of French" was fueled by the fact that in October 1910 "the minister of war undermines the fact that the holders of a baccalaureate which included Latin teaching were granted additional points, for the admission to the École Polytechnique[9]". But the roots of this controversy and the many commitments that it gave rise to regarding the defense of the classics are to be found long before this episode: as soon as 1899, during the consultations on the bill for reform of high schools teachings, and after 1902 and the passing of the bill.

The controversy was back in 1906 when a reform of the French language was started, in order to simplify it. Marcel Boulenger (1873-1932) published a book, *La Querelle de l'orthographe* (The Quarrel of spelling), and initiated a petition to defend the classical French language, which was in jeopardy[10]. In its edition of July 1, 1906, the newspaper *Le Temps* devoted to both information a long article full of literary references (and irony!) and wrote that Henri Poincaré had already signed the petition, most of which is reproduced in the article:

> "To the Minister of Education and Fine Arts, For a hundred years, spelling was practically fixed in this country. The noblest geniuses of the nineteenth century have accepted it. The great classical models themselves appear in a form that is familiar to us. A decree, suddenly disrupting traditional spelling, would give a strange of archaic aspect to all the masterpieces published since the seventeenth century, even the contemporary ones. A higher barrier would be standing between the crowd and the men of letters, and it would eventually jeopardize all the formal

---

[8]Charles Christophe, *Ferdinand Brunot et la défense des modernes*, literary theory workshop for the Fabula project: http://fabula.org, 2005.

[9]*Ibid.*

[10]Boulenger Marcel, *La querelle de l'orthographe*, E. Sansot, Paris, 1906.

beauty of our language and thereby be harmful to the universal prestige of French literature. The undersigned wish that this project is not pursued, for it would soon endanger the national Letters."

From 1906 to 1911, there were more and more initiatives and petitions to defend the humanities, French language and Latin. Poincaré committed himself again by signing in December 1910 one of the petitions entitled "The French language crisis".

12.3   The New Mechanics

During the summer of 1909, Poincaré made a lecture before the French Association for the Advancement of Science in which he presented his *New Mechanics*. Although we have no place to detail and to discuss Poincaré's last work here, it is interesting to notice how the American press reported this event. On August 8, 1909 *The Washington Post* entitled his article like this:

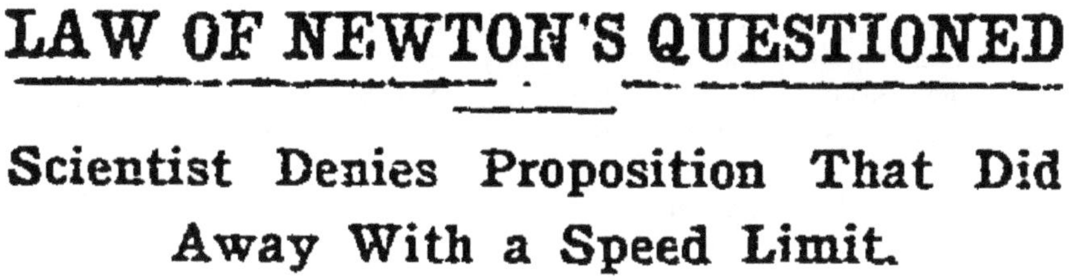

LAW OF NEWTON'S QUESTIONED

Scientist Denies Proposition That Did Away With a Speed Limit.

Fig. 12.1   *The Washington Post* of August 8, 1909.

The day after, the title *The Sun* is even more amazing:

DOUBTS NEWTON'S SPEED LAW.

Prof. Poincare Tells Some Features of the "New Mechanics."
Special Cable Despatch to THE SUN.

Fig. 12.2   *The Sun* of August 9, 1909.

> PARIS, Aug. 7. – Prof Henri Poincaré lecturing before the Association for the Advancement of Science, today announced that one of Newton's fundamental laws of mechanics was now questioned by scientists. Newton laid it down that the effect of a force on a moving body is independent of the speed which that body has already acquired. If a certain force acts on a moving body for one second it communicates a certain speed. If it acts again for another, a new increase is equal to the first, and so on, so that by repeated applications of the force for a sufficiently long time great speed could theoretically be attained. Partisans of what is called "the new mechanics" question this principle. They say that the increase in speed in the second is less than that given in the first still less for the third second, and generally less in proportion to the speed at which the body is moving. Hence there is a limit to the speed that can be produced an this limit is the speed of light, from which they argue that the mass of a material body is not constant but increases with the body's speed. The Newtonian principles also state that whether the force for acts on the moving body in the same direction or at right angles it produces the same acceleration but the new theorists say that if the moving speed be extremely great its resistance will not be the same in each case. Prof. Poincaré allowed that it was difficult to establish the new theories for want of a body by moving at sufficiently high speed. Automobiles making 100 kilometers an hour were, from this point of view snails, and heavenly bodies like Mercury at a hundred kilometers a second did not suffice; but radium supplies three three kinds of ray one of which is appealed to as affording proofs of these new theories

Obviously, this "new mechanics" is strongly related to the fundamental concepts of "Relativity Theory" and also to an old quarrel of priority between Poincaré and Einstein. But this is not the subject of this book.

12.4 An Educational Commitment: "What Things Say"

If we look at what Poincaré actually published himself for the general public in the press, we can see that it comes down to a few things only: *Les sciences et les humanités* is in fact his single significant contribution in this public space, the others being only responses to some attacks or petitions signed here and there, and some rare interviews. Can a weekly journal for children published by Hachette, a publisher that widely spread his books and periodicals in the society of his time, be considered a "mass-market journal"? If we say yes, then it is clear that the second most important contribution of Henri Poincaré in this form of dissemination consists of five articles that he wrote in 1910-1911 in *Au seuil de la vie* (On the threshold of life). This journal, aimed at children of upper primary schools (about thirteen years old), was planned from the start (the contract between Hachette and Poincaré can vouch for it) for a period of twenty weeks, from November 1910 to April 1911. The scholar had to contribute to it in the section entitled "Ce que disent les choses" (What things say) devoted to science, and he shared this section with his friend Paul Painlevé and the naturalist Edmond Perrier. Besides, all three agreed to talk about their science in the journal, but they also allowed the publisher to republish their texts in a full book similarly entitled "Ce que disent les choses" which was effectively published soon after.

> "The goal is to give these young people, along with a taste for personal study, the desire and means to improve and expand their education. This will be achieved if they are presented, methodically and in an attractive form, some talks on various teaching subjects, which kindle their curiosity and make them observe and be attentive[11]."

Let's borrow from Gabriel Compayré his definition of a "lesson on things" in the "Dictionnaire Buisson[12]":

> "The preface and prelude of all experimental studies, the initiation to physical sciences, to geography, to natural history, to all knowledge that are patently obvious and that have to be observed through the senses."

These three wide fields of knowledge are present in *Ce que disent les choses*: natural history and in some way geography (in a broad sense, including geology) in Perrier's texts, physical sciences in Poincaré and Painlevé's texts. Even the chapters devoted to technical subjects also allow the authors to reveal "the most hidden actions of natural forces": *Les mines* (Mines) and *L'industrie* électrique (Electrical Industry) (Poincaré),

---

[11]Publishing contrat: extract from the original left at the Henri Poincaré Archives in Nancy.

[12]Published for the first time in 1887 under the title *Dictionnaire de pédagogie et d'instruction primaire* (Dictionary of Pedagogy and primary education), then *Nouveau Dictionnaire de pédagogie* (New Dictionary of Pedagogy) in 1911 by Hachette, this work is a landmark in the history of pedagogy. We owe it to Ferdinand Buisson (1841-0392), Nobel Peace in 1927, and one of the co-authors of the reforms called "Jules Ferry' when he was director of primary education.

L'aviation (Aviation) (Painlevé). Poincaré chose to deal with five subjects. The titles of his contributions are: "Les Astres" (The Stars), "En regardant tomber une pomme" (Watching an apple falling), "La chaleur et l'énergie" (Heat and Energy), "Les mines" (Mines), "L'industrie électrique" (The electric industry). This was therefore a nice educational effort, particularly in the chapter "En regardant tomber une pomme" where he wrote a kind of theater scene that involves three players, one teacher and two students: the game that he created between the characters to make the readers of his text understand the difficult concepts of gravity, through some precise and humorous dialogues, are indeed a fine example of what a high-ranking scientist can produce in such a context. Yet, when reading these five chapters, it is interesting to note that two of them have obviously been written with an ulterior motive.

We have already seen why in the case of the chapter "Les Mines": thirty years after his painful experience as an engineer in the coal mines of the region of Vesoul, the emotion was still there and he wanted to show it to the children he wrote for (and their parents) and inform them about what awaited many of them and the precautions to take when being a miner. In the chapter "Les Astres", the intention is much less obvious to those who are not aware of the long episode of the controversy over the rotation of the earth in which he was involved for nearly ten years and of which we talked about earlier. The informed reader will understand that he still had a score to settle with those who had taken up what he wrote in Science and Hypothesis, for example here in this journal for teenagers, after asking the question "Is it the celestial vault that rotates, or is it us?"

> "The answer cannot be doubtful. The stars are at enormous distances; if they are not tied together, they cannot move without the patterns they form being blurred; if they are tied together, how huge must be the sphere on which they are fixed; and this heavy machine would have to rotate fast enough to make, in 24 hours, an enormous turn that even light, which travels at a speed of 300.000 km per second, would take several years to accomplish. This reason, which is peremptory, is not unique. To explain the movements of the planets in the hypothesis of the immobility of the earth, Ptolemy was forced to have recourse to the most complicated assumptions. Each planet was circling around an invisible point which was rotating itself; and by a curious coincidence, for all the planets without exception, one of these revolutions lasted exactly one year. There is no chance; every time a scientific theory requires to rely on chance, then it

is a wrong one. On the contrary, Copernicus explained everything the simplest way: the Earth rotates on its axis, 366 times
a year. The Earth also revolves around the Sun once a year,
and this is why the sun seems to move on the celestial sphere.
The planets, like the Earth, revolve around the Sun, and this
is sufficient to explain their seemingly erratic movements. One
of the apparent motions is real, the moon does revolve around
the earth: the moon is indeed the smallest."

So here again he repeated all the arguments of the controversy, and he
even cited Ptolemy and Copernicus, as if he wanted to respond one last
time to these ideological appropriations he had to deal with, for example in
the article by Bishop Bolo entitled "Le Christ est-il Dieu?" (Is Jesus Christ
God?) published on the front page of the Matin on February 20, 1908:

" ...I have professed science and philosophy, I admit that
philosophers are very honest and pleasant entertainers, that
scholars are wonderful workers. But that is all. As soon as
science wants to decree, or (equivalently) dismiss dogmas, as
soon as philosophy seeks to impose systems, I cannot take it
seriously anymore; you think that I am retrograde? Not at all:
I am simply well informed. (...). I have not yet seen half a
dozen qualified philosophers agree on one philosophical system,
nor a scientific dogma that has not been demolished by the latest scholar. Poincaré, who is the greatest mathematician of the
century, blames Galileo for his obstinacy..."

Poincaré has not took on the role of popular scientist that much during
his lifetime. Even his best-selling books are, as we have seen, some reruns of
texts originally intended for specialists, and even if he did simplify them, he
never actually wrote them in a spirit of popularization. Maybe Poincaré finally seized the opportunity offered by Hachette and his periodical *Au seuil
de la vie* to undertake a real work in this specific genre, coupled with the
educational concern that such an enterprise required. In addition, the title
of the section (and of the book that followed) refers quite explicitly to the
"lessons on things" very much in vogue since the beginning of the Third Republic. Besides, the concept of the illustrated edition that popularized and
even glorified science was one feature of that time, from Louis Figuier and
Camille Flammarion's works to the many journals devoted to the wonders
of science and technology. Poincaré agreed to take part in the movement,
not in a journal meant for adults, but in this children's newspaper. He popularized science, he showed some teaching skills, and he placed this work in
the tradition of the publications devoted to "lessons on things". But can

children leaving primary school understand what Poincaré is telling them, especially when the paragraph in question is entitled "reality and appearance" and that it reveals some very personal and philosophical conceptions about the place of chance in the world and in knowledge? In addition, the paragraph ends with this sentence, that refers to all of his beliefs on the relative motion of the planets and thus the fact that these movements will always be uncertain: "One of the apparent motions is real, the moon does revolve around the earth". We can see then that Poincaré considered *Au seuil de la vie* as an forum open to a wide readership, in which he could defend himself again from the attacks (public ones too) he had to go through. We can thus consider this journal for children as being part of our subject: *Henri Poincaré in the press of his time.*

Chapter 13

To Conclude: *the Poet of Mathematics*

As we have said in the foreword, this work is obviously incomplete and fragmented. Having collected a large number of documents, we had to choose some, often reluctantly, and every choice, even done as impartially as possible, ends up cutting the final result: it is not exhaustive, of course, but it certainly also sometimes lacks the maximum objectivity that the completeness would have precisely allowed. But it was also necessary, in order to remain reasonable on the volume of our production, to leave aside some secondary events of Poincaré's life, although these events have sometimes been cited in the press: so in this case also, a choice was made, and the same implications on the final result followed.

We have also already specified that it is still impossible today to consult all the press of the time, to speak only of the national press, and it is likely that further discoveries will refine or even invalidate some of our writings: we can only hope that the first consequence will widely prevail over the second one. We have encountered another great difficulty during the writing of this book: the problem was how to establish a boundary between the "general public" press and the specialized press. The rather confidential journals, and those of difficult approach were not a problem, which was not the case for periodicals such as the *Revue de Métaphysique et de Morale* that we have sometimes cited (it had to be mentioned, for some very important texts were published in it), but that yet did not reach quite the same public that the dailies and periodicals distributed in the newsstands. The reader would surely have noticed that this journal is not the only example of us stretching the rules of our initial project. But in the end, Poincaré himself "had it both ways" for, as we have seen, his philosophical works meant for the public consisted of articles and lectures originally written for specialists.

Finally, the political or ideological orientation of certain newspapers, very marked at the time, was a problem too, regarding the balance between the various tendencies when it came to partisan debates involving Henri Poincaré, most of the time unwillingly. We were able to better understand these directions by relying on the help of specialists of some of these papers: Dominique Pinsolle, for example, has very spontaneously gave us information on *Le Matin* thanks to his thesis and the book he has just devoted to this newspaper. The difficulty of finding the right "balance" between the periodicals tendencies was aggravated by the fact that some of them sometimes radically evolved under the leadership of their directors or successive editors: the case of the evolution of the *Figaro* during the twelve years of the Dreyfus Affair is a striking example. In addition, the reader should not be surprised that, depending on the times and topics, some newspapers appear more than others. What we did was only conforming to this true fact: one subject could, occasionally, be written about only in some part of the press; on the subject of the dispute over Latin and French for example, the *Journal des débats politiques et littéraires* was the main periodical to have spread the ins and outs of this case through long articles.

It is quite hard to bring a conclusion to such polymorphous book. We chose to do so through the very spirit that was at the source of it and guided it: by coming back to an example of a "general public" newspaper writing about Henri Poincaré. This newspaper is the *Revue illustrée* (the illustrated journal) and more particularly the edition of April 5, 1908. The title of this bimonthly is consistent with its content: it does have the richest iconography ever published on Poincaré.

Fig. 13.1   *La Revue Illustrée* of April 5, 1908.

Under the title "Henri Poincarré. Un mathématicien à l'Académie" (Henri Poincaré. A mathematician in the Académie), a large and long four-page article, extremely illustrated, written by Jehan Soudan, reported the event of Poincaré's election to the Académie française in 1908. We will see that this article is worth our attention for several reasons.

First, the grandiloquent style of its author. Viscount Jehan Soudan of Pierrefitte was a socialite whose friendships with Sarah Bernhardt and Alphonse Allais won him some recognition in the literary world of his time. His only real claim to fame (very relative fame if one refers to the quality of the work in question) was to have co-authored with Allais "Dans la peau d'un autre" in 1907, a mediocre vaudeville which plot is based on a hypnotism session, the subject being very fashionable at the time, pecisely in the society world. Amusing detail, he then took advantage of his article on Poincaré to mention (but not really at the right moment) his friend, Alphonse Allais. But his style was finally, with hindsight, quite inimitable. After telling us that the Académie "devoted itself entirely to the poets" first by electing Jean Richepin, he added:

> "The Académie, with its glories of 1908, wanted to offer a chair to an illustrious man: Henri Poincaré, the famous poet of French Mathematics and world Astronomy."

Is the poor reader capable of understanding the importance of the work of this "famous poet"? Jehan Soudan seemed to doubt it:

> "But does the crowd here, or elsewhere, possess an intuitive divination that goes beyond its instinctive respect for the mystery of science? Can it really sufficiently understand the eternal beauty that shines over men without them knowing of it, thanks to the creative thinking of a true scholar?"

He then quotes a well-known extract from a text written by Poincaré, published in the Journal de l'École Polytechnique, where he discussed the similarity between the feelings of a scholar and those of an artist:

> "A scholar worthy of the name, when facing his work, has the same impression as an artist. (...). We work less for these positive results that the common people think is so important to us, than to feel this aesthetic emotion and communicate it to those who are capable of feeling it."

"Mr. Henri Poincarré" in this "involuntary confession," says Jehan Soudan, "has betrayed the poetry of his Science, has shown what is beyond his thinking as a scholar." It is surprising to see Poincaré support such article, since it was at first an interview he gave to Jehan Soudan, during which he even signed a portrait of himself for him, his signature being followed by the famous "*e pur si muove*" of which we have seen the importance in the question of the rotation of the earth, and which issue will be dealt with again here. Singing the praises of the man of science is then a stylistic monument as could be produced at the time, and since it involved the Académie Française, science and poetry merge at the end:

> "For ten years, Mr. Henri Poincaré has been teaching mathematical physics at the Sorbonne. His courses have reviewed the most daring theories, "grandiose or bizarre and fruitful," imagined throughout the world of foreign researchers. He has rectified, corroborated, completed English Maxwell, German Lorentz on light, on electricity, he has prepared wireless telegraphy. There is no progress due to the discoveries which are profoundly changing the modern life of our civilized capitals, which are revolutionizing the industry in the new world of the twentieth century, not one of those amazing inventions that did not have as preface, as basis, as guide, no progress that was not the result, an application, a realization of the teachings professed by this modest, hardworking idealistic French scholar: Henri Poincarré. His transcendent work are summarized in the pages of two master books: *La Science et l'Hypothèse* (Science and Hypothesis); *La Valeur de la Science* (The Value of Science), which are works of considerable impact. Two poems of pure science that the Académie has "crowned" by offering the chair of the poet Sully Prudhomme to the poet Poincaré."

Poincaré and the international, English, German research . . . A photograph illustrates this, on which he can be seen on the deck of the ship bringing him to America (Henri Poincaré and Paul Langevin were sent in 1904 to the Congress of Arts and Sciences of St. Louis in Missouri, as representatives of France.). And it is after this praise that Jehan Soudan comes back to the controversy over the rotation of the earth – but also to the passage on conventionalism in geometry – which had happened four years earlier:

> "Poincarré's assertions are – said the academician Emile Faguet – "breathtakingly, outrageously" audacious, for his fellow scientists who follow the beaten path. Hear this one: "To say that the Earth rotates does not make any sense.". And this one: "Geometry is not true. It is convenient. It is advantageous." Strictly speaking, is it not a reversal of the beliefs that

we, the ignorant, imagined to be absolutely certain? In these blasphemous and revolutionary cries, it pleases us to admire the malicious modesty of a true scholar, and to praise the poet as well. (...) They are irresistible impulses of the independence of his thought. And he did not neglect to tell us that the "truth of science" lives only when expressed in terms, when translated into words. How clear and radiantly simple are the words of this learned academician!"

It is quite sure that Jehan Soudan has not really gone into the subject in depth and that it was only a pretext to practise his own style, reducing it a *minima* to some assumed nominalism form. He then proposed an excerpt of the interview that Poincaré gave him (and this is where he managed to indirectly mention Alphonse Allais):

"How subtle is the good-nature of Poincaré when he corrects his scandalous blasphemers with an intimate speech! One must hear his famous paradox on the movement of the Earth in a low voice, and comment it with a smile: – You can, he says in a deadpan tone (which could remind me of Alphonse Allais, if it was not too disrespectful) You may safely take the risk to repeat it: "The earth moves! Galileo was right! *E pur si muove.*""

We are thus reassured regarding this stormy chapter that deals with the interpretation of the master's writings on the relativity of the earth movement. What is noteworthy here is the fact that Poincaré took part in this activity, as he will again two years later on his own initiative in the children's book that we mentioned above: this again proves that he was deeply marked by the controversy in question, that had happened four years earlier. But the comparison with Alphonse Allais, although put into perspective by Jehan Soudan, is anyway part of another Pantheon than the one considered today for the scholar.

We shall see that Poincaré devoted himself to this exposure activity even more on the occasion of his election to the Académie française. One can imagine without risking too much that he provided the photographs which illustrate the article himself, including the one just below, on which he can be seen with his family at his house in Claude Bernard Street (house in which he gave the interview.) The picture is blurred, but this is due to its reproduction in the journal (See Fig. 13.2).

In the text of Jehan Soudan then comes Poincaré's family history, once again with very "poetic" overtones. The scientist's family is described

Fig. 13.2   *La Revue Illustrée* of April 5, 1908, p. 245.

as "a clan of good intellectual health" who made "the conquest of Paris and of the world of science through the École Polytechnique." From the "drug-making" grandfather, he goes to all the grandsons "uprooted from their homeland (Lorraine) to better honor the great one." And what is more, Poincaré now lives in a "sweet family home" in the peaceful Claude-Bernard street ("a name worthy of him"), "in the neighborhood of serene studies, where, since the century of Abellard, the effort of Youth towards Knowledge has crystallized, at the top of the sacred mountain of Science which crown is made of: the Sorbonne, the College de France, the faculties, not far from the Pantheon of Voltaire and Rousseau, which are next to the bones of St. Geneviève, the patron saint of Paris. The scientific Doubt and the Faith of the Shepherdess." The reader certainly understood by reading the foregoing why it seemed interesting, and admittedly amusing, to finish a book which is about how the life and work of Poincaré were dealt with in the press of his time, with this almost caricatural example from the *Revue Illustrée*. But as we have already said, the scholar obviously lent himself to that little activity and even seemed to enjoy it. And he did so even more when he gladly replied to a discussion obviously initiated by Jehan Soudan on the question of God and ethics in science: we can see that this is the second issue that the "journalist" (and the public opinion?) seemed to be concerned about, after the incomprehension of his writings regarding the rotation of the Earth. This theme, as we know, gradually developed in

Henri Poincaré's work will be taken up by him in the lecture he delivered in 1909 on the occasion of the seventy-fifth anniversary of the Free University of Brussels, which was entitled "Le libre examen en matière scientifique" (Free examination in science). He even wrote an article on this question in the Catholic journal *Foi et vie* (Faith and life) in 1910, which included a text entitled: "La morale et la science" (Ethics and science). We can see then, with his involvement in favor of classics over the same period of time, that he adopted a position that was that of a man of letters as well as a man of science: his election to the Académie Française and the people he was associated with there certainly had something to do with this change.

In the article from the *Revue Illustrée*, when Jehan Soudan asked him whether "the scholar moves away from the idea of God or gets closer, through these elevated paths of Thought," he answered freely, was able to reconcile what at the time seemed irreconcilable to some (getting closer while moving away), and even came back to the terms ending with "ism" attached to his thought forms, and which we have listed in the chapter on philosophy. It therefore seemed worthwhile to give his entire answer here (or at least, of course, what Jehan Soudan was willing to transcribe in his article, see the breaks in the text):

> "A profession of faith? This is a lot to ask of a man of numbers! But Pasteur was Catholic. The good poet F. Coppée is admirably Catholic ...I too was born into a Catholic family ...But I am entirely devoted to Science, without any religious concern ...One speak of "Ethics of science? ..." Ethics and Science do not touch each other, do not penetrate each other ...There can be no unethical science, no more than there can be scientific ethics ...Men ask their gods to prove their existence with miracles. But the true "wonder" is that miracles do not always happen. And this is why the world is divine, for this is why it is harmonious. If it was governed by vagaries, what could prove us that it is not governed by chance? ...I am no materialist ...No spiritualist either! You really want an *ist* word? There is deist ...But there is *idealist* which I like more."

Poincaré here summarized what he wrote elsewhere at that time (*Science et Méthode* (Science and Method), *Le libre examen en matière scientifique* (Free examination in science), etc.). Science and ethics must be separated: there can be no unethical science, and there can be no scientific ethics. We know how this belief, widely shared among scientists, in a form of neutrality (or even innocence) of science has been contradicted by history: as we know, the debate got increasingly impassioned with the double-edged advances in fields as diverse as genetics, the atom, new technologies, ecology, etc.

And he finally reveals the only "ism" to which he identifies himself: idealism. Of course, it came within the connection between science and both God and ethics. But could he not have said it on the other chapters of his scientific thinking and approach, to which were attached so many other "ist" adjectives since that time? In any case, he added, "transcendental science, acquired through hard work, is made only of conventions, of hypothesis": his conventionalist and idealist approach can be noticed simply by reading these words, even though they too briefly summarize a work where he has put into perspective or even fought the conventionalism of some, or where he has defended his own conventionalist vision of geometry, and often placed the scholar's approach – and more specifically the mathematician's – to an almost Platonic idealistic level.

Jehan Soudan made him further clarify his thinking by asking him about what he thought of astrology, "the science of the connections that could exist between the celestial bodies and the fate of human existence." We should not be surprised to find this issue here: astrology was very popular at the time, and its scientism was claimed by some recognized people, in the academia as well. Karl Popper, one of the greatest epistemologists of the twentieth century, even built his philosophy of refutability by going by the questions that several disciplines – or theories – claiming that scientism aroused in him in the early 1920s: Einstein's theory of relativity, Freud's psychoanalysis, Adler's psychology, the Marxist theory of history, but also, he admitted, astrology, "with its large corpus of empirical evidence based on observation – horoscopes and biographies.".

Poincaré too spoke about the fact that people sought to "make Astrology popular again". His response to Jehan Soudan was clear: it is only "pure dreams", some "too inconsistent matter" which would absolutely not be taught "at the Sorbonne and the College de France", and to serve his argument, he used the classic example of Tycho Brahé only to say that he practiced astrology with the sole purpose of pleasing princes, and thus could take care of "the budget of his observatory". The fact that he answered so accurately and with such conviction proves how important this question was at the time.

Poincaré himself finally helps us conclude this work with what he wrote about his own philosophical vision of knowledge and thought. As soon as 1905 and the publication of *La valeur de la science* (The Value of Science), he said that "all that is not thought is pure nothingness," but that, considering "geological history", and for "those who believe in time" (strange condition here ...), "Thought is only a flash of light in the middle of a long night; but this flash is everything." Jehan Soudan took up these words, as if he wanted to summarize and praise one last time Henri Poincaré's ingenuity and philosophy: Poincaré had certainly approved of this quotation, and even recommended it. With this great confidence in the power of thought, which overshadows everything that does not come within it, and the statement that preceded on a claimed idealism, he seems to close a philosophical debate where his vision of the world had been described with multiple terms seemingly contradictory.

And he did it on the occasion of his election to a prestigious institution, through a journal that was not meant for experts only, as if calling all the French people to witness after trying throughout his whole work to discuss with his peers, namely specialists in questions of philosophy as well as the various sciences he was able to study and enrich thanks to his exceptional and universal mind.

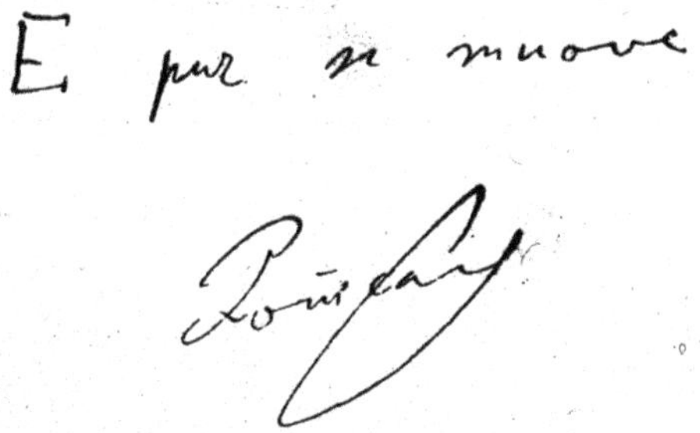

Fig. 13.3   *La Revue Illustrée* of April 5, 1908, p. 243.

Bibliography

Appell, P. *Henri Poincaré*, Librairie Plon, Paris, 1925.

Audureau, E. "Le conventionnalisme, conséquence de l'intuitionnisme," *Philosophiques*, vol. 31, N° 1, p. 57-88, 2004.

Barrow-Green, J. *Poincaré and the three-body problem*, AMS-LMS History of mathematics, Providence, RI, 1997.

Béguin, F. "Le mémoire de Poincaré pour le prix du roi Oscar" (Poincaré's memoir for the prize of King Oscar), in The Scientific Legacy of Poincaré, ed. Charpentier, Ghys, Lesne, History of Mathematics, 36, Providence: AMS, 2010.

Bell, E.T. *Les Grands Mathématiciens*, Simon & Schuster, New York, 1937.

Bellivier, A. *Henri Poincaré ou la vocation souveraine*, coll. "Vocations" n° IV, Gallimard, Paris, 1956

Bernheim, H., Benoît, C. & Vallois, L. *Docteur Léon Poincaré (1828-1892) : Discours prononcés à ses obsèques, le 16 septembre 1892*, Berger-Levrault et Cie, Paris, 1893.

Biezunski, M. *Einstein à Paris : le temps n'est plus*, Presses universitaires de Vincennes, 1992.

Binet, J.M. "Sur le mouvement du pendule simple en ayant égard au mouvement diurne de la terre," *Comptes rendus hebdomadaire des séances de l'Académie des Sciences*, t. 32, p. 197-205, 17 février 1851.

Borel, E. *L'évolution de la mécanique*, Flammarion, Bibliothèque de Philosophie Scientifique, Paris, 1943.

Bottazzini, U. "Poincaré : philosophe et mathématicien," *Les Génies de la Science*, novembre 2000.

Boulenger, M. *La querelle de l'orthographe*, E. Sansot, Paris, 1906.

Brenner, A. *Les origines françaises de la philosophie des sciences*, PUF, Paris, 2003.

Briot, C. & Bouquet, J.C. "Recherches sur les propriétés des fonctions définies par des équations différentielles," *Journal de l'école Polytechnique*, 36e cahier, vol. XXI, p. 133-198, 1856.

Deligeorges, S. *Foucault et ses pendules*, éditions Carré, Paris, 1990.

Desachy, P. *Bibliographie de l'Affaire Dreyfus*, Édouard Cornely et C°, Paris, 1905.

Duclert, V. *Alfred Dreyfus, l'honneur d'un patriote*, Fayard, Paris, 2006.

Duclert, V. *L'Affaire Dreyfus*, Larousse, Paris, 2009.

Dugas, R. *Henri Poincaré devant les principes de la mécanique*, in *Revue scientifique*, T. XXXIX, 1951.

Eneström, G. "Ist es zweckmäßig, daß mathematische Zeitschriftenartikel datiert werden?," *Bibliotheca Mathematica, Zeitschrift für Geschichte der Mathematischen Wissenschlaften*, p. 196-199, 1904.

Fonvielle, W. *Démonstration populaire du mouvement de la terre à l'aide du pendule de Léon Foucault*, éd. Spectateur Militaire, 1887.

Foucault, L. "Démonstration physique du mouvement de rotation de la terre au moyen du pendule," *Comptes rendus hebdomadaire des séances de l'Académie des Sciences*, t. 32, p. 135-138, 3 février 1851.

Flammarion, C. "Le problème des trois corps et le triomphe de M. Poincaré," *Bulletin de la Société Astronomique de France*, n° 7, p. 265-268, 1889.

Flammarion, C. *La fin du monde*, Librairie Ernest Flammarion, Paris, 1894.

Gérini, C. *Henri Poincaré : Ce que disent les choses*, Hermann, Paris, 2010.

Gilain, C. *La théorie géométrique des équations différentielles de Poincaré et l'histoire de l'analyse*, Thèse de Troisième cycle de l'Université de Paris I, 1977.

Joly, J.S. *Léon Poincaré (1828-1892) : Un nom célèbre, une œuvre oubliée*, PhD Thesis, Université Henri Poincaré, Nancy I, Mai 2000.

Langevin, P. *Henri Poincaré*, Librairie Félix Alcan, Paris, 1914.

Laskar, J. "A numerical experiment on the chaotic behaviour of the Solar System," *Nature*, 338, p. 237-238, 1989.

Lazare, B. *Une erreur judiciaire : la vérité sur l'affaire Dreyfus*, Brux., imprim. Monnom, 1896.

Lebon, E. *Henri Poincaré : biographie, bibliographie analytique des écrits*, Gauthier-Villars, Paris, 25 mai 1912.

Lechalas, G. "Sur la réversibilité du monde matériel," *Revue de Métaphysique et de Morale*, vol. 2, p. 191-197, 1894.

Le Roy, É. "Science et Philosophie," *Revue de Métaphysique et de Morale*, vol. 7, p. 375-425, p. 503-562, p. 706-731, 1899 et *Revue de Métaphysique et de Morale*, vol. 8, p. 37-72, 1900.

Loisy, A. *L'évangile et l'église*, Picard, Paris, 1902.

Mach, E. *Die Mechanik in ihrer Entwickelung historisch-kritisch dargestellt*, Leipzig, F. A. Brockhaus, 1883, 1888, 1897, 1901, 1904 et Mach, E. *La Mécanique. Exposé historique et critique de son développement*, translated from the fourth German edition, preface of Émile Picard, Paris, A. Hermann, 1904.

Mannheim, A. *Transformation des propriétés métriques des figures à l'aide de la théorie des polaires réciproques*, Paris, Mallet-Bachelier, 1857.

Mannheim, A. *Cours de géométrie descriptive de l'école polytechnique*, Paris, Gauthier-Villars, 1879, 2e éd., 1886.

Mannheim, A. *Principes et développements de la géométrie cinématique*, Paris, Gauthier-Villars, 1893.

Mawhin, J. "La terre tourne-t-elle, a propos de la philosophie scientifique" d'Henri Poincaré, in Stoffel Jean-François (éd), *Le réalisme, Contributions au séminaire d'histoire des sciences 1993-1994*, Centre interfacultaire d'étude en histoire des sciences, Louvain-la-Neuve, 1996, p. 215-252.

Mawhin, J. "Les fondements de la mécanique en amont et en aval de Poincaré : réactions belges à l'expérience du pendule de Foucault," *Philosophiques*, vol. 31, n° 1, p. 11-38, 2004. http://id.erudit.org/iderudit/008932ar

Michelson, A.A. & Morley, E.W. "On the relative motion of the earth and the luminiferous ether," *American Journal of Science*, 34, p. 333-345, 1887.

Miller, G.A. "M. Henri Poincaré," *Science, New Series*, Vol. 36, N°. 927, p. 425-429, (Oct. 4, 1912).

Moulton, F.R. "M. Henri Poincaré," *Popular Astronomy*, Vol. XX, N°. 10, p. 620-634, (Dec., 1912).

Nabonnand, P. "Rougier et l'histoire des sciences," *Philosophia Scientæ*, n° 10-2, 2006.

Nordmann, C. "Henri Poincaré, son œuvre scientifique, sa philosophie," *Revue des deux Mondes*, vol. 11, p. 331-368, 1912.

Pasquier, P. "À propos du pendule de Foucault," *Revue des questions scientifiques*, vol. 53, p. 501-515, 1903.

Pinsolle, D. *Le Matin, Une presse d'argent et de chantage (1884-1944)*, Éditions PUR, Rennes, 2012.

Poincaré, H. "Démonstration nouvelle des propriétés de l'indicatrice d'une surface," *Nouvelles annales de mathématiques*, vol. 13, p. 449-456, 1874.

Poincaré, H. *Sur les propriétés des fonctions définies par les équations aux différences partielles*, Thèse de la Faculté des Sciences de Paris, 1879.

Poincaré, H. "Sur les courbes définies par une équation différentielle," *Comptes rendus hebdomadaire des séances de l'Académie des Sciences*, t. 90, p. 673-675, 22 mars 1880.

Poincaré, H. "Sur les courbes définies par une équation différentielle," *Journal de mathématiques pures et appliquées*, Série III **7**, p. 375-422, 1881.

Poincaré, H. "Sur les courbes définies par une équation différentielle," *Journal de mathématiques pures et appliquées*, Série III **8**, p. 251-296, 1882.

Poincaré, H. "Sur les Fonctions Uniformes qui se reproduisent par des Substitutions Linéaires," *Mathematische Annalen*, XIX, p. 553-564, 1882.

Poincaré, H. "Sur les courbes définies par une équation différentielle," *Journal de mathématiques pures et appliquées*, Série IV **1**, p. 167-244, 1885.

Poincaré, H. "Sur l'équilibre d'une masse de fluide animée d'un mouvement de rotation," *Acta Mathematica*, vol. 7, p. 259-380, 1885.

Poincaré, H. "Sur les courbes définies par une équation différentielle," *Journal de mathématiques pures et appliquées*, Série IV **2**, p. 151-217, 1886.

Poincaré, H. *Notice sur les Travaux Scientifiques de Henri Poincaré*, Paris : Gauthier-Villars, 1886.

Poincaré, H. "La logique et l'intuition dans la science mathématique et dans l'enseignement," *L'enseignement mathématique* 1, p. 157-162, 1889.

Poincaré, H. "Notice sur Halphen," *Journal de l'école polytechnique*, Cahier LX, p. 143, 1890.

Poincaré, H. "Sur le problème des trois corps et les équations de la dynamique," *Acta Mathematica*, 13, p. 1-270, 1890.

Poincaré, H. *Les Méthodes Nouvelles de la Mécanique Céleste*, Paris, Gauthier-Villars, 1892-93-99.

Poincaré, H. "Le continu mathématique," *Revue de métaphysique et de morale*, vol. 1, p. 26-34, 1893.

Poincaré, H. "Le mécanisme et l'expérience," *Revue de métaphysique et de morale*, vol. 1, p. 534-537, 1893.

Poincaré, H. "Sur la nature du raisonnement mathématique," *Revue de métaphysique et de morale*, vol. 2, p. 371-384, 1894.

Poincaré, H. "Réponse à quelques critiques," *Revue de métaphysique et de morale*, vol. 5, p. 59-70, 1897.

Poincaré, H. "Les idées de Hertz sur la mécanique," *Revue générale des sciences pures et appliquées*, vol. 8, p. 734-743, 1897.

Poincaré, H. "La mesure du temps," *Revue de métaphysique et de morale*, vol. 6, p. 1-13, 1898.

Poincaré, H. "La logique et l'intuition dans la science mathématique et dans l'enseignement," *Enseignement mathématique*, vol. 1, p. 157-162, 1899.

Poincaré, H. "Sur les principes de la mécanique," *Bibliothèque du Congrès international de philosophie*, Armand Colin, Paris, vol. 3, p. 457-494, 1901.

Poincaré, H. *La Science et l'Hypothèse*, collection "Bibliothèque de Philosophie scientifique" de Gustave Le Bon, Flammarion, Paris, 1902.

Poincaré, H. "La Terre tourne-t-elle ?" *Bulletin de la Société astronomique de France* p. 216-217, mai 1904.

Poincaré, H. "Sur la dynamique de l'électron," *Comptes rendus hebdomadaire des séances de l'Académie des Sciences*, t. 140, p. 1504-1508, 5 juin 1905.

Poincaré, H. *La Valeur de la Science, collection,* "Bibliothèque de Philosophie scientifique" de Gustave Le Bon, Flammarion, Paris, 1905.

Poincaré, H. "Le Hasard," *Revue du Mois*, 3, p. 257-276, 10 mars 1907.

Poincaré, H. *Science et Méthode,* collection "Bibliothèque de Philosophie scientifique" de Gustave Le Bon, Flammarion, Paris, 1908.

Poincaré, H. *Ce que disent les choses,* cinq chapitres publiés dans la revue pour enfants Au seuil de la vie, Hachette, Paris, 1910 et repris par Hachette en 1911 dans l'ouvrage éponyme *Ce que disent les choses.*

Poincaré, H. "La morale et la science," *Foi et vie*, N° 3, Paris, p. 323-329, 1910.

Poincaré, H. *Leçons sur les hypothèses cosmogoniques*, Paris, Librairie Scientifique Hermann, 1911.

Poincaré, H. "Analyse des travaux scientifiques de Henri Poincaré faite par lui-même," *Acta Mathematica*, Vol. 38 (1), p. 3-135, 1921.

Poincaré, L. *Leçons sur la physiologie normale et pathologique du système nerveux,* Berger-Levrault et Cie, J. B. Baillière & Fils, Paris, 1873-1874 (2 volumes).

Poincaré, L. *Le Système Nerveux Périphérique au point de vue Normal et Pathologique,* Leçons de Physiologie, Professées a Nancy, Berger-Levrault et Cie, Paris, 1876.

Poincaré-Boutroux, A. *Vingt ans de ma vie, simple vérité, Journal intime, 1892-1913* (Coll. priv.). édité par Laurent Rollet, *Vingt ans de ma vie, simple vérité. La jeunesse d'Henri Poincaré racontée par sa sœur* Hermann, Paris, 2011.

Poinsot, L. "Remarques de M. POINSOT sur l'ingénieuse expérience imaginée par M. Léon Foucault pour rendre sensible le mouvement de rotation de la terre," *Comptes rendus hebdomadaire des séances de l'Académie des Sciences*, t. 32, p. 206-207, 17 février 1851.

Rageot, R. *Les Savants et la Philosophie*, Felix Alcan, Paris, 1908.

Reinach, J. *Histoire de l'affaire Dreyfus* en 4 volumes, Librairie Charpentier et Fasquelle, Paris, 1905.

Rolland, R. *Sur la vie de Tolsto*, Hachette, Paris, 1921.

Rollet, L. *Henri Poincaré. Des mathématiques à la philosophie*, PhD Thesis, Université de Nancy 2, advisor: Gerhard Heinzmann, 1999.

Rollet, L. *L'université et la science* in Vincent Duclert et Perrine Simon-Nahum (éds), *Les événements fondateurs : L'affaire Dreyfus*, Paris : Armand Colin, pp. 195-208, 2009.

Rollet, L. *Des mathématiciens dans l'affaire Dreyfus ? Autoforgerie, bertillonnage et calcul des probabilités* sur le site : http://images.math.cnrs.fr/, article numérique publié le 17 juillet 2010.

Rougier, L. préface de l'édition de *La valeur de la science*, Éditions du Cheval Ailé, Genève, Suisse, 1946.

Samueli, J.J. & Boudenot, J.C. *Henri Poincaré (1854-1912) : Physicien*, Éditions Ellipses, Paris 2005.

George Sarton, "Notice nécrologique de Henri Poincaré," *Ciel et Terre, Bulletin de la Société Belge d'Astronomie*, XXXIVe année, n° & n°2, 1913.

Schiavon, M. "Les officiers géodésiens du Service géographique de l'armée et la mesure de l'arc de méridien de Quito (1901-1906)," *Histoire & mesure*, Numéro XXI - 2 (2006), en ligne : http://histoiremesure.revues.org/1746.

Schmid, A.F. *Henri Poincaré. Les sciences et la philosophie*, L'Harmattan, Paris, 2001.

Schmid, A.F. "Conventionnalisme" in *Dictionnaire d'histoire et de philosophie des sciences*, Dominique Lecourt (Dir.), PUF, Paris, p. 244, 2003.

Sil'nikov, L.P. "A case of the existence of a denumerable set of periodic motion," *Sov. Mat. Dokl.* 6, p. 163-166, 1965.

Sapiro, G. "Défense et illustration de l'"honnête homme". Les hommes de lettres contre la sociologie" in *Actes de la recherche en sciences sociales*, N° 153, 2004-3, Le Seuil, 2004.

Toulouse, É. *Enquête médico-psychologique sur la supériorité intellectuelle : Henri Poincaré.* Paris, Flammarion, 1910.

Yoccoz, J.C. "Une erreur féconde du mathématicien Henri Poincaré," *Gazette de la Société Mathématique de France*, n° 107, p. 18-26, 2006.

Name Index

Subject Index

absolute space, 84–86, 90, 92, 96–99, 105–107, 122
absolute time, 99, 106
Académie des Sciences, 19, 39, 40, 46, 48, 51, 59, 60, 75, 87, 91, 96, 98, 111, 117, 153, 173, 188–190, 192
Académie française, 37, 197, 209
Académie française, 3, 44, 124, 134, 187–192, 195, 202, 219–221, 223
Alsace-Lorraine, 14, 27
anti-nominalism, 135

baccalaureate, literary, 14, 16
baccalaureate, scientific, 15
Bachelor of Science, 23
bifurcation, 13

Celestial Mechanics, 48, 53, 74, 108, 177, 192, 203
chance, 126, 127, 129, 132, 180, 183, 184
chaos, 53
Concours, général, 16
conventionalism, 116, 117, 121, 133, 135
conventionalist, 117

Davy lamp, 28
deist, 223

Ecole des Mines, 20, 22, 23
Ecole Normale Supérieure, 16, 17, 23

Ecole Polytechnique, 4, 16–18, 20, 22, 23, 27, 39, 43, 45, 49, 59, 97, 122, 143, 169, 172, 192, 210, 219, 222
empiricism, 115, 133, 205

Foucault's pendulum, 86–88, 92, 96–98, 105, 106, 108, 191
Franco-German war, 13, 27, 37
Fuchsian functions, 35, 36, 38, 39, 43, 45, 193

genealogy, 3
Grand Prix des Sciences, 39, 48

homoclinic, 53

idealism, 133, 224, 225
idealist, 224
idealistic, 220, 223, 224

Kleinian functions, 35, 37

materialist, 223
meridian, fight for, 67, 71
meridian, Greenwich, 67–69, 71
meridian, Paris, 71
meridian, Quito, 73
meridian, reference, 67
monist, 127

nominalism, 133, 135, 137, 221

www.ingramcontent.com/pod-product-compliance
Lightning Source LLC
Chambersburg PA
CBHW070346100426
42812CB00005B/1440